CUNARD

❖❖

Library

Out of respect for your fellow guests, please return all books as soon as possible. We would also request that books are not taken off the ship as they can easily be damaged by the sun, sea and sand.

Please ensure that books are returned the day before you disembark, failure to do so will incur a charge to your on board account, the same will happen to any damaged books.

www.oceanbooks.com

NATURAL SELECTION

DAN PEARSON

NATURAL SELECTION

A Year in the Garden

First published in 2017
by Guardian Books, Kings Place, 90 York Way, London N1 9GU
and Faber & Faber Ltd, Bloomsbury House,
74–77 Great Russell Street, London WC1B 3DA

Typeset by Donald Sommerville
Printed and bound by GGP Media GmbH, Pössneck, Germany

A CIP record for this book
is available from the British Library

ISBN 978–1–78335–117–6

2 4 6 8 10 9 7 5 3 1

To Mum and Dad, for your encouragement and constancy.
And to Huw, for sharing the vision.

CONTENTS

LIST OF ILLUSTRATIONS

INTRODUCTION

It has been interesting to look back over the best part of ten years of writing for the *Observer* and see my gardening time mapped in words. In that decade my evolution as a gardener has been transformed by a move from London, where for fifteen years I had a long, fenced-in garden in Peckham, to Hillside, an eight-hectare smallholding in Somerset. In London I created a world which provided me with a haven in the hubbub. Here at Hillside my boundaries are distant and the eye can travel. The move was perhaps the greatest change of my life, in gardening terms, but one that was necessary and inevitable. I needed to feel smaller and less in control of my environment and to develop a new way of gardening that allowed me to be closer to the land and its rhythms. The move – the need for which was best explained by a friend who equated my London life to being pot-bound – was also part of a process that every gardener embarks upon when they make the commitment to garden. You cannot help but evolve, for a garden is never static and inspires you to keep pace and develop.

Writing has helped to pull my gardening journey into focus. While the articles in this collection have been selected from a decade of observations and a variety of locations, they have been chosen to cover the twelve months of the year, so that the shifts in the seasons – and in place – are mapped in thoughts and activities. One of the great joys of the gardening year is the fact that the garden forces you to pay attention to the here and now. Every week is different from the next, but there is also reassurance in the repetition; the inevitability of spring blossom, and the flare of the berries at the other end of the growing season. A single year's experience is like the growth that accompanies it. It builds and layers and enriches.

My own path as a gardener was set at about five years old when my father and I made a pond in the orchard. It was a rectangle of just a couple of metres, but in planting it and watching its evolution through a watery lens, I discovered the alchemy of tending living things and the reward that comes from that process of nurturing. Some describe this as having 'green fingers', but to me gardening is a unified combination of skills that is actually not remotely mysterious. It is an ability to observe and to notice the needs of a plant (or combination of plants) and then to respond to those needs. As time goes on and the process continues, we become wiser as gardeners and more confident. We learn that it is possible to break the rules and, indeed, to make up our own. We evolve, we get wilder or neater or more accepting about the nature of weeds.

I feel I had a head start in learning to garden so young, and

I was luckier than most because I grew up amongst people who were fascinated by gardens and had an enthusiasm for growing things. My mother, who was brought up in vicarages and whose father had grown produce to eat during the war, tended our kitchen garden. My father grew the flowers and, although I wouldn't describe Dad as an instinctive gardener, he had a great eye. He also had a way with colour; he was never afraid of it, and we used to spend hours comparing notes while working on a pair of borders on either side of a path, one of which was mine, the other his. It was safer that way, for even then I had an insatiable appetite for plants and was hungry for more ground, and would have happily taken his border too.

Our neighbour Geraldine was also a great influence. A naturalist at heart, but a lifelong and committed gardener, her garden gate was always open to me. She gardened on the wild side, and from her I learned early on that a weed is only a plant in the wrong place. She was never discriminating on that front, and weeds were as welcome in her garden as choice plants, and they all came with fascinating stories of their provenance: the *Fritillaria pyrenaica*, for instance, collected on one of her travels to the Pyrenees and wrapped in damp, foreign newspaper in the boot of her car for the long journey home. In the garden she would part the weeds like curtains, to reveal her collected treasures, and then the stories would begin. Although my training at the RHS garden at Wisley was the polar opposite (and would soon teach me a very different set of rules), her influence instilled in me an openness to the blur between the world of the garden and the wild ground beyond it. In my late teens it was Geraldine's stories that set me off travelling to see plants in the wild. Her stories were the inspiration, but it was only when I saw plants growing in their natural settings for myself that everything fell into place.

My mother, who has always been driven as much by a project as by a story, was responsible for our family's move to a house with half a hectare of long-forgotten garden. Hill Cottage had overwhelmed the old lady who had lived there in its ruins and, by the mid-1970s, when we acquired it, the garden was several decades gone. Trees sprouted from the cottage's chimney and akebia vine had got under the skirting boards and wound around the furniture. We moved there when I was ten and spent the next seven years, until I left home, clearing the garden and discovering the treasures that lay submerged in the undergrowth. It was there that I learned to garden *with* and not *against* nature, for we were gardening as we cleared and with only as much energy as we had to keep the wilderness from closing in behind us.

At ten I was a child with a narrow frame of focus. While classmates were reading Enid Blyton and Alan Garner, my reading consisted of plant catalogues; my entire world was the garden. I started, but never finished, creating an illustrated book about Hill Cottage and made diaries with diagrams and drawings of plants and combinations that I'd been inspired by. Beth Chatto's catalogues were a paradise of description and anecdotes. At school I kept my secret to myself, for I knew that it was strange to be so committed to a pastime that was seen as the domain of an older generation.

Joan Wiggins, my English teacher at that point, was trying to get me to read more broadly and it is her whom I thank for showing me the connection between words, plants and the process of growing. She encouraged my writings, which, once they were on track, poured out with stories of the wilderness we lived in and the natural world that was my domain.

By the time I was thirteen she had introduced me to the books of Christopher Lloyd and I became hungry for the written word and the wider gardening world it connected me to. Christo's words, of course, came out of a real place and from decades of experience. Later, when I visited his garden, Great Dixter, with my father, I came to love it. As I stood under the Mount Etna broom he had described so vividly, his writings and my imaginings came together and combined. I wrote to him as a teenager and he gave me a tour of his meadows. He was a man who saw the importance of sharing his experiences. Later I came to read the late Vita Sackville-West, whose garden was by then in the hands of her gardeners. Although it had become something else entirely – clipped where it was once voluminous, and chic where it had probably been shabby – the romance was still there in her writing. I never dreamed then that I would one day be writing in her shoes at the *Observer*.

Today my gardening time is precious and well guarded. The garden is a place in which I can lose myself as I did when I was a child, with a disregard for time that can easily see two hours turning into an afternoon or even longer. It is a sanctuary of sorts and one that allows me to combine mindfulness with the purely physical. It is a place that opens up ease of thought. In fact the juxtaposition of discovery and disappointment is often a better education than a delight easily forgotten. It is all part of an evolution, of the growing and the enrichment that comes from doing and looking. And the writing helps to pin it down.

As an adult, I have found that writing and gardening have become inextricably linked. I put aside one solitary day a week to write and the day will often start with a walk to visit my subject matter. I used to think of this as procrastination, but the hour or so lost, when I might be drawn into a task I hadn't planned for, is all part of the ritual. It is then that my ideas come together and I get a purchase. A posy picked allows me the opportunity to really describe something in intimate detail. Making notes in a notebook is the other method I employ to get something onto the page.

The thoughts which I have when I am gardening may well be born of a repetitious task and appear to be equally weighted, but when I examine them alongside what has gone before and what is yet to come, they are layered. What I like about writing is the act of capturing the process of gardening, of distilling these experiences in words. Some thoughts draw to conclusions and are satisfying as a result, but others are equally interesting for remaining in flux. The writing might interrogate a colour, a feeling or a place. It might capture a moment that I know will only happen once, perfection existing for minutes and then passing: the experience of standing under a cherry when the very first blooms are opening, or the perfume of a solitary lily. Writing helps to keep those experiences present and alive and in the memory.

I hope that some of my thoughts are inspiring, be it to the imagination or as dirt under the nails and the growth that comes with the act of doing and discovering for yourself. In writing these articles I have also felt the responsibility – a delightful one – of sharing my ongoing process and enlightenment with you, the reader.

JANUARY

J

Because the first month of the year is the darkest, you might think it is the most inert in the garden, but January is not a month in which everything drops back into inactivity. Our benign climate means that there is always something pushing against the season to draw us out into the garden as witnesses. The foliage of celandine against bare earth, the perfume of witch hazel: each holds your attention and ostensibly has the floor to itself; but look again and the garden is full of intrigue. Low, raking light catches seedheads from a season spent, and plant skeletons provide a spectacular framework for frost if you let them stand, as I do, in the belief that it is good to see the garden run the full course of its cycle.

I love our four seasons, and winter is never one to fear, for it is then that there is room to think. The frenzy of activity that comes with the growing season is absent and you can look up and around and take in your surroundings without the burning feeling of the yard-long list of tasks. You can see a tree's structure and history in its naked branches, just as you can see the plants that are ready for winter pruning.

Pace yourself with the winter work and use this time to plan for building in change, to keep a garden feeling vital and refreshed. Tasks map the season, but although we have several weeks ahead of us to revitalise and re-do, there is time in January to embrace the winter garden.

1 January, *Hillside*
FIELDS OF DREAMS

———

Above ground and in the cold and the low light of January, the garden is at its quietest moment. The rust-coloured, velvety buds are yet to break on the hamamelis, and though the catkins are formed on the hazel they are clutched tight and sensibly waiting. Even the snowdrops are showing little above the ground, and for the first time in ages I feel I have the time to think.

I can see now what my neighbour meant when she said that she looks forward to the slower pace of winter, for the growing season was frenetic: the rush of sap and weight of growth never abating once the tide had turned in the spring. Hunger and exhaustion finally drove me in with the revelation that I had sometimes gone a whole day without ever stopping to look at my surroundings.

I can afford that luxury now that the weeds are in stasis, turning my back on the kitchen garden for a little and starting my day down by the stream, walking the length of it where it slips along the boundary. From here I can look up to the slopes where the garden will one day be and amble through what we have achieved in the first year here. I lost only two of the 400 hedge plants and saplings that went in last winter – and I'm asking myself if it was the beneficial mycorrhizal fungi in the Rootgrow that were added while planting that got them through the drought in spring.

The newly planted fruit trees also recovered after they were stripped of foliage by the sheep. Their willingness to return suggests they already had a well-developed root system. I also experimented this year with not incorporating muck or compost into the planting holes of the trees and shrubs. Current thinking goes that as long as your soil is in good condition, it is better not to give the plants a false head start, as over-nurtured plants can refuse to move beyond the 'comfort' of the planting hole. I stand by the importance of improving your soil if it is poorly drained or impoverished, but I am simply adding the Rootgrow for now.

I could see the blaze of Californian poppy (*Eschscholzia*) in the meadows from the other side of the valley in June and I completely fell in love with the *Linum grandiflorum* 'Rubrum'. The red flax danced on its wire-thin stems, each flower rimmed with a darker eyeliner at the edge of the petal. I'm wondering how the self-sown mix will do this year, as the seedlings of the *Eschscholzia* have already found their way into the cracks of the yard, softening the concrete of the farmer's footprint.

I will oversow with seed saved from the flax and start some experimental mixes with umbellifers such as the delightfully lacy *Orlaya grandiflora*. They will be teamed with Shirley poppies, creamy corncockle 'Ocean Pearl' and the giant dandelion clocks of *Tragopogon* to mark a new palette for the upcoming year.

Stretching ahead of us is the planting season, and what could be more appropriate for a new year than planting trees? I have ordered *Malus* to make a huddle of crabs on the slopes behind us to complement the blossom wood. *Malus transitoria* has filigree leaves and tiny golden fruits and has a wild look about it, while *M. hupehensis*, the tea crab from China, is a more ornamental thing and can come closer to the house. This Chinese species is arguably one of the best crab apples, forming an upright tree in its youth to spread out comfortably in middle age. The flowers are deliciously scented, the branches laden with dark red fruits.

It is a good time for pondering the exact positions for your new plantings to ensure they have room to make their journey to maturity. I find myself planting more than I need so that they can protect each other in youth, but I will have to be a disciplinarian later and thin them to prevent them from spoiling each other. These are dilemmas I am allowed to ponder for now, but it won't be long before the snowdrops are giving us the nod that the resting period is over.

LEAVE AND LET LIVE

———

After the past couple of weeks of inertia, the temptation to sweep out the detritus of the old year to welcome in the new is considerable. I want to be out there building a bonfire or clearing a patch of rough ground to greet the new year, but it is so worthwhile taking time to think about what really needs to be done. Our instinct to tidy should be curbed. More and more I find myself urging people not to clear a garden too rigorously or too early because, however small, these plots of land are oases to a slumbering ecology. Gardens are stripped, made up, and turned down like hospital beds far too frequently, and homes to hedgehogs, ladybirds, slug-eating ground beetles and lacewings are swept aside in the process. So much beauty can be lost in a clear-up and so little gained for things looking spruce and pukka.

I am not advocating leaving everything in a shambles, but a gentle transition to neatness and readiness for the spring is a much better option than blitzing it all now. To appreciate this you need to take time to tune in to the subtleties of winter – looking is just as important as the acting on it. The ghosts of the last season may be a shadow of their former selves but, when you take a closer look, they are as beautiful in a different way.

The rhythms of decay have their own pace, and a good reason for taking the time they do. Next time you are out there, crouch down to see how the fallen leaf litter is being pulled back into the ground by earthworms. The first time I saw this,

I couldn't work out why all the leaves were pointing up from the ground with one end pulled in, but leaves are food for the worms, and the bacteria and the decomposed leaves provide much needed humus for the soil. Then turn your eye to what the last season has left behind as skeletons. Like miniature cities reaching skyward, many are home to insects and a host of other living things, and as structures they are often one of the most beautiful aspects of the winter garden.

Look to the hedgerows, roadside embankments and waste ground and it is easy to argue that this is their best season, with the colour pared back now that the greens have receded. I love green, but in the winter months you realise that the predominance of green often prevents you from registering the detail – and the winter skeletons are all about detail. Bleached grasses strike their pale vertical lines into the landscape like a mirage when you see them en masse. Some spent stems crisscross as they weaken at the base to break with the upright, but it all has its charm with tangles of vetch hanging in blackened nests and dots of chocolate brown marking the presence of long-gone moon daisies. High above the grasses are the last of the umbels – wild carrot, hemlock and sweet cicely, with its sooty seeds hanging in pale cages.

Despite appearances, winter is also far from monochrome, and the range of browns, buffs, cinnamons and oranges seem infinite in their informal weave. The rusts heat up when it is wet, and the blacks darken so that teasel is as dark as coal in a smouldering grassland. When it is dry, the parchment tones of the grasses whiten and bleach to silver on a rare bright day. That's one good reason for leaving some rough ground if you have the room, and certainly a rich inspiration for what you can bring together for winter interest in the garden.

When planning perennial planting, I always choose a good percentage for their ability to leave behind something of note for this season. Some, such as tradescantia and many of the geraniums, wither back to nothing, their foliage dragged to earth by the worms to leave only the expectant crown. But many leave behind the woody structure they formed in the summer, devoid of foliage perhaps and transformed into something quite new and magical. These forms are just as interesting as the summer garden if you play with them in this so-called 'down time'. They provide a framework on which frost and snow (if we have it) can alight, and on which sunlight can be caught where it might otherwise fall to ground without interruption. Many of the spent stems are also rich with seeds. If these are left standing, you might find your garden a-flurry, with blue tits feasting on the fennel seeds or picking over the russety heads of the *Phlomis russeliana*.

Each skeleton has its own level of endurance – fennel and many of the grasses persist until they start to look out of place among the March newness, so I edit them back only when they lose their will and succumb to inevitable decomposition. The silvery stems of *Perovskia* also go right through, being reduced only by the need to give them a hard prune in March, but some are as fragile as they look and will last just long enough to be worth it. The eryngiums in my garden are a good example. The tall stems of *E. agavifolium* make a valiant start, with their cinnamon stems held high above the remnants of their neighbours, but they have all toppled by January and lower the tone of the bolt upright miscanthus nearby. Their cousins, *E. giganteum* (aptly named 'Miss Willmott's Ghost'), have a little more endurance, but it will not be long now before their silver crowns go from net to nothing. The reference to the ghost in this case has nothing to do with their skeletal forms, but to the charming story that Ellen Willmott, a nineteenth-century gardener, used to scatter the seed surreptitiously in other people's gardens as she was shown around, for it to appear magically the following year. I leave mine until they topple and only remove them to the compost heap at the last moment.

It is easier to be casual in a larger space, but many of the best skeletons take up little room and stand bolt upright. *Calamagrostis* 'Karl Foerster' is a classic example of a grass that endures almost everything that a winter can throw at it, and during that time it will be the best armature for frost and the wick for low slanting winter light that blazes on its stems. The *Miscanthus* are also hard to rival, continuing to rustle in the wind and bleach to a variety of natural colours that range from bone whites through to spicy browns. Those that hold their plumage, such as *M. sinensis* 'Silberspinne', are bright enough on a sunny day to erase any melancholy in an instant.

The sedums form a low-level horizontal plain of rusty seed-heads. I like them more in the winter time without the colour of flower. As plants get older and more lax their tendency to open out in the centre to form a cartwheel is revealed in all nakedness, with the fat buds for next year waiting in the centre. In a group this is amazing to look at, and it always reminds me of coral in a reef or Catherine wheels spinning. Good old-fashioned *Sedum* 'Autumn Joy' (aka 'Herbstfreude') stands at about 30 cm, while the much larger-growing 'Matrona' often forms a wheel as much as a metre across. You need to wade in at the end of March to remove the remnants, as they keep going if you let them, but by that time they are tinder dry and light as a feather, snapping easily from the rosette. I often scatter opium poppies as a complement and their pods teeter on leafless stems high above the sedums, and in snow each has a hat of white.

Clearing can be hard to resist, but the longer you leave it the more of a chance there will be for anything that can rot to make its way back into the ground to improve it in the coming growing season. Some plants, such as angelica, just can't keep it together for the duration and are quickly toppled by winter rot and wind. When the stems totter, you should resist the urge to have that winter-warming bonfire and give any interlopers a chance to see the winter out in comfort. Break the hollow stems and you will often find little colonies of ladybirds still sleeping there. Best to find a rough corner for these, or at least give them a chance on the compost heap. In spring you will thank them for their efforts to eradicate the first wave of aphids, but in the meantime, you can have the pleasure of knowing you are providing their winter quarters.

GHOST TREES

———

Look up and you will see one of the best things this coming season has to offer in the bare branches. Every tree has its own character – the beech slender and steely; the oak twisting and gnarled, its growth showing exactly how long it has taken to attain stature. Distinct among any group or thicket is the birch. On elderly *Betula pendula* – though elderly may be not much more than fifty or sixty years, as they are fast-growing trees – the branches will hang gracefully to catch the wind. An old tree, now black and white where the bark has cracked dark as charcoal, will show its age in the trunk, but the finely spun limbs will always retain the grace of their youth.

The birch is a pioneer among trees, the scaly wafer-thin seed being light enough to blow from the branches for quite some distance. Happiest on acid soils but content in most, they will often be one of the first trees to grow in newly disturbed ground.

You might think this was the behaviour of a weedy species, and I have pulled a few in my time, but birch is a tree that it is easy to welcome. In three years from seed they will be slender whips, but in seven their russet-coloured bark will be showing white and the branches reaching high enough to cast you a dapple of shade to stand in.

Being pioneers, our native birch suit their own company and the nicest plantings of *Betula pendula* are en masse, so you can enjoy the repeat of their chalky stems. The groves planted not so long ago between Tate Modern and the Thames are even beginning to cope with the scale of the building behind them as they mature. Birch is not a tree I'd use if gravity were needed, but their veil of twiggery is one of the nicest ways of concealing something you might not want to see without blocking it entirely. This is why they are good for fraying edges and for stopping a boundary from feeling final.

The heightened ornamental quality of the species from China and the Himalayas makes them fine stand-alone trees. *Betula utilis* var. *jacquemontii* is perhaps the whitest of them all. It lacks the delicacy of our native *B. pendula*, but packs a punch in the right place. There are several forms that are as good, and of them 'Silver Shadow' is one of the best.

Betula ermanii is unusual among the group for bark that is touched with salmon pink. The pink-and-red-coloured forms of *Betula albosinensis* are more colourful still, and 'Kenneth Ashburner' or var. *septentrionalis* have bark that peels away like paper as the stem stretches from season to season to reveal new colour underneath.

The latter are smaller in stature as trees and useful for a smaller garden, as is the much-underrated *Betula nigra*. The river birch is a tree for wet places, the pale bark flaking as it ages until it is frilled and feathering the trunks. Team it with fiery-coloured *Salix* for the winter and you will find the dark months are something you positively look forward to.

NEW YEAR'S HONOURS

———

A new year stretches ahead of us and already I am ring-marking space so that things I failed to do last year don't slip through my fingers again. I want to visit the Atlas Mountains to be part of an early spring and to witness the plants I love most growing in the wild and in context. There are garden moments too, the erythroniums at Knightshayes and the magnolias at Caerhays in Cornwall. Of course this is a distraction from the cold muddy beds and the plants that are in retreat here in my wintry garden, but it is good to have plans.

The art of gardening lies so much in the planning. You have in your mind the tree that you will be standing underneath when you plant the whippy sapling and you can smell the *Chimonanthus*, even though you know it will be at least three years before the wintersweet flowers. The sheets of scarlet poppies vibrating in summer sunshine are vivid in the mind's eye as you throw the seed on to the dirt in deepest January, but you know that the frost will help to break the dormancy and that you have partaken in something wonderful by starting the cycle off for another year. Though the January garden might look its most inert, a new year is a year full of promise.

With a planting season extending through into March, I am promising myself that I will plant more magnolias. I have two gardens on site in Devon and I know that magnolias will enjoy the West Country with its slightly milder climate and plenty of moisture. Though one tends to think of magnolias as woodlanders, and indeed, most hail from the forests of China and North America, they are remarkably adaptable as garden trees. Given moisture at the root and a position that isn't blasted by wind, they are happy out in the sunshine. That said, *Magnolia* × *loebneri* and its starry-flowered cultivars are proving to be really quite tolerant of wind down by the coast, but the larger-flowered forms will be torn to shreds in a gale.

The extra light of an open position will reward you with sun-ripened wood and more plentiful flowers as a result. The winter outlines of trees are often more interesting than the summer ones. The flowering magnolias are a good case in point once the leaves are down, the bare branches glistening with buds. Next month, Cornwall will see the first tree magnolias blooming but most of us further up country will have to wait. The wait is made that much easier, though, with such anticipation mapped out in bud. Velvety textured, and primitive in appearance, they capture the light in a silver pelt that covers them for protection. Some forms are a rich russet brown, and on closer observation you will see that they are more animal than vegetable, like a paw with a downy covering.

In terms of waiting, we are gardening in good times. It takes a good fifteen years for a tree magnolia such as *M. campbellii* to flower, but we now have the Jura and the Gresham hybrids, which have all the assets of their parents but the precociousness of breeding. Before it is taller than you are, you will be reaping the rewards of a tree such as 'Iolanthe' or the aptly named 'Star Wars'. In terms of getting the year off to a good start, I make every effort to get the woody plants in on this side of winter. The unspoken rule goes that they should be planted by Christmas so that the roots have as long as possible to make contact with their new environment, but the late start to winter, followed by the wettest November I can remember, has already thrown out good intentions. No matter, whenever the ground is dry enough for it not to stick to the spade, I'll be pushing for things to get in the ground.

Planting should never be thought of as a chore. An hour spent preparing a hole is nothing in the life of that tree and the duration of the time you will have together. A hole should always be twice the width of the root ball and a good spit deep. Current thinking goes that it is not necessary to dig deeper than a spit as a deep hole can act as a sump in heavy ground. Break up the base of the hole with a fork to ease drainage and work in some organic matter to improve the backfill of topsoil and you will be off to a good start.

One of the first areas to be planted out this January is a catkin wood for a client. We will be employing very simple techniques as the young trees are no more than whips and these can be slit-planted into a 'V' cut into the ground with a spade and then closed again with your heel once the roots have been inserted into the slot. This simple method of planting is time-saving and is all that's needed with the more vigorous native species. I follow through with a mulch mat to keep competition at bay in the first couple of years, and recommend rabbit guards if the critters are in your area.

The little wood is an excuse to welcome the year in with branches that illustrate the first stirrings, and alder, willow species and hazel have been chosen for their early movements. In just a few years' time, we will be able to walk under their branches and look up to see the first signs of life against grey skies. Silvery and expectant, and dusting the air with the first pollen of the year, they are something worth planning for.

11 January, *Peckham*
HAPPY HOLLY DAYS

———

January is the beginning of what would once have been a long, hard winter, which not long ago would have meant food was scarce and heat was something that had to be managed with care. You would have had to hunker down very seriously, prepare for the long nights and the inclement weather, and plan ahead with military precision.

With the luxury of heating and a full fridge, we can enjoy the spartan nature of winter outside. In the garden, I also feel the need for winter foliage to ease the bleakness of the next few weeks. It has been the supporting act for three seasons of activity, but now that the garden is dormant it comes into its own. I am always surprised by its reappearance; and to find the ivy again – running fast and furious up tree trunks and encrusted in voluminous flowering bracts along the tops of walls – is a treat. It is a safe haven for the birds in the winter, as the berries ripen when food is scarce elsewhere. The birds are the reason it appears as frequently as it does, and apparently always in the places that suit it, and the seed is scattered as the birds move from tree to tree.

Though there are 400 species found globally, of all the native evergreens the holly is perhaps my favourite. *Ilex aquifolium* is a fine tree, compact enough, and a home for wildlife when deciduous trees become transparent. I like the way an old tree that has not had its skirts lifted will sweep to the ground to tickle the leaf litter. If you look hard at an undisturbed tree you will see that it is only the foliage within reach of foraging animals that is undulating with prickles. Out of reach and the leaves are mostly restricted to a single needle at the apex.

Although the holly is by nature a woodlander, thriving in quite dry conditions, where it sows itself and has time to delve deep before making top growth, it is just as happy out in the open. A deep, loamy soil will bring the best out of it, but a holly is just as contented on sand or chalk and quite heavy clay, as long as it doesn't lie waterlogged. Planting is always best carried out in the early autumn to give the roots time to take hold, or in late winter, so that the foliage doesn't dry out in winter winds.

I have also had a lot of success with holly near the sea, or in polluted environments where other evergreens, such as yew, might fail. *Ilex* × *altaclerensis*, a cross between *I. aquifolium* and *I. perado*, is the best for these conditions, and it has broader, larger leaves. Try to get the plain, green-leaved form if you can, as it drops back so much more nicely than the variegated selections more readily available. The beauty of evergreens is that they are happy to be at the forefront in winter but will settle into the shadows once the leaves are out elsewhere. If you need winter colour, much the best route is to opt for some *Cornus alba* or coloured-stemmed willows.

Having said that, the fruit of a holly is half its appeal. Not all trees produce fruit, because there are male and female trees and one needs the other to provide a show. If your tree never fruits, it is probably because it is male. So it is always worth seeking out a female form, because it only takes one male to pollinate several females, and a male is rarely so far away that the pollen cannot be distributed. One of the most reliable is *I. aquifolium* 'J. C. van Tol'. This is a self-fertile female, so you are guaranteed fruit. The stems are dark purple and the leaves almost complete and without prickles, so it cuts a clean, shiny outline. Left to its own devices it will form a broad, upright tree, and to keep it bushy when it is young I tip the branches late in July. Holly makes a good hedge and responds well to regular cutting, but it will always take some time to regenerate if you cut too far into the old wood. Little and often is the key.

Of the female forms selected for their berries, 'Bacciflava' and 'Amber' are worth considering, as the birds will go for the red berries first and leave you with the yellow-berried forms for at least another month. A shot of yolky yellow in the winter is lovely scattered throughout the dark foliage.

A male worth having, if you are prepared to forgo the berries, is the hedgehog holly, *I. aquifolium* 'Ferox'. This is considered to be the oldest surviving cultivar, dating back to the seventeenth century, and it does have an ancient demeanour. Each leaf has bristle upon bristle once you refocus your eye. When the rest of the garden is sleeping, it is good to know that there's support in the shrubberies.

14 January, *Peckham*

THE LION IN WINTER

———

At the dimmest point in the year, when life in the garden seems at its most still and inert, my *Hamamelis* 'Jelena' breaks its first buds. The cinnamon-coloured beads, held in tight clusters up the stem, have been swelling since the foliage dropped in the autumn; now, one at a time, they open like sea anemones awakening in rock pools stilled once the tide has gone out. The tendrils of petal break bud, unscrunching themselves but not quite, so that each petal is crimped. They gather momentum as one catches up with the next until the whole bush is covered from top to bottom. I look out on a dim day to see the terrace illuminated with a rusty-coloured glow, and it is 'Jelena' that gets me out there to see what else the garden has to offer.

My neighbour Geraldine used to have the Chinese witch hazel, *Hamamelis mollis*, in the jumble of treasures that made up her garden. You always knew it was out even though it was tucked away in a gloomy corner because she would pick a tiny sprig for a jar on the kitchen table. The posy was part of an ongoing installation – a microcosm of her garden, captured and intimate, so you had to study the detail. The witch hazel was the star of the dark months. You'd be spurred on to venture out around the side of the house. Anticipation would build as you passed the *Iris unguicularis* at the bottom of the wall and the *Cyclamen coum* spreading out into the lawn. You had to push under a big *Magnolia grandiflora* to get to the clearing, and there the *Hamamelis* took your breath away. Its luminous branches filled the clearing with a delicious sweet perfume.

When I was studying at the RHS's Wisley Garden in Surrey, just a short walk from our halls of residence were the witch hazels that grew on Seven Acres. I was rather intimidated by them because they were old and twisted and roomy. Their magnificence seemed to be unattainable, like a beautiful but expensive item of clothing in a window. When you are younger, as is the case a lot later in life, it can be inhibiting to think that you might have to wait too long to get the benefit or never see a plant mature, so for years, until moving to my own garden, I looked at them with admiration and from a distance. The fact that I was stung with a couple of plants that I failed with at Home Farm in Northamptonshire, where I studied for a time, made me doubly reticent. I put them in the woodland garden on a bank so they would drain freely in the heavy soil, but I had no idea that the winds whipped around the corner of the house. The wind did for those two plants, burning the young foliage early in the season and finishing them off in a dry spell when I was away and the bank cracked open like a crusty loaf.

Winter gardening is something that I have grown into as I have matured. I used to view spring through to autumn as the time that the garden did its thing, and winter as the time to prepare for the action. But increasingly I will try and work towards there being a framework of plants that 'do' in the winter and those that have their season now: the *Hamamelis* have come high up the list. In my own garden here in London, I have got around the issue of there not being adequate space to grow a decent-sized bush by growing them in pots. Then they take on the fascination that Geraldine's posy had, for you can see them up close and move them near the windows to be displayed in winter quarters. In the summer, I heave them back up to the end of the garden, where they are put in a holding area by the compost heaps. In the cool under the neighbour's trees there is less risk of drying out and their summer foliage, which is modest, like a hazel, can blend into the background.

Alongside the trusted 'Jelena' – one of the earliest to come into bloom – I have several hybrids on my own trial in an effortless effort to get to know them better. Between them I have flower for almost three months, one variety picking up where the last faded, and when they get too big, they will be found a home in a suitable garden. *Hamamelis* × *intermedia* is a cross between *H. mollis* and the smaller-flowered *H. japonica*. Both parents are highly scented and worth having for that alone – it is a pity that the hybrids miss out here, but the crosses make up for it in the incredible range of colours. From the gold of 'Arnold Promise' through to warm, glowing-orange 'Aphrodite' and on into spicy-red 'Diane' (also famed for crimson autumn foliage) and bloody 'Livia', they are worth seeking out in a collection so you can make the comparisons. Many of these hybrids were raised by the De Belders's Kalmthout Arboretum in Belgium, where there is one of the best collections in the world. I have vowed to go this winter to see the woodland there glow like it is on fire.

Each year, my obsession grows a little, so last February I sought out one of the national collections, grown by Chris Lane in Kent. Chris is the writer of the superb monograph *Witch Hazels* (Timber Press), and I was keen to see them all together to single out the best. They were set out in orderly rows in an exposed field, the conditions far from what you might expect if you have read the textbooks. *Hamamelis* like good living: a deep, well-drained soil with plenty of humus and some shelter, as they hail from scrub and edge-of-woodland conditions in the wild. They hate waterlogging, so a high water table or heavy clay soil should be avoided, but here on the free-draining slope it was the heavy acid soil that enabled them to be out in the open, as it held the moisture in the summer. Though many books say that they need acid soil, this rule can also be bent, and I have had success with *Hamamelis* in limestone soils in the Cotswolds. The secret is to get a good-enough depth of topsoil enriched with humus and to ensure that they never dry out in the summer.

Looking back in my notes that were jerkily scrawled with a cold hand in that field last February, there are a bewildering number of varieties to choose from, but not so many that stand out from the crowd. It is worth seeking out the best varieties of *H. mollis* if you want a gold-flowered witch hazel. These are still the most gloriously scented, but look for a named variety such as *H. mollis* 'Boskoop' or 'Jermyns Gold', as they can be variable. *H. mollis* 'Pallida', a marvellous sulphur-yellow, has been re-grouped with the *H.* × *intermedia* hybrids, and that is where you should go for the best range of colours. I would pass on *H. vernalis* and *H. japonica* and its varieties in preference to the hybrids and to *H. mollis* because the flowers of these two species are smaller. The true witch hazel, *H. virginiana*, will bloom with autumn foliage in October and November, but it is a subtle thing that I would only ever plant if I had room enough. I prefer to play to their strengths and to use the best of the winter-flowering varieties.

Large plants establish better than smaller plants, so seek out a ten-litre plant over the standard-sized three litres if you can afford it. Sometimes where plants are concerned it is worth going short elsewhere. Imagine yourself right now being able to glance at a blaze of flower out there in the grey of winter. In a few years you may have invested enough time to be able to bring a sprig inside to remind you to get out there into the cold. Believe you me, the wait is worth it.

16 January, *Hampshire*

GLOOM RAIDERS

———

I remember very clearly the first time I came upon *Viburnum × bodnantense*. I must have been ten and we had just taken on a long-forgotten garden that had engulfed the house and the old lady who had planted it. It was early winter and I was bashing about in the remains of the thickety orchard that lay in the lower parts of our plot. There was a crumpled greenhouse in which the old lady had encouraged a solitary camellia, and as we had not been there for long, the path she had trodden to stoke the boiler was the path we took to gather windfalls.

The leaves were recently down and I remember the surprise in the monochrome when coming upon the sweetly smelling flowers. They were the palest pink imaginable, but it was the perfume which drew me to them first. Sweet and smelling slightly of cloves, it hung on the cool, damp air and mingled with the windfalls from the previous season. The shrub must have been fifty years old, but thirty-five years later it is still rewarding my parents with a steady but spasmodic supply of flower through to the end of January.

Viburnum × *bodnantense* is most usually offered in a sugary-pink selection called 'Dawn', but I prefer the pink-budded 'Deben', as it fades rapidly to white. They are angular shrubs when in youth, softening in outline as they age, but today I prefer to plant *Viburnum farreri* 'Candidissimum'. I first saw this shrub in the winter gardens at Anglesey Abbey in Cambridgeshire, where its clear white flowers shine among dark mahonia. Winter whites are easier to place at this time of the year, and this is one of the best – brighter and showing up the creaminess of winter-flowering honeysuckles, and easy to use with fiery hamamelis. Its summer lumpenness, for it is an 'ordinary' shrub in summer, can be forgiven, as its heavily perfumed flowers continue for a good eight weeks in the darkest months. I have used it as a bright focal point in the newly planted Winter Garden in Battersea Park.

The family *Viburnum* is large and wide-ranging and I have included the native wayfaring tree, *V. lantana* and the bloody-berried *V. opulus* in a list of whips to bulk up my native hedges this winter. The former is common in hedges on chalky ground and is particular for its lily fragrance, but I also love the latter for its lacy flower heads in June. In the Mediterranean areas of Europe, *Viburnum tinus* takes the reins and weights the winter landscape with evergreen. I use it frequently in gardens in the UK, as it looks relaxed and informal and is more than happy to sprawl about in dark corners. 'Eve Price' is a compact-growing form with carmine buds. Though unperfumed, the flowers appear from autumn until March and are often seen in tandem with the previous year's metallic-blue berries.

If you were to keep going east through to China and then Japan you would continue to find the tribe in its subtly shifting guises. Some are modest in appearance, but most offer up something, be it berries, good-colouring autumn foliage, or evergreen. *Viburnum davidii*, a plant that is unjustifiably out of fashion today, is still one of the best low-growing evergreens, with pleated foliage that smothers a low, shade-tolerant mound. Creamy domes of April flower are berrying a wonderful turquoise blue in the winter months, if you get a male and a female plant to ensure pollination. Similar, but growing into a loosely domed shrub, is *Viburnum cinnamomifolium*, a plant that has real potential as a winter mainstay.

Of the perfumed members of the tribe, the semi-deciduous *Viburnum × burkwoodii* remains a firm favourite as it picks up late, in March, when the early-winter forms have finished. It forms a large, open-structured shrub with glossy foliage that glints and refracts in winter sunshine. It is adaptable to being wall-trained, and there is a compact form called 'Anne Russell', but I like to leave it to grow naturally and with room around it so that it can find its own shape. In time you can use the shade it casts to tuck winter-flowering hellebores under its skirts. Find it a sheltered corner where the perfume will linger and hold you spellbound, as it held me all those years ago.

19 January, *Peckham*

WORKING TOGETHER

––––––

The celandines are already pushing through, the mild weather providing a window for early growth. The first of their foliage lies flat against bare earth. They make me feel optimistic and, though it will be a while before they flower, the buds wait expectantly.

Close by, our native lords and ladies is up and also seizing the window of growth. I have the marbled form *Arum italicum* 'Marmoratum' in my garden. It is an old favourite, which I grow for exactly this moment. Unless it has flowered and left berries behind in the summer you all but forget about it once it is dormant. The autumn rains are the trigger for renewed action and by deep midwinter it is at its finest with the foliage like a spearhead and veined with silver to catch the light.

Right now the arum is king and a delight for being the foil to winter companions. Slip it among winter-flowering Algerian iris and *Cyclamen coum* and drift it through evergreen ground cover to lift the coppery tones of *Tellima grandiflora* 'Purpurea' or use it to provide flux among the sombre fronds of *Polystichum setiferum*. A solitary leaf, picked for the table, will support a sprig of witch hazel or honeysuckle. It will also enliven a drift of snowdrops in a gloomy corner and remind you that, in combination, one makes the other stronger.

When I plan winter corners that are connected, I see the combination as a layering exercise. Most of the best plant combinations are one thing juxtaposed with something that shares the same requirements or provides for its partner. The space under a shrub is valuable, the shrub providing cover, the understorey support in a dull moment. Ground cover in turn is the foil against which emerging bulbs can be placed. Winter-flowering honeysuckle is lovely when its scented creamy flowers spangle bare branches, but it's a dull thing in summer and all the better for an evergreen *Epimedium* × *versicolor* 'Sulphureum' at its feet.

Close by, the textured foliage of *Viburnum davidii* might provide the contrast of a change in leaf scale and the benefit of blue berries. Team it up with early-flowering Tenby daffodils. The shady places are often the areas where winter performers do best.

Ground cover is also a way of connecting spaces in winter, a sweep of the winter-flowering *Vinca difformis* moving easily in the areas that remain overshadowed in the summer, yet drawing the eye in winter to pools of other plants that emerge to puncture this layer. *Helleborus foetidus*, with dark-fingered foliage and lime-green bells, and evergreen *Iris foetidissima*, with its rupturing seedpods exposing the tangerine seeds, will provide colour, textural relief and contrast.

Winter may be a long season, but you could never say that it is one that is lacking in interest.

20 January, *Tokyo*

QUEEN CAMELLIA

———

Recently I made a visit to monitor progress with my commissions in Japan. I am working on an eight-hectare project in western Tokyo where the developers are building a 'garden city'. The land has an interesting history, and when I first saw it two years ago, it was being used as a sports ground. It is an extraordinary thing for this much ground to have survived as open space in a city where space is the ultimate luxury, but here it was, a vast green expanse of beautifully maintained pitches and running tracks ringed with giant *Zelkova* and established shrubberies. The developers showed me images taken just a hundred years ago, when Japan had a very different economy. A scruffy stream ran alongside little paddy fields, but in the twenties, once Tokyo started to develop at a pace, the landowners built an ocean liner of a lido and sent someone to Wisley to study the plants to make a collection befitting a burgeoning interest in the West.

As a Wisley boy, it was fitting I should be asked to help to move the land on into the next chapter, and we spent some time looking over the plant material that could be reused. Vast *Kalmias*, complete with their 1929 labels, rhododendrons and giant cherries were all to be moved, and it was my job to decide how they could be reintegrated so that the feeling of maturity could be retained in the garden city.

It is a rare thing to work with developers who see the value in greenery, and rarer still to see so many specimens prepared for new homes rather than simply replaced. Some of the fully mature cherries had already been reduced to thin their crowns in readiness to be moved. The roots were severed at a safe distance and then the root balls wrapped in hessian and rope to hold them in one piece. These sculptural wrappings were far too beautiful to be covered over again, but the trenches were backfilled for a year to encourage the hair roots needed for the specimens to be moved successfully.

The development has moved on considerably in the past year and most of the trees have now been transported to their new positions, but this time I was to choose new trees which will complement the old and help us to establish a series of forested courtyards that will nestle the buildings into the site.

We set out early in immaculate vans, with a small army of businessmen and a boot-full of pristine white wellingtons, to walk the nurseries that lie on the outskirts of Tokyo. The nursery visits are one of the favourite aspects of my job, and I will never tire of walking the rows to select the right specimen for a chosen position. Each tree has its own character that can be matched to a chosen position: a branch that will lean over the door into the spring courtyard; a group that will work perfectly together to provide dappled shade elsewhere. It is as if they are waiting for you, and it is just a case of taking the time to find the right plant.

On our final day we retreated into an old farm building in the middle of a field of magnolias for lunch. It is customary that the clients are treated to a meal, and a feast of autumn vegetables and mushrooms had been prepared for grilling in the fire pit that formed the centre of the sit-down table. Hot sake was produced in utensils that had been made that morning from giant bamboo stems. It was a vivid moment, and before long we stumbled out into the dimming light to see the last of our selections.

It was then, on the way through a grove of Japanese umbrella pines, that I chanced upon the surprise that until that point had eluded me. And there it was in the gloom, a white, autumn-blooming *Camellia sasanqua*. Its delicate branches had formed a perfect dome four metres high and swept down to knee height to fan out as if it was doing a curtsy. Each leaf, a slim twist of the darkest, most lustrous green, reflected what light there was left in the afternoon, and along its branches was the peppering of flower. Pale and pure glistening white, the five-petalled blooms flared informally away from a golden boss of stamens. Where most camellias look like they have been cut from cloth and fashioned by a dressmaker, these were informal and light on the bush. There were buds and fully blown flowers spotting the branches, and under the tree in a perfect circle, like an inverted halo, was a luminous ring of fallen flower. I pointed out this diversion, and we stood around in a ring and marvelled at its beauty.

C. sasanqua is a relatively new plant for me and one that came to my attention a few years back when Stuart Barfoot, the head gardener at the 'Italian Job' – a project I continue to work on near Ninfa – bought some for pots up by the house. They had charmed him because they bloom in the very first part of the winter, and ahead of their spring-blooming cousins by a good three months. This is valuable stuff in a garden, when many of us are beginning to feel the impact of losing the autumn colour, so I made it my mission to find out more. The reason, it transpired, that they are rare in this country is that they are less hardy and need the warmth of an urban microclimate or the shelter of a frost-free conservatory to thrive. A prolonged frost will see them defoliate and in time weaken and die. Interestingly, and unlike the spring-blooming *C. japonica*, which likes a cooler position, they also prefer some sun, which is necessary to form their flowers.

Stuart had tested them to the limit in southern Italy, where it gets unbearably hot in the summer months, and found that they thrived in pots if he moved them into the shade once the heat got into the sun. They can be grown in pots here as well, left out like citrus in the summer months and brought into a cool conservatory for the winter, or at least up by the shelter of a house. Great news, too, if you have an alkaline soil, but in London, and in many of the warmer counties, they are perfectly happy out in the open. There are some fine plants in the shelter of other trees in the woodland garden at Wisley, so I suspect that it is simply that they have not been put to the test as yet.

Most forms that you find in this country are pink or dusky red. I am trying 'Hugh Evans' with winter-flowering cherry in Guernsey. It is a soft, single flower, rose-pink. We are also trying the darker rose 'Hiryu' there. They are slender in stature and I have great hopes for them as a backdrop to a small woodland garden, where they will fill a slot at the end of the year, and in a mild year last long enough to welcome in the new one. But I have a pot I have to fill for home in which I am hankering for the pure white form that I saw in Japan. I think it is *C. sasanqua* 'Narumigata'. It will be kept with the hamamelis at the end of the garden and brought down to the terrace once the autumn foliage is down on the camellia. I brought one of the sake jugs home for just this moment.

22 January, *Hillside*
RISING FROM THE ASHES

———

The Tump is the roundest, plumpest field on the farm. It forms the horizon line from the house, but when you mount it the views open up both up and down the valley. There is a solitary ash that sits off to one side in splendid isolation. The old man who lived here before us pollarded the tree in the year he died, and now we have the growth that came after his demise. From the lower slopes the pollard takes the form of a limbless lady standing her ground and looking out.

This is our oldest and finest tree, and it represents a long line of self-sufficiency. It is traditional in the area for ash to be allowed to grow up in the hedges and you would have a number of hedges on your land to provide you with pollards. This way the fields could be kept open, the shade falling in the hedge lines and the grass left free of competition. Leaving the trees for a decade between pollarding allows them time to replenish their resources. By that time the limbs are the perfect size for dropping and logging, and as ash is one of the few woods that burns green, it is a valuable piece of the puzzle.

When you get your eye in, you can see the history in the pollards as they become increasingly gnarly. They stagger up the valley like an army of old ladies, and though you might not think it when you see how they age, pollarding extends the life of a tree considerably. Many have rotted so that they are hollow within, creating habitats for wildlife. Bats and sometimes owls make their homes there, while the gaps between the toes of their twisted roots provide the perfect spot for burrows.

As part of the plan for the farm, we are looking at how we might provide ourselves with fuel. We have eight hectares, and although I do not want to change the character of the landscape too dramatically, a proportion of the land should provide us with firewood.

The pollards are the answer, and I am keen that we keep up the tradition, while also restoring our rundown farm to productivity. I like the idea, too, that a whole new generation of ladies can grace the slopes.

We made a start once the leaves came down before Christmas. A friend with a chainsaw and arboricultural experience came to help, and a second tree was reduced back to a crown above the grazing height of the cattle. It was a tree that had been left for some time, but it was good to keep up the rotation. Elsewhere we have singled out the ash saplings that can become future hedge trees in the hedge lines. They were tagged before the hedges were cut, and I'm estimating that they will be ready to pollard in under a decade.

Ash seed is wind-blown, with wings to carry it a distance away from the parent, and as it is a pioneer by nature, it is the first tree to punch through cracks or a forgotten patch where the brambles grow.

Though you might not want to introduce our native *Fraxinus excelsior* into the confines of a garden setting, the family offers a good range of adaptable cousins. In the main these are fast-growing. They are late to leaf, allowing you light underneath for woodlanders and their shade is never too dense. I use two species with regularity. The southern European *Fraxinus ornus* is a tree you are more likely to find in France and northern Italy and, for those who know the landscape painters of the eighteenth century, it is surely the tree you see arching from cliffs and overhanging a ruin. Loose-limbed and flowering in early summer, it sports a plumage of creamy, sweetly scented panicles.

It has pretty autumn colour, too, but not as good as the American *Fraxinus americana*. This is a delightful species with a myriad of tiny leaves that move like shoals of fish in the breeze. 'Raywood' is a fine selection – never too big, but substantial enough to sit under, and colouring deeply with plum and an undercurrent of hotter embers. I can see it here, within the confines of the garden-to-be, nodding respectfully to its cousin on the hill.

25 January, *Peckham*
HEART IN HAND

———

My old friend Geraldine slipped away on the winter solstice. She was ninety-six and due to turn ninety-seven this month. It seemed entirely fitting that she chose to die on the shortest day of the year, as she was the person who had introduced me to the natural world, and through it we maintained a friendship that lasted the best part of forty years.

Geraldine was one of those people who enters your life to open a door. In her case it was a door that was as real as it was metaphorical, and it was always left ajar. She lived just a few houses down our lane and I was welcome to make my way through the garage, where there was an entrance into her garden. She was a naturalist to the core and combined her love of the natural world with an idiosyncratic way of gardening that was free and uninhibited. A small lawn outside the back door provided room for a bird table and a deckchair in which she was often to be found reading, but beyond this semblance of order was a world that to a small boy was filled with treasures.

My trips over there were frequent, and when I was five I would spend hours peering into her pond, fascinated by the life that teemed within the crudely assembled plastic liner. Geraldine was never precious – her paths were made from cinders and she embraced weeds. The fruit cage trapped as many blackbirds as it kept away, and if the lolloping vegetable patch looked a shambles, the object of the exercise was always beauty or pleasure. She had her own fruit and veg in the pantry, a chest of dangerously volatile elderflower 'champagne' and the luxury of peaches in a good summer.

She had the knack of combining plants that would be happy in each other's company. *Nerine* against the hot wall with Algerian iris; wild poppies and annual *Adonis* with *Eschscholzia californica*, and electric-blue *Anchusa* and *Fritillaria pyrenaica* (smuggled from one of her many trips to the mountains of Europe in the back of her Morris) never happier than in the grass that sprang up in the rockery. Though Geraldine's plants were not conventionally grown – she had her own pruning style and never bothered if a plant got moth-eaten along the way – she understood how to get the best out of them.

Every day of the year there would be a posy to greet you on the kitchen table. Pushed at random into a little pot or suitable utensil, the posy would be there come rain or shine, and in it there was the reward of adventure, the fruit of labour or the chance happening of something one of her many birds had brought to the garden. In this posy were mapped the weeks of the year. A sprig of *Hamamelis* and *Galanthus* in January, or a tuft of old man's beard and rosehips come the autumn. Her posies were the garden distilled in a jam jar, and often she would pluck a sprig that you might admire from the assemblage and push it into your hand as the makings of a cutting. She shared her gardening well, and to this day I try to keep a posy from my own garden.

The posy is not something you should think about too much in its construction, for it is more the act of pulling things together for closer observation that is the objective. Christopher Lloyd talked about bringing what you are writing about up close. I do the same at the beginning of my writing days, gathering my subject as a means of gathering my thoughts and then having it right in front of me to keep me on the spot and in focus. It is amazing, too, when you look into the detail, how much more you might notice than you do in passing outside – the way a flower is put together and how it sits on the stem, or a perfume that up close yields just enough to add another layer of interest. You can witness the passage of bud from opening to demise, see how the colour is infused and then diluted, or in some cases intensified by ageing. The seed and the berries and even the skeletons, come the winter, are of just as much interest.

The posy is also a means of throwing up surprising combinations of plants that are separated in the garden but sit just right in the pot. When the growing season is in motion – and it won't be long now, because it is already easier to gather a collection rather than individual specimens – the unexpected also comes together. You might suddenly find that the magenta *Cyclamen coum* is the perfect partner to the rust-orange *Hamamelis* 'Jelena', or that the *Crocus* 'Ladykiller' are hard to better than with the first of the violets. I have moved many plants around the garden through discoveries such as these coming together on the kitchen table.

On the morning that my mother called me to give me the news that Geraldine had not survived the night, I looked into the front garden to find the first of the *Iris unguicularis* 'Mary Bernard'. Their violet flowers are darker than the sky-blue 'Walter Butt' that Geraldine grew. I remember she used to pick them in bud and then watch them open inside in the heat. This is something that happens in minutes when the buds are ready, the falls springing back to reveal the finely penned interior. Often the smallest of gifts is the most enduring.

FEBRUARY

Despite its actual length, February can feel like the longest month of the winter, caught between the openness of January and the surge that becomes evident in March. To pine for signs of life is not a bad thing and planning ahead in autumn is always time well spent. Winter would not be quite the same without pots of early bulbs to steal a march on the season. A pot of *Iris reticulata*, pushed on a little in the cold frame, and then brought into the warmth of the house to enjoy up close, is a reminder that life is just around the corner.

It is important to get out there, and with this in mind I have begun a snowdrop trail, which is designed to light up this moment. Since first writing about the idea when we moved to Somerset, I have extended it yearly in a ribbon that is now snaking up the lane and way out beyond the comfort and confines of the garden. It is already showing enough to entice my neighbours, who have offered splits of their own plants to unravel it further, and has become something quietly shared with the community.

Making room for the winter garden is every bit as important as managing a garden for summer, and I have learned to accommodate the plants that draw your attention in the dark months. *Cornus mas*, for instance, with its cloud of acid-yellow flower, or creamy hazel catkins, both lighten up the gloom. The scarcity of winter flowers can lead to obsession, and it is hard to imagine that the Lenten roses would provide such diversion in another season. Every year my own collection grows and with it the excitement of the first flowering of seedlings that have self-sown here in Somerset.

But all at once February is over and the industry of winter gardening already fills the daylight hours. It is time to shape and mould the fruit trees for the future, prune out the dead and the diseased, and plan for fruit and flower. There are wisterias to untangle, seeds to order for the summer garden, and a list of things to split and acquire and improve upon in the months to come.

2 February, *Hillside*

UP WITH THE EARLY RISERS

———

When the January snow slowly eased its grip, slumping off the cold frame, pulling away from the molehills and the banks, an altered landscape was there to greet us. The changes were tiny – angelica skeletons pushed to an angle and long grass flattened

– but there were signs of activity, too. I had looked for the snow-drops beforehand and found nothing, but here they were, the first flowers tilting free of their foliage. One day I would like to have the common-or-garden snowdrop not just close up by the house in clumps but in ribbons of early life in the hedgerows. It's a project I began last year: in time, the trail will mark a snowdrop walk which will leapfrog from hedge to ditch to watercourse, to move us out of the comfort of the house.

Early bulbs remind us that, in this country, the dormant season is more a perception than it is a reality. In all but the coldest snap there is usually something stirring and with this in mind I have earmarked a sunny bank behind the house for some early risers. Though they are still small, my *Cornus mas* are showing promise. Tight buds, wide and sculpted with a pointed hat, looked expectant over Christmas and showed some colour against the snow, then broke with the thaw to bloom with the snowdrops. The flowers, which are tiny, are a mass of acid-yellow stamens, but en masse the bush is bright and alive.

I bought a handful of *Galanthus* varieties after visiting the Snowdrop Theatre at the Chelsea Physic Garden a few years ago. I'd been inspired by witnessing them up close, displayed against black velvet so that you could see the detail in the flower. Although I loved the experience, galanthophilia is a condition I'm not keen to contract and I remain a firm believer that you need to be able to spot the difference between one snowdrop and another while standing up.

I am gradually adding to a small collection: 'Atkinsii' is one of the first, with tall stems and good vigour. 'Magnet' has similar qualities, the length of the pedicels allowing the flowers to dance in the breeze and it's that movement as much as anything that is distinctive. I also have a couple of good unnamed doubles that will be placed close to the path so that their flowers can be upturned to examine their green-rimmed petticoats.

I always grow a few of the early-flowering *Iris reticulata* in pots as they are easy and dependable. Growing them in pots allows you to bring them into the house where, if you get the timing right, you can actually witness the flowers popping open from a tightly speared bud. They will last for a few days in the artificial heat and you can get up close to take in their perfume and exquisite colouring. In a cool room, an unheated conservatory or on an outdoor windowsill you can savour them for a week or two. I have learned over the years not to put too many in a pot so that you can reflect upon their beautifully drawn lines and colouring. Out in the ground, *Iris reticulata* and *Iris histrioides* tend to be short-lived, but planting them deep and in a free-draining position helps prolong their lives – by deep I mean at least the length of a pencil. Planted in grass, as they will be on my bulb bank, they should be up and out with the first of the primroses, and certainly with the violets.

When content with their surroundings, *Anemone blanda* and *Crocus tommasinianus* seed themselves freely and begin to move about where they like the lie of the land. Both are happy planted in dappled shade, but they prefer somewhere that lights up their flowers with sunshine. I like them combined, the tall-necked crocus rising up above the starry anemone. On a dull day they will wear the deeper colouring on the reverse of the petals – violet on the reverse of *Anemone* 'White Splendour', and soft lavender on the reverse of the crocus. Sunshine will see them blink open, winking bright centres and coloured pollen to make you pleased that you braved the elements.

5 February, *Bath*
MAGNIFICENT OBSESSION

———

In the last week of January I caught up with an old friend in Bath who is working a twenty-five-hectare farm in the steeply sloping valleys outside the city. We set out into the muddy fields not long after letting the horses out, cracking our way through the ice that had formed in the muddy depressions around the field. The light was silvery-grey and the morning was still, in contrast to the wild week before. There was evidence of the storms as we picked our way along the dark hedgerow to the top of the field: branches and dead wood cast a shadow of litter, tracing the direction of the gales, and on the brow of the hill whole trees had been ripped from the hedgerow.

The aim of our walk was to find the green hellebores that grew in the woods. It had been mild until this cold snap and we were sure there might be signs they were stirring. On our way up the hill the cowslips were already forming their rosettes in readiness, and nearby were the first shoots of the bee orchids. On the edge of the woodland, under a canopy dripping with hazel catkins, the first primroses were already in flower. Pure and pale, but luminous in the milky light, they marked the transition from open ground to woodland.

The land on the northern slope of the hill was far too steep to farm, and many hundreds of years ago it had been put down to hazel coppice, with old oaks left as canopy trees and for their long-term timber. The precipitous slope and the slew of long-fallen branches meant no one had been into the coppice for decades. Moss had colonised everything that had stayed still for long enough, and the first shoots of dog's mercury confirmed the ground had been this way for a long time.

To start, there was little more to see than the first of the wild arum and celandine foliage but, just above the spring line, where limestone shale meets clay, we came upon the first leaves of the hellebores. The first we saw, nestled into the mossy crevices of a fallen branch, could not have been arranged more artfully, but as our eyes became accustomed to the search a seam of hellebores revealed itself, running down the hillside. A few were showing bud, exactly the same shade of pale green as the foliage, and we rearranged ourselves lower down the slope so we could see into those that had already opened. When we tilted the lantern up they revealed a boss of creamy anthers and a tiny stain of red at the base. In another month their subtlety will be eclipsed by the growth of the dog's mercury, wild garlic and bluebell foliage, but for now they were queen of the woods, and an indicator that winter was beginning to loosen its grip.

Markers are important in the year, which is one reason why I have always grown hellebores. As Christopher Lloyd once said, they are the stuff of obsession. They make the first RHS shows at Vincent Square in London worth going to, and it is almost impossible to leave empty-handed. They are one of the first perennials to show life, and as soon as there are enough flowers to pick, I float them in a bowl on the kitchen table, face up, to see them as you never do out in the cold.

You might struggle to grow the lime-loving *Helleborus viridis* if your conditions are not to their liking, but there are others far less choosy. *H. foetidus*, the stinking hellebore (which never stinks to the point of it being a problem, but has a musky odour), is another plant you might find wild in this country, although it is always confined to chalk land. I have seen it in the mountains of northern Spain, where it grows in limestone shale among scrub of broom and myrtle, forming the perfect foil for miniature *Narcissus*. In a garden setting here, it prefers it on the cool side, but it is just as happy out in the open, and I have grown it on acid sand, heavy clay and in most places as long as the soil doesn't lie wet in the winter. It is one of my favourite winter evergreens, forming a solitary trunk in its first year and a great splay of many divided, lustrous, dark-green leaves.

At some point in the early winter of its second year the centre of the ruff fattens and arches over, and the great spray of flower begins to emerge. By the end of January it will have produced the first of several hundred green bells. They are fertilised by the bees and form bladder-shaped pods that, if left on the plant, scatter enough seed for a rash of seedlings come the autumn. This great performance can seriously weaken the plant, so at the end of March I cut out the whole stem to the shoots forming at the base to give the plant a chance to recover for the summer. Even with this treatment, this species is only at its best for the first four or five years and then needs replacing. 'Wester Flisk' is a form that has a just-red rim to each bell and a slightly blue cast to the foliage.

H. argutifolius, the Corsican hellebore, is very similar in habit, but this is a hellebore that really prefers to be out in the open. It is a longer-lived and more spectacular plant than the stinking hellebore – the old stems fall out in a great cartwheel at flowering and wither away in early summer if allowed to seed. The growth is often as much as a metre across, the large green bells in clusters at the end of the stems, but some time in late spring, after you have enjoyed it with other Mediterraneans, such as *Euphorbia characias* and pedunculate lavenders, last year's flowering stems should be cut to the base to make way for new growth. In six weeks or so it will be back, fresh and lovely, as a foil for summer plants.

The Christmas rose, *H. niger*, is another hellebore that really likes it out in the open, but in my experience it is a fussy thing – it either likes you and thrives or hates life and sulks. It rarely flowers at Christmas and its pure white flowers are best if protected by a cloche to prevent winter damage. The hybrid with the Corsican hellebore, *H. × nigercors*, is reportedly a fine plant and much more reliable. I have no experience of this plant in my own garden, but have it on my list to grow one day.

I expect that 'the stuff of obsession' refers to *H. × hybridus*. Formerly known as *H. orientalis*, they are a little later than *H. niger*, blooming usually in February and into March. With the mild weather, they have been in flower in my garden in London since the turn of the year, the buds pushing up from a rosette of coarse foliage. The splay of leaf is larger than you might think, forming a mass easily 60 cm across when the plants mature. They are also incredibly long-lived, though hating disturbance, but being more than happy in most conditions, as long as they don't get too much sun in high summer. Black spot can be a problem. The affected foliage should be removed and burnt in late autumn and mulching kept away from the leaf bases to keep the plant airy.

There are seductive selections of Lenten roses and, interestingly, they are now sold mostly in colour ranges, as they cross-pollinate so freely. Each plant within a range is slightly different. Slate-grey hybrids are just that, and they move through plum reds to pink to pure white. I have restricted myself to the best of the spotted forms and the picotee whites, which have a blood-rose stain to the petal edges. I also have some green forms with grey-green spots within. I interplant my darkest plum forms with white snowdrops, as they easily get lost against the dark soil. My dilemma this year is I'd really like to try the primrose-yellow hybrids. I want to trial a few in readiness for a planting that will combine them with primroses and celandine under hazel. Obsessed? Yes, I freely admit it.

7 February, *Peckham*
WHITE MAGIC

––––––––

It all came at once this winter. Rain dashed the autumn in what seemed like an endless deluge of five or six weeks. The tulips remained in the shed, their plumpness a little less so each week I looked in on them. One weekend after the next it was wet, too wet to garden, until one Sunday in early December the skies cleared enough to get out there and finally trowel in the tulips among the toppled persicarias. Though the garden had been crumpled by rain-laden gales the nasturtiums rallied, until one day in the middle of the month the temperature plummeted. The sky was clear by the time I got home from work, the garden already glistening with frost.

The next day, things looked wretched and, as the sky darkened, a fine dusting of snow settled upon the wreckage of the night before. I went outside, because there were Christmas trees in the windows and it is a rare thing to see them in tandem with the real stuff on the ground. Of course it didn't last long, and as I was putting the tulips that the squirrels had thrown up to the surface back in the ground, I had that usual feeling of loss. Loss of a growing season, the threat of the bulk of the winter ahead, and the unnerving question that I always ask myself at this time of year: what is it all for, and why do we push against the natural order of things in our efforts to garden? I know by now from having done it for the greater part of my life that this is a recurring theme, and I rootled around instinctively in search of the snowdrops. Sure enough, there they were, their hardened tips spearing frost and now-dirty snow. My mood lifted in an instant.

A month on and despite the freeze the snowdrops at the front of the house are up and readying themselves to flower. Certain plants are there for a reason: bluebells to light up wood-land with just-sprung green; night-scented stock for those few heady nights in summer, and apples and sunflowers to remind us that it has been a good year, a full one with rewards in their plenty. The snowdrops indicate that the earth is turning, turning towards a new growing season, even though it feels like there are weeks to go yet. Pushing decisively from the leaf mould, they will light up any dark woodland where they have colonised and claim a moment in deepest winter as their own.

The thought of winter blues was very much in mind when I chose the early flowering *Galanthus* 'S. Arnott' for a position just an arm's length from the basement window. From the warmth of the kitchen I can chart their every movement: the first spears pushing up among the cyclamen foliage and the partially formed flowers developing as they ascend. Until meeting 'S. Arnott', I had never understood the galanthophiles' obsession with this humble winter flower. Snowdrops, it seemed to my uninitiated eye, came in just a handful of species, and the differences between the varieties were so minute that I was happy to leave those to the collectors. But the Snowdrop Theatre revealed something different, with its dark, velvety interior and ranks of shelving to show the plants to their best. And though I vowed not to join the obsessives, I must admit to having begun a small collection.

'S. Arnott' is easily identifiable among the crowd, growing larger than most and holding its flowers on wire-thin stems that arch to set each bloom into its own space. The first few days of flower see the drops hanging heavy, but a sunny day will trigger the petals to open, where they are held wide, in the equivalent of an early morning stretch. Everything is that tiny bit larger, more slender and elegant than a common hedgerow snowdrop, and this is why the bulbs will cost you. A stand selling the early varieties at an RHS show in Vincent Square will shock you, with as much as £25 a bulb charged for some varieties that are slow to increase. I have resisted such temptation because I like my snowdrops in abundance, and so far I have dabbled only with varieties that are obviously going to be 'doers'.

'Magnet' is one of the largest, growing to almost 30 cm tall but losing none of the essential delicacy. 'Galatea' seems to be one of the strongest, and a single bulb sent to me by a friend a couple of years ago is already showing athletic potential. I have three or four other selections held in pots so that I can bring them up close to the house. 'Wendy's Gold' has an almost yellow rim to the inner hoop and there is a good form of the double, old-fashioned 'Flore Pleno'. Turn the flower up and it will reveal whirls of petticoats.

I keep my pot-grown *Galanthus* in a cool position while they are dormant, to keep the bulbs moist in summer. Their fast and early season means that they are adaptable bulbs otherwise, growing quite happily under deciduous plants and among perennials. Moisture while they are growing is key, and they are best moved and divided immediately after flowering 'in the green' to get the best results. To have them drifting through the garden is the ideal, so each time you divide, pull the clumps apart to replant five or six bulbs in each position. So much to give for so little effort, and an ally against the winter blues if ever there was one.

A SMALL GREEN PARADISE

———

Our studio in Waterloo was the nursery to a Victorian school and when we took it on in 2009 we made the changes we needed to make it our own. As garden-makers, it felt imperative for us to have a green space, and the garden is already proving its worth as an oasis. The roar of buses on the other side of the wall is rapidly diminished once you step inside – not so much by the rustle of foliage but because you feel 'recalibrated' by the greenery. By the time you get to our front door you are already a chapter away from the bustle of London.

The garden is not large, running 12 m in length along the north side of a tall wall. The wall protects us from the busy Westminster Bridge Road and the garden is wedged between it and the school building. The garden was not a thing of beauty when we arrived. A poured play surface surrounded a stunted cherry tree, and where the play surface was peeling at the edges the buddleia had taken hold. There was no soil, and when we pulled up the rubbery covering there were signs of an old building which had been demolished. An ugly fence wrapped the two remaining sides.

Despite the challenge, the sun pours in over the wall to split the garden in two. I like this opportunity, for it gives us a range of conditions to play with. After removing the old cherry, we put a generously sized terrace in the wider end of the wedge. This provides room for a table and chairs in the sunshine. Against the hot wall of the school we placed three oversized planters containing *Thamnochortus insignis* – a South African sedge to harness the wind, and minty pelargoniums to brush past on the way to the front door. The thinning end of the wedge was split with a path that wends its way to the bicycle racks and a tiny terrace under the dappling of *Cornus* 'Gloria Birkett', which provide privacy.

We made three big investments to make the best of the space. First, the bed spaces were excavated to 45 cm, the rubble removed and backfilled with topsoil. Soil is the very foundation of a garden, and as I knew I wanted it to be heavily planted, good preparation was an imperative. Our second investment was in choosing a pale Jura limestone for the paving, which bounces the light back into the studio. Our third investment was to clad the ugly fence with a hardwood screen and add a tall garden gate that gives complete privacy and reveals the surprise once the door is opened.

Though I am not a fan of planting large trees, the cherry was replaced by a 4 m multi-stemmed katsura to avoid any sense of loss. It provided instant presence and set the tone with its soft green foliage. The tall wall has been clad with climbers to take the limited planting space on the ground up into the air. Scented *Trachelospermum jasminoides* are interwoven with *Fuchsia magellanica* 'Molinae', which has been trained as a wall shrub and flowers from April to December. Scarlet *Tropaeolum speciosum* enjoys the cool roots and the reach up into sunshine.

I wanted the garden to feel fresh year round, and the flashes of red are supported by *Jasminum* 'Clotted Cream' and primrose-yellow *Rosa chinensis* 'Yellow Mutabilis'. *Hakonechloa macra*

'Allgold' at ground level gives us the feeling of dappled sun in the shade of the katsura even on a grey day.

A water bowl provides dipping for the birds and is home to a yellow waterlily. The water is a focal point and its reflective surface brings the sky into the garden. The feeling of sanctuary works. The rub of scented pelargonium, the wind in the foliage and the feeling of being surrounded by green make this little garden feel like a world of its own and make our working days richer. Quite simply, we could not be without it.

10 February, *Hillside*
UP AGAINST THE WALL

———

Tight against the walls, life is beginning to stir. The *Euphorbia characias* are arching their tufted necks, the cluster of lime-green bells already visible. I planted a huddle of seedlings gathered from a particularly good form in a client's garden and this is their first year to flower. They are a sign that things are moving, and I am grateful, for just inches away it is still deep midwinter.

Walls are an asset, but there are few here that are plantable. My ladder from London, which I used to fear to roll out to its full height, is redundant, sailing over the gutters. I can pamper and enjoy the wintry forms of a couple of wall-trained pears which I will train out laterally, a tier a year, to either side of the door, and carefully between the windows. I have five pear trees already growing heartily in the new orchard, but the heat of these walls will suit a 'Beurre Hardy'. The flower will be there to greet early bees in the first warm sunshine and we will pick fruits warmed by the heat reflected back by the stone.

Bare stems neatly ordered against architecture are almost better naked than they are when clothed in summer. A fan-trained or espaliered apple will mark the artistry of the gardener in its branches. So will the twist of wisteria, stag-headed and gaunt, or the arch of a rambler rose ready ahead of the rest of the garden and a contrast to the disorder in the beds. Walls, whichever way they face, should be savoured, but not all walls are for planting. Some – and you are lucky if you have them – are just too pretty, with lichen marking time and providing more than enough interest. Others are too short and if they are to be planted need to be teamed with well-adapted winter jasmine or *Chaenomeles* and not a climber that will outstrip them to wave uncomfortably in the breeze.

My father grew a *Chaenomeles* on the cool wall of a big wooden shed. You passed it on the cut up through a hole in the hedge that connected us to the outside world. It was a pink named 'Apple Blossom' and it prevented that little corner from looking gloomy early in the year. The buds swelled in February, pale against the blackened wood of the shed. Blush to the outside, the flowers opened to reveal a boss of stamens within the pearly interior. In certain years the fruit from the previous season would appear in tandem, a quince by common name only and, as I later learned, a far inferior fruit to the true *Cydonia*.

Winter quince hail originally from south-east Asia, and in Japan the name for *Chaenomeles japonica* roughly translates as 'stupid plant' because of their gangly growth. Sure enough, as a free-standing shrub they appear not to know which way to grow, their branches crossing and re-crossing. But ordered and tied to wires they will make something of a cool east- or north-facing wall. Bring a branch into the house once you start to see the buds swelling and you can steal a march with the blossom opening weeks in advance. Grow *Chaenomeles* against a warmer wall and you can have them in flower by the end of the month.

I have planted a cool, north-facing wall with a nice range of *Chaenomeles* for picking. We have 'Crimson and Gold', the dark-ness of the petals throwing the yellow of the anthers into relief, and 'Nicoline', a brave orange-red. 'Nivalis', a white too vigorous for this setting, is replaced by the slower-growing 'Jetfire' and 'Lemon and Lime' for white and off-white respectively. The latter two plants are weaker by nature and appreciate the extra attention a wall gives them, for you need to treat wall shrubs well if they are to look the part.

Garrya elliptica is a shrub that suits wall training. Its evergreen growth has a blue-green cast and catkins that are at their best in January and February. 'James Roof' is the best form, with the longest catkins. A summer-flowering *Clematis* at the base of the *Garrya* will ascend from tight pruning to add another layer of flower when winter is gone.

THE GIVING TREE

———

There are a handful of hazel trees down by the stream in the shade of the neighbouring copse and I have just gathered a bunch of catkins to remind me that spring is on the way. Hazel is one of my favourite British trees, its catkins already formed by the end of the year and lengthening now to provide us with one of the first signs of movement. The branches are arching over the water, the creamy catkins hanging almost vertically once they are elongated and producing pollen.

When we were first looking at the property, I noticed that they were the ideal host to Herb Paris, ferns, wild garlic and bluebells, but they are a well-behaved tree in a domestic setting, too, modestly proportioned and easily curtailed if they over-reach themselves. Their roots are non-invasive, so they also associate well with other woodlanders, such as epimedium, hellebore and snowdrop, and once they are in leaf their foliage is soft, cool on the eye and light enough to dapple shadow.

Though it is hugely tolerant of a wide range of conditions, hazel is a woodlander by nature, favouring the cool, moist atmosphere where ferns and mosses grow. Plant a hazel in open ground and it will sulk for five years before it gains enough reserve in the root to start increasing its canopy, but in the company of other trees its limbs will grow long and slender, several dozen from the base. Their willingness to multi-stem is why they make such excellent trees for coppicing and why for the best part of a thousand years they have driven an industry of woodsmen here in the British Isles. Cut to the base on an eight-to ten-year rotation, the 'rods' can be split for poles for hurdle-making and the brushwood has multiple uses too, for besoms, faggots and pea sticks.

For the most pliable wood, and to save the energy in the bowl of the tree for re-growth, it is best to coppice hazel in the first half of the winter. The cuts are made low and close to the ground to encourage growth to push up and away straight from the base and where there are deer or rabbits or livestock, the re-growth can be covered with a 'dead hedge' of offcuts so the new stems are protected. In the right conditions these will make almost two metres in the first year to rise out of harm's way and replenish the roots with energy.

I could count my own hazel trees on one hand, but I would like to have several dozen so that I can coppice four or five a year on a rotation to keep me in poles for my beans, twigs for the peas and kindling to light the fires. I have earmarked a section of one of the lower fields that feels like it might be a good place to start, for it is sheltered and already in the influence of the neighbouring woodland, and I am already looking forward to clearing this area of bramble so that I can set them out come next autumn.

Up on the sunny slopes I will also be sure to include a few to feather the garden-to-be seamlessly into the hedgerows, but I will be tempted to include *Corylus avellana* 'Purpurea', the purple filbert, as the catkins are stained darkly with smoky-pink. The newly emerging foliage is as dark as damsons and ruby red with the light through it later in the season. It is also a more elegant option than the more usually offered *C. maxima*

'Purpurea', as there is space in the branches, which makes the general impression of darkness appear lighter.

Hazel rarely seems out of season, its cool summer foliage giving way to hazelnuts, which are clearly visible by August, but you will have to be vigilant if you are to get there before the squirrels in September. The fruit ripens before the foliage turns a buttery yellow, and if you do manage to fill a bowlful before they are poached, you will notice how very different the nuts are to shop-bought fruits. They are wet and milky, gently sweet, and wonderful raw as a crunch in a peppery watercress salad.

It is hard to see why this humble native isn't better integrated into our lives, but after all these years of admiring them from a distance, I feel a lightness at being able to live with them up close. I have coppiced my first tree to set the cycle in place, hauling the wood away to be divvied up into its various uses, and I cannot tell you how good it feels to plan them into my future.

14 February, *Peckham*
ROOM TO BLOOM

———

This year I am planning two cutting gardens for clients. The first and smaller of the two is to be planted this month; the second is being built this winter, with the aim to have it up and running for annuals by the summer. In many ways a cutting garden is an extravagant idea, because cutting flowers is the most luxurious way of enjoying them at close quarters, but I have no intention of either of these gardens feeling like an indulgence. They will be workmanlike and take their aesthetic from the vegetable garden or the allotment. You should be able to harvest flowers as you would a row of beans, and leave with an armful – and not the slightest twinge of guilt.

A friend and fellow designer in America has been making cutting gardens for some time, simply by fencing off an area from the garden proper. Within these vermin-proof enclosures, Edwina's vegetables, herbs and flowers are lined out in rows, with paths wide enough for a barrow to pass between them. The paths are mulched with pine needles in her own garden, as she has a wood of pine at the back, but it could just as easily be bark to keep things simple. Everything is reduced down to the most practical way of growing things: the tallest plants are at the back, so they don't put the shorter plants in the shade, and there is little regard for colour – if Edwina likes it, it works. Where most garden owners would never dream of trusting you with a pair of secateurs to pick a posy for the house, it is a different thing for Edwina, and it is standard practice to be issued with a couple of buckets – one to fill with spuds and beans, the other with as many flowers as you see fit to liven up the table for lunch.

In planning my cutting gardens I have enjoyed a certain freedom, with plants that are not easily worked into the garden proper. Because as soon as you pick a flower and take it out of context, it becomes an object that you can look at for itself. Dahlias with stripes suddenly become an option – if the stripes don't work this year, then something else will next. Likewise, if you want to grow 'Blue Moon' roses for their scent and curiosity, then do so – a solitary flower will be a delight in a bedside jug.

Having a brief is important, because the cutting garden needs to work hard if it is to be truly productive. The larger the area is, the more relaxed you can be about plants that might bloom only once. Bearded iris can be enjoyed without having to worry about the remaining eleven months of the year, when they are doing little more than leaf. And if you have enough room for peonies, there's the creaminess of the 'Duchesse de Nemours', which, picked in bud, will rupture to perfume a room. In a decent-sized cutting garden, a whole row of once-blooming *Anchusa azurea* 'Loddon Royalist' can easily be accommodated as a luxury, but in the main the plants should be 'doers', and able to come again after they have been harvested.

Planning for a long season of flowers (or several seasons) is important, so I am using modern English roses from David Austin to extend the season. I have chosen varieties that are disease-resistant, as we want to run the cutting gardens on organic principles because they are close to the fruit and vegetables, but I have been free with colour as long as there is scent. I am also intercropping, using lines of *Alchemilla* under the roses, as lady's mantle is a good filler in a vase.

The rest of the perennials are set out in rows one metre apart. Within the rows they are planted in a double line, 30 cm apart, and the gaps between the main rows are planted with bulbs, so you can fill a jug with tulips and not hold back – or worry that they might not come back a second year. The tulips can be dug out after they have flowered and replaced with annuals – *Scabiosa atropurpurea* 'Chile Black', wild gloriosa daisies (*Rudbeckia hirta*) and mixed cosmos where a mix would never do in the flowerbeds. Whereas the perennials might take a couple of years to come to cropping well, the annuals will provide for you in a matter of months.

The smaller of our two cutting gardens is in the country, so I have decided to go two ways with the brief. The first is to use highly ornamental flowers that are in contrast to the rest of the garden, which feathers to hedgerow. There are lilies in rows that can easily be picked over for lily beetle, blowsy chrysanthemums and dahlias for the autumn. In contrast, the second route is to use plants that have a super-nature quality about them: vivid thistles such as *Eryngium* 'Electric Haze' and *Cirsium rivulare* 'Atropurpureum', and the peachy-flowered recurrent *Geum* 'Princess Juliana' to work in among a bundle of native grasses or cow parsley. There will be giant daisies such as *Leucanthemum* 'T. E. Killin', larger-than-life *Scabiosa caucasica* 'Blausiegel' and rows of Michaelmas daisies so that you can fill a room with them come the autumn.

It is an exciting prospect planning a garden with freedom in mind – my very own trial ground and a place where gardening can break the usual rules.

15 February, Peckham

DOGWOOD DAYS

———

You need a lift in February when the winter takes its toll. So, with the backdrop of a yew hedge and behind that the red of a tile-hung house, I set out a garden with coloured-stemmed *Cornus* as its base.

Elsewhere in the garden we have the winter-flowering Cornelian cherry, *Cornus mas*, popping acid-green flowers. But the *Cornus* in the new planting were selected specifically for their stems. Coloured-stemmed varieties are often used in car parks, but don't hate them because of that. Grown well – and this is down to good pruning – they are easy and reliable garden plants. All they need is a sunny position and hearty soil. Removing a third of their growth to the base at the end of the winter will encourage the newest stems with the most brilliant colour.

Cornus alba 'Sibirica' is bright crimson but, en masse and in bright sun, it shines flamingo pink. I have combined it with the black-stemmed *Cornus alba* 'Kesselringii' to keep things smart. The stems of 'Kesselringii' are charcoal black. In their own way they are as dramatic as the red, but they need the right partner if they are not to be lost. I have grown them with white hellebores at their feet in the past and among straw-coloured grasses, such as *Stipa* 'Karl Foerster', to heighten their darkness. They also look wonderful against a pale wall or with the white of birch as a backdrop. Black and white in winter is always rather wonderful.

The lime green of *Cornus stolonifera* 'Flaviramea' is at the other end of the colour spectrum from 'Sibirica' but easily as intense. I would never put them together for fear of an almighty clash, but I would love to see the green with the black of 'Kesselringii'. You need lots of space to try these experiments and I still have this one up my sleeve, using the acid green of the *Cornus* with the brown and rust of chestnut-stemmed willows and sedges. *Salix daphnoides* 'Aglaia' and *Carex testacea* would look wonderful. The white-stemmed *Rubus thibetanus* 'Silver Fern' would also work well.

I am growing our native dogwood, *Cornus sanguinea*, as a shelter belt and in hedges where the ground is too wet for hawthorn. The winter stems are a rich mahogany brown. 'Midwinter Fire' is a fine selection, which channels its native vigour into an extraordinary blaze of orange stems tipped with coral to heighten the spectacle further.

Regular pruning is the key to promoting good colour. I like to wait until the end of winter when I see the buds just beginning to swell before stripping out a portion of the growth. Some books recommend coppicing to the ground every year, but I prefer to keep the structure and thin out the eldest stems by a third. A good feed after pruning and a mulch will encourage regrowth under the cover of summer greenery. As the leaves drop, the colourful stems flare just when you need them.

18 February, *Peckham*
MAKE IT SHARPISH

———

Two pairs of secateurs have just returned in the post. In an annual ritual, I release them from their bubblewrap to find the blades protected by tissue paper. When it is removed, new steel is revealed, smelling of oil and glistening like razors. This is a luxury that I look forward to every year, because I myself have never been able to sharpen them as keenly as I would like and, after a couple of years, I feel they have earned a good service. I have four pairs of Felco secateurs, though it is rare that they are ever all in the same place at any one moment. Spread between the car, a ledge in the kitchen and somewhere in the ever-evolving chaos that is the garage, the theory is that there is always a pair to hand and that at least one is sharp. I don't like to be out in the garden without them and my gardening jeans always have a hole in the back pocket as proof.

I never aim for my garden to look like it has been over-manicured, but I like good structure in a plant and to know that it has been well set up in life. No doubt this came from my Wisley training where, in the first three months of the two years I was there, I was sent out into the orchards. Firstly it was to harvest the apples, for the year started there in September, but as soon as the leaves fell we moved on to pruning.

Hayden Williams was our lugubrious foreman and he had an incredible knack of appearing from nowhere despite the fact that the orchard was laid out in a grid, so we worked hard and competitively, starting at the head of a row and slowly making our way through the 650 or so varieties. That was where we were taught about the importance of structure. My grandfather had alluded to it once on one of his trips down from Yorkshire. He was no gardener, and a gruff man at the best of times, but he stood at the base of our wayward trees at home and announced: 'You should be able to throw a cap between the branches!' At Wisley we learned how to encourage a tree to do what you wanted it to do for maximum yield, and we applied it not only to the apples but to the currants, soft fruit, figs, pears and fan-trained Morello cherries. We also learned about the importance of keeping your tools sharp so that the wood was never damaged by a cut. 'Never strain a cut with a tool that's not up to the job' was one of Hayden's mantras, so we would sharpen and oil our blades, starting with the pruning knife and moving through the secateurs, the nimble Grecian saw and then on to the loppers. To this day, I keep the same range of pruning equipment so that I am equipped for most situations.

On site, when planting up a garden, I take secateurs at the very least. They are used to prune whips to half their height to encourage branching and bushiness low down in a new hedge. New trees are laid out on the ground before they go in so that the branches and the structure can be examined, and trimmed, with ease. Damaged wood is removed and a leading shoot selected if the tree is to form a standard. Shaping up happens at this point in a multi-stemmed specimen or shrub so that crossing branches that might rub or become problematic later in life are removed.

Pruning is an enormous and complicated subject and it can strike the fear of God into an inexperienced gardener. Whether they are old hands or not, you can see a person's personality when they prune, and I would urge anyone who wants to learn to do so from someone experienced, as there is nothing like first-hand knowledge. It was Mrs P. at my Saturday gardening job who encouraged me to be confident and not to 'fiddle about'. She explained why you prune the flowering wood out of *Philadelphus* after blossoming in June to promote new wood for the next summer. She taught me some of the tricks and explained why you pruned *Philadelphus* 'Belle Etoile' that way for flower and why with *P. coronaria* 'Aureus' you sacrificed flower by pruning hard in winter to promote plenty of coloured foliage. You never forget if you have a mentor.

The key to pruning is only to do it if you have good reason. The three Ds are helpful. Dead, Diseased or Damaged wood are your first port of call. Knowing why you are doing it should be second. Are you wanting to encourage spur growth for fruiting, or are you after larger flowers or lush foliage? Some plants, such as the spring-flowering clematis, flower on last year's wood, most of the summer-flowering clematis on the same year's growth, so you need to know what you have got before you start chopping. Do you want to keep a plant within bounds and orderly? Honeysuckle and Virginia creeper, let alone ivy, will very quickly set about claiming your house by getting into the gutters. You might want to keep a hedge a certain size, but when is the best time to do that? Deciduous hedges need a cut after the first extension growth in high summer and then a tidy-up in winter, but evergreens are best pruned in spring and summer only, as they need their foliage when dormant.

If you prune hard, you will get a strong reaction if the plant is healthy, and you can end up with a plant just as big again in a season. So pruning lightly and regularly might help to maintain a better balance. Of course, hard pruning can be used to advantage with willow and *Cornus*, promoting good winter stem colour, but you will get better reactions if it is accompanied by a good mulch to compensate for lost growth. Basics underpin the art, as always.

I will start the winter pruning in February when things are at their most dormant. First are the *Clematis*, which this year are growing away far earlier than they should in the mild weather. Those that flower on the current season's wood such as *Clematis viticella* and the *C*. 'Jackmanii' types are pruned back hard to a bud at knee height. You need to get in before energy is lost, so I use the *Clematis* as the litmus test for the sap beginning to rise in the garden. Next are the vines, because they are prone to bleeding if you cut after the sap is moving. I have the strawberry grape (*Vitis vinifera* 'Fragola') on my brother's house nearby. We need to get that done first because it is on a south-facing wall, but my *V. coignetiae* can wait, since it is north-facing and is slower to get a move on. Both are pruned to within one bud of a framework that we have laced over the buildings, removing all last year's wood once the framework is the size it needs to be.

My wisteria is the job I save for a special day in February, and I savour every moment of making the slow progress over the back of the house. This was the first plant I put in the garden after moving here nine years ago and I have taken my time establishing a weave of limbs. Wisteria sets the flowering spurs that you need if the limbs that soar skyward in the summer are re-trained horizontally to create the main framework. When that is established, summer growth is cut back to eight buds in August and then to two buds now. The *Parthenocissus henryana* that is lacing itself through the wisteria is taken back from the roofline, the spent stems of the *Cobaea* pulled away to avoid congestion in the summer. By dusk, my secateurs will have lost their edge, but not before order is restored in readiness for the year ahead.

20 February, *The Studio*

CITY SQUARES

————

The little garden that is attached to my studio in Waterloo is contained on all sides by walls, which divide this tiny oasis from the rush of the Westminster Bridge Road. There are no views out, save the one up to a window of watery London sky. That said, it is a place that keeps us going and through it we can feel the seasonal changes. Grey skies and the hiss of wet roads matter less when the snowdrops are spearing the ground. We have two good selections – 'Magnet' and 'Galatea', as there is only room for the best – and some yellow hellebores picked by hand from the excellent selection at Ashwood Nursery in the Midlands.

I planned this garden to have something for every week of the year, but these first few signs of life are of particular importance. An evergreen layer forms the foundation and I have made a point of weighting the garden with foliage in the deepest moments of a British winter. Against the evergreen of *Cyclamen hederifolium*, *Viola labradorica* and *Epimedium* we can enjoy fleeting moments caught in flower, and the interludes between the flower are rarely dull with the texture of foliage as a backdrop.

The tall, north-facing wall has been clad in *Trachelospermum jasminoides*, which scaled to the top last summer. Evergreen jasmine is happier on a warmer wall where it will remain clothed to the base, but with careful pruning to keep it bushy it can cushion us from the raw expanse of London brick. Though they are tiny yet and slower to get off the blocks, I have laced them with shade-loving ivies that will cover any gaps which might arise as they reach for the sun. If the *Trachelospermum* feel stressed, either by exposure or winter drought, they will colour bronze and red in the winter. Yew and box are prone to the same behaviour if caught out by cold winter winds, but all three will green up again come the spring.

In the shade of the wall is a remarkable *Euphorbia* called 'Roundway Titan'. It is bigger in all its parts than its parents, *E. mellifera* (the honey spurge), and *E. stygiana* (a smaller-growing shrub with strappy, emerald-green leaves). In a couple of weeks and with this early push of growth it will start to give way to sprays of rust-orange flowers, which will be at their peak by May.

I grew the honey spurge in my Peckham garden where it overshot the fences, but I have no idea how this giant will grow here yet. I first saw this plant at Spinners Nursery in the New Forest, where it colours copper and orange in the winter and it is pretty hardy considering its exotic appearance, coming back from the base like a *Melianthus* if it is felled by frost in the winter. These shrubby *Euphorbias* can be coppiced every five years or so in late winter if you find they outgrow their position.

Daphne bholua 'Darjeeling' keeps most of its foliage in winter and, as I write, the first of the flowers are perfuming the courtyard. They are the palest pink in this form, fading fast to white. They are youngsters yet but they are fast growing if they like you, reaching 1.8–2.5 m – though they are skinny and can easily be squeezed into a narrow position. Shelter from the fiercest wind and coolness at the roots will emulate their

Himalayan heritage, where they dwell in the foothills; but they are happy in a warm position. I have the white form here, too, a more compact grower – and plan to use it by the boot-room door in Somerset so that in the wilds of February we can be greeted with this intoxicating perfume.

The *Iris unguicularis* have been spearing flowers since November whenever there is a mild spell. I have the silvery-blue form called 'Walter Butt' and have saved the sunniest wall to make sure they have the reserves in their rhizomes to provide us with wintry delights. They like poor living, hailing from the boulder-strewn hillsides of Syria, but I have also integrated *Iris lazica* in the shade. This beautiful winter-flowering iris is similar in habit but happier in the cool. It provides lush, strappy evergreen foliage and the pale blue flowers will help us to make it through this home stretch to the growing season.

MARCH

M

The clocks change at the end of this month, the gloom eased by an extra hour of gardening time. Life is suddenly happening: pale primroses on the banks and the perfume of violets caught for a moment in the warmth of the first spring sunshine.

Do not be fooled, however, as March is a month of contradictions. All too often a warm start sees a cruel end to the month, whipping young growth and withering your first attempts at gardening. Better that the winter keeps its grip for a while, though, to remind us to hold back from being overly optimistic. The ground is cold and it takes a while to warm, so pace yourself with sowing and put energy into the remainder of the planting season. Bare-root plants should really be in by the end of the month so that they have time to settle their roots before the light and warmth trigger their top growth.

I make a point of planting not just for the coming growing season, but for longevity. It never takes as long as you think to be able to look up into the canopy of a tree that you have planted or to lie in the shade of your efforts. Everyone should plant a blossom tree specifically for this moment, to light the spirits and the skyline, and to bring spring into the garden with a broad brushstroke.

Regardless of the weather, the sap is up and the signs of life are unstoppable: lungworts busy with bees and crocuses flinging their petals open at the first hint of sunshine. Over time, gardening with the long view has taught me the importance of refining. I want to be greeted by just the right plants after the long wait, so I am happy to build slowly towards identifying the best that spring has to offer and not to suffer a host of golden daffodils when there are altogether more delicate varieties available. March is the time to make way for this new life, to clear away the skeletons that were welcome just a month ago and give the garden a clean sweep so that it is ready for the off.

5 March, *Peckham*

QUICK MARCH

———

A mild start to the month encourages the soft growth on the epimediums, so soft it's like a layer of coppery skin. The flowers are up just before the foliage and both will be bashed by cold, dry winds that can so often hit the turning point from this month into April. It seems harsh that new life could be given such a hard start, and I remember many years when a walk in the garden at the end of March inspired nothing but anxiety: first seedlings standing still in fear, magnolia blossom turned to the consistency of chamois leather. I remember one hard frost that hit at the end of March up at Home Farm, while I was studying there. The dicentra melted, the new growth on the roses was seared as if a flame-thrower had been through the garden. Even the comfrey was burnt black. Burgeoning blossom was lost, the orchard barren for a year, but I think that it did the trees very little harm. New growth was back within weeks and the trees liked a year off from fruiting, and proved it by over-compensating the following year. In the most part, the majority of things survive.

A cold start to the month always feels more appropriate to me, because it is better to go slow when there is so much to do and so much to take in. I prefer the feeling of caution that is engendered when there is a beast waiting in the wings – it takes away the assumption that this might be the start of spring. A case in point was the mild winter a few years ago, when my cobaea managed to keep going through the season. This is a plant that, in a mild climate, is at its best in the cooler months at the beginning and the end of the summer, and I was over-confident, thinking that I could cut it back to the new shoots that were emerging at the end of February. The lion whipped those off pretty fast in a cold, wild week that year – growth that would have survived if I had left the cutting-back until a more gentle April.

I wait to sow seed until I am sure that the ground really is warm enough to sustain growth. A line of rocket sown in the middle of March will not have much advance upon a line sown at the start of April. Nasturtiums will rot in the ground if the mild days in the month deceive you into thinking that spring is already here. Potatoes may do the same if planted too early, and if they don't, their first shoots will only get clipped by frost. That is, of course, if we have any. Things catch up and equalise in just a short time once light and warmth are on our side.

I also take my time with tender plants that by now are beginning to strain in their winter quarters, reaching for the increased light. Too often I have cleaned up the pelargoniums and potted them on in a mild March then, once they were watered, put them out in the sunshine to get a breather. But it can be too much too soon. Leave them out, if only in a mild spell, and they may well get a chill that undoes all your winter cosseting. Better to keep them on the dry side, inside, and not disturb them too much until the beginning of next month. The same can be said of plants that you had the foresight to give protection to last autumn. Though the young shoots may be coming away at the base of the melianthus and the tops may be looking terrible after the winter, it is best to leave the yoke of bracken or straw, or whatever you may have used to protect the growth, in place until the month is over. Wraps on the *Musa basjoo* and piles of mulch put down to protect the cannas and dahlias that you might have left in the ground are better left in place.

Life can be kickstarted inside, if you have the room and the inclination to sow half-hardy annuals and perennials. They need a good six weeks to two months of growing time before they are put out, once all risk of frost is past. So, now that the light levels are improving, I will be sowing the likes of nicotiana, cleome and bidens, casting the seed finely on to the surface of the compost. Anything finer than ground pepper should be left without a covering and the pot covered with a sheet of glass. Anything larger can have a sieved covering no greater than the depth of the seed. It is vital to sow thinly so that you do not get seedlings overcrowding, as they are most prone to damping off and rotting when there is no room for air movement around them. A pinch of most seed is enough. Seeds that are large enough to count, such as ipomaea and sweet pea, can be put two to three to a 7.5 cm (3 in) pot and then thinned down later as necessary.

Outside, I start to clear the garden in earnest now, for most hardy plants can cope with whatever the month has to throw at them. Starting with the toughest first and those that are showing signs of early growth, I make my way around the garden pulling thatch off the ground where it comes away easily and cutting stiff growth on perennials back hard, so that it doesn't catch you later in the season when you might be weeding among the plants. It is the perfect time for division of those perennials that might need it more regularly, as the growth is just stirring and they will get to grips with life again fast. Bergamot, fast-growing asters and achilleas are the candidates for such treatment. It is important to be hard-hearted: only take the best new growth from the outside of the clump; the rest can be put on the compost heap.

Once the perennials are pared back, I move on quickly with a spring mulch to smother any weed seedlings that might be thinking of setting up home in the beds. Mulching is a favourite job – it protects the soil from the elements, feeds it and improves its texture. An eiderdown of compost, chipped bark, manure or cocoa shell also makes the garden look instantly shipshape, so that whatever the weather, some things feel certain.

7 March, *Peckham*
WHAT A LOVELY SPREAD!

———

I returned home from three weeks in the Far East in mid-February to find the garden transformed. The crocuses were up as if from nowhere, dazzling and brilliant in the cold sunshine. I'd left the garden as long as I could so that the goodness from last year could be pulled back to the ground, but the bulbs demanded attention now. The yet-to-become-compost from the top of the heap was turned into the empty one beside it and the wreckage of last year piled high as it came off the beds. The roses were pruned and the dead leaves pulled from the hellebores, and in no time at all the garden was naked. Red buds pushed through on the peony, the celandines were clear to breathe, and the soil had warmed just enough for a rash of opium poppy seedlings to venture out.

Bare soil has always made me uncomfortable, and where the deciduous perennials are pulled away it is important to protect it again against the elements. Where I grew up in Hampshire, with its thin, acidic sand, mulching was a necessity, for the soil dried as soon as you turned your back, but not before the chickweed had taken you hostage. Living in woodland, we used leaf mould from the previous year among the precious plants and leaves among the shrubs and ground cover to keep the soil covered. The eiderdown protected and nourished as it was pulled down by the earthworms, and precious moisture was locked in.

When I was at Wisley, I was introduced to the luxury of spent mushroom compost, which at that time was cheap because it was still seen as a waste product. We learned that the lime content meant it should not be used for more than two or three years consecutively, and that it should be kept from acid-loving plants, so we kept a stock of composted bark as a substitute. Bark lasts for a couple of seasons, but it needs at least a year to rot down before it is applied, if it is not to rob your soil and plants of nitrogen. Still, it is lovely to work with and easy to spread among newly emerging perennials.

The soil at Home Farm, which was my next port of call, was a sticky, yellow clay and could not have been more different. With annual mulching we transformed the soil over five years into a friable loam. Where it had sat heavy, cold and wet in the winter, the organic addition pulled in by the worms allowed it to breathe. It warmed quicker in the spring and gave us the opportunity of growing a wider range of plants. In London, I continue to mulch with whatever is light: recycled green waste, cocoa shell (beware if you have dogs, as it can choke them) and, of course, my own homemade compost have saved me hours of summer weeding and watering.

Now is the ideal time to mulch, as there is moisture in the ground and the soil is warming. You should only ever mulch on ground that is clean and free of perennial weeds, or you will be feeding the weeds in the process. Seedling annual weeds will be smothered, or indeed prevented from germinating, once they are incarcerated in darkness, and you will need a consistent covering of 5 cm or so to make it worthwhile. Energy expended at the beginning of the season will free up time for other tasks later, and the garden will never look neater and better cared for than under this blanket of goodness.

8 March, *Hillside*
SPRING'S MAGIC CARPETS

———

Last February I was allowed to choose a collection of *Galanthus* from another garden. I went for varieties I could recognise from a few paces away – I don't see the point in obsessing about a detail you need to be on your hands and knees to observe. I've enjoyed their reappearance in the stock beds, partly because they're different from the common forms we have already, but also because at least half have flowered a month earlier than my natives. 'Mrs McNamara' was already with us at Christmas, and since then I've picked a posy for the house that has gathered in complexity with witchhazels and Algerian iris and early willow catkins braving the cold.

The first bright days in February saw the *Crocus tommasinianus* spring open on the banks behind the house. I grew this beautiful species under a *Cercis* tree in London, but their pale flowers would fail to open on all but the brightest of days. It would make me feel a little sad that they had made all that effort and never got to see the sun, but here on the sunny bank they are a different thing altogether. Spearing the grass to muscle their way into the light, they are all but invisible until that first bright day of readiness. When they open, suddenly and with absolute joy, they fling their petals as if they were stretching in the morning.

C. tommasinianus is one of the few crocuses to naturalise readily in this country. I prefer the straight species with its lilac outer petals and silvery-mauve interior to the named forms that are darker and sit less lightly in the turf. 'Ruby Giant' is violet-mauve and 'Whitewell Purple' has a mauve exterior and paler interior. Both are nicer by far than the blowsier Dutch varieties that you see more often.

I have a couple of pans of the *C. tommasinianus* 'Albus' that I am keeping separate from their mauve cousins to curb any promiscuous behaviour. They are pure and elegant and make the larger white varieties look voluminous and vulnerable, like brides and bridesmaids caught in a storm. Though the white form doesn't have that delightful contrast between dark outer petal and silvery inside, their saffron anthers inject a shot of colour.

For more intensive colour after a winter's grey, the *C. chrysanthus* varieties are a delight. Christopher Lloyd planted a wonderful selection. He delighted in the way they spangled the turf, like sweets cast on the ground or myriad butterflies. The best selections have a marked contrast between the interior and the exterior so that when closed they register very differently from when they are triggered open in sun.

C. chrysanthus 'Gypsy Girl' is gold with quite a contrast in the liquorice stripes to the reverse. 'Blue Pearl' is silvery-blue with lavender outer petals, while 'Cream Beauty' is cream both inside and out – but it does have gold in the throat as compensation, and just being there to herald the spring is enough.

PUTTING DOWN ROOTS

———

Last summer, on a still, bright day in August, the quiet was broken by a thundering crack, followed by a thud which shook the ground. It was one of those rare moments when time moves in slow motion, and as we glanced up from the vegetable garden to the source of the sound we saw an enormous branch crash out of the oak tree on the hill. This particular tree is a stand-alone veteran from another era, with character in its limbs and wide-reaching branches. We walked up there later in the evening, when the shadows were long, to find a limb the size of a tree lying on the ground.

Oaks are said to take 300 years to grow, another 300 to stand in their maturity and then the same again to die, so I felt curiously privileged to witness such change in the life of this tree. It would have been standing on the hill way before any of the houses currently dotting the valley and it will probably see them out, too. The event and the change set me thinking about the legacy of being the custodian of our land and of the glance in time that will mark our own moment.

I like the idea of planting for longevity and find myself increasingly drawn to the idea of planting for the future. A tree will map decades if not centuries in its branches, and though we have no control over what might happen to that tree in years to come, the feeling associated with steering it in the right direction is nothing but wholesome. With this in mind I have planted three oaks this winter, one each on either side of a gate into the field below the veteran. The third has been inserted in a gap in the hedge high on our land in the hope that one day we will be able to sit under its branches and take in the view.

Though you might think of oaks as being slow, this is far from the case, and in thirty years' time these trees will be easily 10 m tall. If you are planting for longevity, though – and this, I might add, should be the case in choosing any tree – it is important to think about their ultimate size. Not all trees that live to a great age are space-hungry with it. If I wanted the character of an oak in a small garden, it would be a black mulberry every time. Where an oak might win on points with the amount of wildlife it would attract, a *Morus nigra* would win hands down in terms of its fruit. Acorns are good for pigs. Mulberries are very definitely the choice of humans.

Another long-lasting tree and another of my favourite natives is the field maple, *Acer campestre*. This is a modestly sized tree happy to grow in almost any condition, be it coastal, wasteland or in a prime position in your garden. Well behaved, slowly attaining a height and ultimate spread of 8–10 m, it can also be coppiced should you require it and, come autumn, the leaves colour a delightful russet orange. I have collected keys (seeds) from another veteran in the valley and plan to give them to clients so that they live on for future generations.

A HOST OF SILVER DAFFODILS

The daffodils have broken ground, emblazoning our parks and gardens. The golden stronghold of 'King Alfred' and his allies marks the break with winter that we have all been waiting for, but I feel a little punch drunk from colour by the end of the month.

Sometime in the past, the orchard here was planted with a mixture of long-forgotten hybrids that over the years mixed with the wild *Narcissus pseudonarcissus*. Pale and not so far in colour from the primroses among them, they were all individuals, with gentle twists in the petals and trumpets as varied.

Once you have tasted good chocolate, it is impossible to eat anything that doesn't measure up. I feel much the same way about 'King Alfred' – there are a fleet of beauties that are far more refined and forgiving: try 'W. P. Milner', 'Minnow', 'Petrel'. I experiment by buying a few bulbs each year, which I keep in pots near the house so I can see what happens over the course of their flowering. Some change in colour as they age – in the case of 'Jenny', from cream with a primrose throat to a bone-white throughout once fully opened. Others, such as 'Segovia', a miniature pheasant's eye, are deliciously perfumed. All have delicate flowers that dance with other springtimers and never dominate.

As I have been looking for varieties that are good for naturalising in grass, I'll pay particular attention to the foliage, which I like to be fine so that it sits well in a meadow. Delicate, creamy 'Hawera', *cyclamineus* forms with their flung-back petals, and perfumed jonquils: all allow you to see the flower and not the foliage. The jonquil *Narcissus* are late to flower and have sweetly perfumed foliage that is a darker green than your usual *Narcissus*.

I love the straight *Narcissus jonquilla*, which are sometimes two to a head. The flowers are no larger than a buttercup, so the fact that they are gold is never dominant. I grow a good hybrid jonquil called 'Silver Chimes'. It is altogether more ornamental, and in my book too showy to grow among the grass, but a bunch will perfume a room. *Narcissus* 'Pipit' must have some jonquil blood, for it is beautifully scented.

I have planted *Narcissus pseudonarcissus* down by the stream, where I hope in time they will naturalise. This British native is a coloniser of woods and coppices and when it is happy it will seed to form drifts. The flowers are no more than 30 cm in height with a rich yellow trumpet and paler outer petals that twist finely forward. 'Moschatus' is a pure white and very desirable.

Over the past couple of years I've been exploring the heritage varieties to see if I can find some that feel like the inhabitants of our old orchard. 'Beryl' is scented and a firm new favourite, and 'Stella', too. Those I like are added to the bank so that one day my crab apples will be complemented by a host of daffodils.

WHAT'S NEW, PUSSYCAT?

It is that time of year again, the *Forsythia* emblazoning front gardens like double yellow lines. Do not ignore, do not stop, keep on moving. Combine *Forsythia* in a rhubarb-and-custard coupling with *Ribes sanguineum* and prepare for all else to be eclipsed.

It is the concentration of *Forsythia* which is the challenge, and it never looks worse than as a hedge, hard-pruned and solid with colour. Leave it to grow out into a loose-limbed shrub; tucked away somewhere woolly at the bottom of the garden it has its uses. Cut a spray as soon as the buds hint at yellow and they will brighten a wintry windowsill in the warmth. Allow them their room so that they don't have to compete.

The tail end of winter should not be rushed. Colour is hard to come by, so why force it? In a matter of weeks we will be overwhelmed by greenery and flower. Few things in the natural world are solid at this time of year; the gauze of deciduous growth allows light and air to filter through, offering glimpses between branches.

This is why I would prefer to come upon the delicacy of a witch hazel or the smattering of acid-green flower on *Cornus mas*. The little group I planted on the bank behind the house is providing me with ample colour already – each pinprick of flower sharp against the monochrome. I am also experimenting with the Chinese *C. officinalis*, which has the upper hand in terms of showiness, with all its parts just that little bit bigger than its European cousin. It is also lovely underplanted with *Crocus* and small-flowered *Narcissus*.

The waxily flowered *Chimonanthus praecox* is a fine example of how I prefer things to gather pace, the perfumed flowers breaking while everything else is still slumbering. Winter-flowering quince also break the gloom with the glistening white of *Chaenomeles speciosa* 'Jet Trail', the delicate pink of 'Apple Blossom' or deep moody colour of *C.* × *superba* 'Crimson and Gold'.

The delightful *Corylopsis pauciflora* is known as starwood in its native Japan because the flowers are suspended naked in bare branches and this is how I favour the wake-up call: to stumble upon it like treasure.

The lift the catkins can give your garden while most of the landscape is slumbering is worth planning for and the hazel and alder catkins are perfect in combination with the pussy willows, the one following on from the next. The pussy willows are having their moment: silver at first and then alive with early insects once they turn gold with pollen. Our native *Salix caprea* is just the tip of the iceberg; the willow is a promiscuous genus that can be found all over the world, taking as its territory the hinterlands or the rough places.

I have a jug of willow wands on the table now and though my plants are just a year old they are already proving their worth. The pregnant buds will be fully formed by the time the foliage falls and in some, such as *S. hookeriana* – the coastal willow from the United States – the buds are like beetle cases, fat and hunkered close on the stems. These burst a glistening silver.

Others, such as *S. daphnoides* 'Aglaia', are as glossy as

nail polish and black or deep burgundy red in bud. *S. purpurea* 'Nancy Saunders' is wire-fine and slender, the silvery catkins like a myriad of light-filled dewdrops in the branches. The catkins are unbelievably soft – you barely feel their downiness. I have a fine form of our native *S. purpurea* called 'Howki' which has moody little catkins of a dusky grey-mauve.

In *S. gracilistyla* 'Melanostachys' the pussies are black, like specks of charcoal among the branches. The pollen of this variety is a rust-orange. The furry protection doesn't last long before the anthers break free and dust themselves with pollen and, at this point, the pussy willows are a Mecca for early bees. Underplant them with comfrey, primroses and violets and the passage into spring is guaranteed to be spangled.

27 March, *Hillside*

BREAKING THE SILENCE

———

It would be difficult to let this moment pass without sharing my delight in the blossom season, for it is a moment that places you very firmly in the here and now. Darkness replaced by light, inertia with movement, monochrome with the first smatterings of colour and then the gathering tide of life. When I have been frantic with spring business, I make it a rule to down tools and make my way to a tree or a place that I know will be marking this transition. The craggy almonds on a Jerusalem hillside, an apple orchard in Kent or a 'borrowed' tree in a park that welcomes with open branches.

I have watched the twilight beneath an ancient cherry tree in Kyoto, illuminated with flaming braziers, a few buds burst, the rest to open in a flurry the next day; and I have marvelled at the self-sown geans lighting up a dark, industrial wasteland with my face glued to the window of a speeding train.

Standing under a twisted amelanchier in my parents' garden on my tenth birthday was probably the moment I first fell in love with this transformation. I can still feel the damp spring air, the moisture and the cool, the softness of palest pink bud and the chocolate fuzz of hair on leaves just about to break. It was an infatuation that has never waned and I have avidly planted blossom trees ever since. Single magnolias in tiny London courtyards, groves of crab apples and apricots where there is an opportunity, and now, for the first time in my life, my own blossom copse on the top field where some ancient terraces crease the hillside.

My dear friend Geraldine left me a small amount of money in her will when she died and it has gone towards this blossom copse. I planned it for the birds when my head was filled with berries and fruits, so the copse has a dual purpose. It will feed the early bees and, in time, it will be the place I gravitate towards when the sap is rising to see it expressed in flower.

With the exception of the cornelian cherry – the acid green *Cornus mas* – which has already been and gone, all the trees are native. They will blend into this rural setting and I have planted them in informal spinneys, which will sit in a tussocky meadow as if they were wildings sown by the birds that will eventually come to feed in their branches.

The first to flower is the cherry plum, *Prunus cerasifera*.

This is a wild plum that has naturalised in Britain and is more usually seen in the copper-leaved form 'Pissardii'. I rarely use this ornamental selection as it is heavy and dark when in leaf, but the wild form is delicate, forming a finely twigged tree the size of a hawthorn. The buds are visible as early as February and come out in a warm spell to smatter the tree at first and then fill out the branches with pale flower. They beat the blackthorn, which follows on shortly afterwards, but if you see them together the creaminess of the blackthorn reveals the pink in the plum. Each flower is tiny, cupped to reveal a dark boss of stamens.

The copse will sit above an orchard, which I plan for the next field down the slope, and the cherry plum will help in the pollination of the early mirabelle plums. The mirabelles are the culinary selection from this same species.

The thorny wild pear, *Pyrus pyraster*, will also help in pollinating any ornamental pear trees I'm growing for fruit. Pears have some of the most delightful of early blossom, each flower registering as an individual, like an origami balloon when in bud. The geans will follow, their flowers clear, bright and held in distinctive muffs at the tips of the branches. The fast-growing *Prunus avium* is a lovely thing where there is room and I have planted several close together to form a colony with the silvery foliage of young whitebeam among them. The flowers last half as long as the double gean, *Prunus avium* 'Plena', which is one of the best white cherries. Bird cherry, service tree, hawthorn and wild apple will follow on, but I'll enjoy the brevity of my trees on the hill for they are part of a team that will keep me in flower for the best part of six weeks. Spring savoured in blossom.

28 March, *Hillside*
HOPE SPRINGS ETERNAL

———

I have just picked a posy of the first flowers to bloom. You can delight in a jar of them, and in searching them out at the end of winter. There are cherry plum with tiny, bright flowers which have the scent of almonds, and primroses smelling of only themselves. I have a suspicion that the sweet violets growing by the house are a florist's selection that were once grown here when this was a market garden. Larger-flowered and longer-stemmed than those on the sunny banks, they appear spontaneously in the lawn. Bury your nose in them and you can smell them once, perhaps twice, as is the way with violets.

Early flowers always have joy in them, and this is why I have been slowly studding the banks behind the house with bulbs and catkin-bearing trees and shrubs: hazel, alder and pussy willows – the first of which into catkin is *Salix purpurea*, with its tiny, dusky pussies. The enormous catkins of *Salix candida* have joined them now. They are alive with bees on a sunny day, when they turn from silver to gold and break into flower. I have planted lungworts at their feet as the bees love to work their profusion of flower.

The lungworts like it here, the heavy soil favouring their preference for moisture-retentive ground, but are easy as an understorey to deciduous shrubs or in a quiet corner as long as it doesn't dry out completely. *Pulmonaria* 'Blue Ensign' is as blue as gentians, but the range is wide, moving to the soft red of the first to flower, *P. rubra*, and on to pinks and mauves.

'Leopard' combines both, while 'Cotton Cool' is a pale icy blue and 'Sissinghurst White' is clean and sparkling.

Their leaves, shaped like a lung and thought once to be good for them by the apothecaries, are one of their great attractions. The elongated leaves of 'Highdown' are freckled with pale spots while the foliage of *P. saccharata* is marked so definitely that the leaf looks as if it has had silver leaf applied between the veins.

In a similar camp and favouring much the same conditions are *Brunnera*, with forget-me-not flowers and rounded foliage. 'Langtrees' has a subtle spotting while 'Jack Frost' is almost entirely silvered. I like the plain green leaf of the white-flowered 'Betty Bowring', and will often team them with the yellow *Epimedium* 'Fröhnleiten' and *Narcissus* 'Jack Snipe', to soften the brightness of spring yellow.

Many of the early-flowering perennials are not only good for being there to bridge winter and spring but also for their ability to seize the window before the leaves pop on the trees. To cope with the ensuing lack of light many have a short lifecycle. *Lathyrus vernus*, a pea with rich purple-blue flowers, and *Cardamine quinquefolia*, wood anemone and celandine are mainstays in this window. They act like a starting gun for the rest of the flowering season, and allow us to breathe easy in the knowledge that winter is now firmly behind us.

APRIL

grew up in a long-forgotten garden. When we took the property on, forty years of decay, neglect and miracles were discovered as we began to clear the undergrowth. April particularly reminds me of this time and I remember like yesterday discovering the soft new growth of an awakening epimedium with its delicately veined leaves and dancing flowers, otherworldly amongst the brambles. Blink now and the moment is gone. To this day I wish I could slow time to take in spring's newness.

April is spring at its best, with the intensity of green being notched up daily until it is as vibrant as it ever will be. It is the time of some of my favourite plants and an opportunity to get to know better those that flourish in this brief window. Magnolias, one of our most ancient flowers, make their glorious reappearance, as do the snakeshead fritillaries, hugely variable as a tribe and adaptable enough in our benign climate for us to forget their Eastern origins. Tulips too have made the leap from their homes on the rocky hillsides of the Middle East and I could garden for another half-century and still be delighted by their flair and opulence.

It is not only the speed with which the garden comes to life that makes it hard to take it all in. April is one of the busiest months, with little time left to prepare for the growing season ahead, and a list of jobs that stretches beyond the time in hand. This is one of the joys of gardening. The clematis are racing away up their supports, the potatoes already pushing through and in need of earthing up. There are seeds to sow and a vegetable garden to plan and to plant, and in the background bare branches being clothed and closing winter's chapter.

2 April, *Peckham*
STILLNESS IN THE CITY

———

I have long been interested in the idea of the garden providing sanctuary; for when it sings, a garden will have the power to transport and to lead you to a place that is magical. It can transcend its surroundings or conversely allow you to tune in to them, to draw your eye to a view or your ear to the sound of a stream.

Gardens have long been used as oases, quite literally in the case of the gardens of the Middle East, which turned their back on the deserts around them to order nature and heighten an interior world. Although I have never seen the original Persian gardens for myself, I have found the Moorish influence in southern Spain a powerful influence and the gardens of the Alhambra in Granada remain some of my favourites. Room upon room gives way to a sensuous world with a sky ceiling, the cooling influence of water and the smell of lemons, jasmine and roses as a companion.

The gardens of Japan are among the most spiritual spaces I have ever visited, offering sanctuary for thought and contemplation. In the chapel-like stillness of the gravel enclosure at Ryoanji, your mind is free to imagine the mud wall as a range of hills, the gravel an eddying sea among the rocks. The contrasting soft, mossy woodland of Saihoji will be etched on my memory forever with its stepping-stone path forcing you to walk slowly, to focus your eyes on the texture of mosses at your feet or a crimson camellia fallen and left with purpose.

These were places that grounded me and rooted me in the moment, while giving cause to explore the landscape of my imagination. Being in the here and now is a rare thing in these times of rapid communication; although we might move too fast, we can depend upon our gardens not having to.

An oasis or a sanctuary need not be a perfect composition, and some of my favourite places have been thrown-together gardens, built from love and passion. The need to nurture can create a world in a window box, and inspire guerrilla gardens in unlikely places. The empty lots in the Lower East Side of Manhattan, converted in the 1970s, proved that you need little more than willpower to make an oasis in hostile surroundings. Chain-link fences were lifted and rubble cleared to make plots large enough to garden and a whole new culture of improvisation grew as fast as the beans through the scaffolding. Many of these plots have since been made into official gardens and will remain there against the odds.

Our allotments are probably our closest parallel in this country. Look out from the window on any train ride through the suburbs and you will see a patchwork of little worlds and sheds, like a shantytown for growing things. It is no surprise that these egalitarian spaces have never been in such demand, with waiting lists decades long in some boroughs.

It was the idea of sanctuary that spurred my Peckham plot. It was a place that produced and provided in response to the hours I put in to nurture it, and it offered a still eye in the city. I discovered a lot there, too: how the evening primroses marked the longest day of the year, and how the rustle in the bamboo baffled the hubbub of the Peckham Road.

The garden was also a magnet for wildlife: the nectar-rich eryngium attracting five or six types of bee, my copper water bowl with its solitary water lily, the dragonflies. The garden offered a still contrast to the city for friends and family, too. You could argue that it was the reason that exhibitions came and went without me seeing them and that I had my head in the earth when I should have been more engaged with urban life. But the payback of tending a garden is profound and restorative. It is an oasis for the creation, available to anyone with a little space and the compunction to get their hands dirty.

5 April, *Yorkshire*

SNAKES IN THE GRASS

———

One of my clients lives in a sturdy stone cottage in the Yorkshire Dales. It sits on the brow of a hill, facing south, with the valley sweeping away as far as you can see to either side. There are dry-stone walls sectioning the land and on the far hills the haze of heather smudges the tops in August. You feel the weather with intensity. When I was last there the January gales made the house shudder and the valley was a pure and glistening white with frost. But now, at the beginning of spring, the most extraordinary thing happens. The midwinter green increases in intensity over a week or so until it could only be described as luminous. It is like nature turning up the contrast so that the fields appear to be pulsing green. Go down into the valley and the hedges will be thrumming with activity. Bristling new shoots on the hawthorn, *Stellaria* smattering the base of the hedgerows and young nettles as soft as they ever will be, at the best moment for making into soup. Cowslips will be gathering in strength in the open ground where the turf is kept short and when the tops of the first new grass are bent over on a bright breezy day, the meadows will literally shimmer with reflected light. This is all good news after a long grey winter and I plan to make the most of this glorious moment. It involves studding the shiny new meadows with sheets of bulbs, not great sweeps of colour-heavy daffodils, but with species bulbs that will scatter colour.

No meadow in early April would really be complete without the *Fritillaria meleagris* and in a week these snakeshead fritillaries will be at their best. Pushing up on wire-thin stalks, they are almost impossible to see until they arch their heads over in readiness to flower. And flower they do in abundance when they decide they are going to naturalise a sward. The sight of them in countless numbers is breathtaking. They like to naturalise low-lying floodplains and there are some incredible colonies in the lowlands of Cambridgeshire, Oxfordshire and Wiltshire. They used to be more common, but with ground drained for agriculture and building spreading as it is, the wild colonies are now few and far between.

Last year I visited a good example just inside the ring road that runs around Oxford. It was odd to be among them, sitting in spring sunshine with the *Juncus* and ragged robin indicating how wet the land lay year round and the traffic hurtling by. Their chequered pattern never fails to delight me. It really is like the patterning on a snake. Mulberry overlaying pale silvery scales in the dusky forms and green overlaying white in the rare but ever-present albinos. The flower looks like it has been made from fabric and starched into position with its high-pleated 'shoulders'.

I have no grass at home in London so I have chosen to keep a couple of dozen bulbs in a pot so that spring doesn't go by without me enjoying them. I am amazed that they do as well as they do because they are a plant that looks so much better in the wild and only really does well where the ground is damp. I do nothing more with them than bring them out from the holding area in the shade when they show and then allow them to feed up their foliage until it withers in early summer sunshine after they have flowered. The pots are filled with *Viola labradorica* so that they are not too bare for the rest of the year and they are completely neglected beyond the watering that is needed to keep the *Viola* alive and kicking.

Establishing *Fritillaria meleagris* in a garden setting is fairly straightforward as long as you remember their requirement for damp ground. This is unusual in a bulb, for most like to be on the dry side when they are dormant. Soil that floods infrequently and in winter will be fine but really they like to draw upon water rather than lie in it for long periods so it is worth bearing that in mind. Though I have had success planting the bulbs in the autumn at two-and-a-half times their own depth, as most bulbs like to be, I have heard that they prefer to be planted deep, up to 15 cm. If you can get plants pot grown, though not the cheapest way to introduce them in numbers, it is the surest way of getting them established. As with any other bulbs grown in grass, leave them for five to six weeks after the flowers fade to seed and store goodness for the following year.

The fritillarias are a huge tribe of wonderful treasures and most hail from Turkey and the Middle East where they bake bone dry not long after the spring rains are finished. It is hard to see many of these in the wild now because grazing has stripped the colonies as has unscrupulous bulb collection, but try and see them in the alpine houses of botanic and RHS gardens. You will be bewitched. Most of these species are beyond me at this point in my gardening history. They need to be grown in frames and given just-so attention, but there are several which are less choosy. The earth-brown and green *F. acmopetala* and *F. pyrenaica* are easy. My childhood neighbour Geraldine had a wonderful clump of the latter growing for years in free draining ground through some low perennial campanulas. Then there is the exquisite *F. thunbergii* from China, with its grass-like foliage, twisted at the tips to haul itself up into the low scrub in which it likes to grow. This is a woodlander that the garden designer Beth Chatto grows well against the odds in Essex. Its exquisite green bells are the perfect companions to *Trillium* and *Uvularia* in her sheltered woodland garden.

In areas of the country where the dreaded lily beetle has yet to make its presence felt or where you can be prepared to pick off the first generation of beetles and grubs, I will always make room for *F. persica*. Tall, at about 90 cm in the strongest selection 'Adiyaman', the whirl of blue-green foliage is up early in March and the grape-purple flowers follow fast behind. This is a plant that loves to bake, so think about it being with thymes and small lavenders, *Origanum* and the like. It will be withered and below ground by mid-summer having lived fast and furious.

The Crown Imperials are closely related but a scale up again in impact. Perhaps they were brought here along with the tulips as part of the trading that used the ancient silk routes. Hailing from Turkey through to Kashmir they must have been exotic treasure, and their provenance explains why you often see them depicted in medieval woodcuts of apothecary gardens and in the floral paintings of the old Dutch masters. The flowers, which hang from a cluster at the top of a waist-high shoot, were said to have not hung their heads when Christ passed them on his way to the crucifixion. They are forever bound to bow their heads as a result. Lift them up and in the base there will be a tear of nectar at the heel of each petal.

The bulbs, which go in as usual in the autumn, have a pungent foxy odour and there is something of that in the glossy leaf. They are happy in a hot spot and in good hearty, free-draining soil. 'Lutea' is a bright chrome-yellow, 'The Premier' a dusky orange and there are brick reds that never look better than when basking in spring sunshine. They display none of the earthy tones of their many relatives, nor the snaky subtlety of our British native, but every bit as much individuality.

8 April, *Jersey*
JACKETS REQUIRED

Back in early January, when a week of bitter easterlies cut across the country, I ventured out to Jersey to look over a potential project. We dipped sharply, through buffeting crosswinds, in a plane that was small enough to make the businessmen scream. I had never visited the island before, and it was surreal to see a landscape wrapped up in plastic and incubating the famous Jersey Royals. The earliest of the crop can fetch as much as £5,000 a tonne.

Last year I almost grew enough potatoes to go commercial. There were eight varieties in total and two rows of each. I'd been tempted by a combination of factors. We had space and it had been all too easy to click another variety that caught my eye on the online catalogue.

Potatoes fall into three main groups: first early, second early and maincrop. First earlies mature after about 100 days, second earlies after 110–120 days, and maincrop after 130 days. If you aim to plant around Good Friday, selecting a range for continuity and keeping, you can give yourself salad potatoes and keepers.

Potatoes are easy to grow. If you have limited space you can grow them in a dustbin or pots on a terrace. In the garden they prefer ground that has been manured the previous autumn. They are not fussy about soil, but scab is alleviated if your soil is on the acid side of neutral and if water availability is regular. Water is important as the young tubers are developing – that's why potatoes grow best in Ireland and Scotland.

Although you can plant shop-grown potatoes as mother plants, certified seed potatoes are virus- and disease-free, so they produce a higher yield. Chitting is advisable before planting – it speeds up establishment. It involves placing the seed potato end up in an egg box on a cool, bright windowsill to form 'eyes' no more than a couple of centimetres long. A 30 cm spacing between tubers is optimal, with rows 60 cm apart, but wider spacing in the row produces a bigger potato, so the earlies are best planted closer for salad potatoes, and the maincrops, which you might save for wintry jacket potatoes and mash, can be spaced 45 cm apart. As soon as the growth emerges above ground, you can start the 'earthing up' process to keep the tubers from greening when exposed to light. Harvest can start as soon as you see the flowers opening.

There are about 400 varieties of potato, so start experimenting. Last year's experience taught me this: you only need as many earlies as you can eat fresh out of the ground; and you need to choose maincrop varieties that will keep. We preferred lighter eating in the summer but came back to spuds for winter.

We had success and we had failure, as the blight caught the maincrops in August. Blight is a fungus, *Phytophthora infestans*, and it needs high humidity and mild temperatures day and night to grow on potato plants. Although I removed the foliage as soon as I saw the infection, it ruined a couple of varieties.

Generally I have chosen varieties that are blight-resistant. Perhaps the best second early is 'Belle de Fontenay', with a smooth, waxy consistency. 'Lady Christl' is a delicious first early, producing numerous disease-resistant pale tubers. 'Orla' (first early) is the most blight-resistant early ever produced and is also good for second cropping.

'Edzell Blue' (second early) was hit heavily by blight last year, but the blue skin and the dry, tasty tubers were superb steamed and mashed or cooked in their jackets. 'Shetland Black', said to be one of the oldest varieties, is a fine jacket potato. 'Pink Fir Apple', a late maincrop potato, is delicious eaten whole and superb re-fried from cold. 'Ratte' is similar but a little earlier.

17 April, *Hillside*

RACE FOR THE SUN

———

From freckled to raspberry red, clematis are the most lovely – and temperamental – of spring's climbers. There is a tiny bed at the front of my farmhouse in which the former owner grew some colour. It contrasted with the rest of the farm, which was grazed back to the base of the hedges, the grass being the focus. I have used the bed this winter to line out my bare-root plants while the vegetable garden is being prepared, but in the last week or so I have made it my own. In pulling out the hardy fuchsias and the remains of last year's pelargonium, I came upon a sickly clematis, baked into submission on this south-facing wall and strangled with bindweed at the root. It is not worth saving, but in consigning it to the bonfire, with the fleshy roots of the bindweed, I have begun to ponder on a replacement.

Though the large-flowered clematis were plagued by wilt in my previous garden in Peckham, the species and the spring-flowering clematis were successful. How nice finally to be able to write about spring flowers, and the first of this temperamental tribe are some of the most lovely. *Clematis cirrhosa* 'Freckles', a large-flowered selection of this Balearic species, love to be on south-facing walls. 'Freckles' starts flowering in November, with smatterings through the dark months and a last push about now.

The evergreen clematis are sun lovers on the whole and in a warm position *Clematis armandii* will already be making its whippy extension growth. These come in tandem with the unseasonably opulent flower, but not before the buds, which are as fat as capers, and the red of cherries have wooed you. How could something so foreign-looking push against the vagaries of a British spring? But here they are, creamy white in an unnamed form and aptly shot with pink in the selection named 'Apple Blossom'.

Clematis armandii is a difficult plant to look after as its fresh, rangy growth overwhelms last year's foliage. The leaves are arguably the finest feature, long and longitudinally ribbed like the wing cases of an exotic beetle. It pains me to see them tatty, but the new growth will soon eclipse the old. For this reason I will give it a position where it can be larger than life, rather than containing it and insisting it behave itself, which simply isn't in its nature. So let it go over a shed or into a suitably resilient tree and, if you have to cut it back, prune it to a new framework of old wood immediately after flowering. You will have to remove new growth along with the old, but it will come back if you get your timing right. Pruning immediately after flowering is the best method with all spring clematis, but I wouldn't encourage such drastic action on more than a five- to seven-year cycle.

Far more delicate and better behaved are *Clematis alpina* and *C. macropetala*. The former tend to be single or semi-double, while the latter are flurried with petals. Deciduous by nature, they like cool at the roots and their heads in light. That said, they are perfectly happy on a shady wall or in dappled light.

C. alpina 'Frances Rivis' thrived for years on a north wall at Home Farm. 'Ruby', a soft raspberry-red selection, is also almost single and a good partner if you fancy planting them together, while the weaker-growing 'White Moth' is a delight.

I like the whites very much as their newly emerging foliage is lime green and delightfully fresh. *C. macropetala* 'Markham's Pink' is double and faded like it has gone through the wash.

For something strong and capable of sending up a tree, it is hard to better *C. montana*. Again, they like cool at the roots, so if you are planting near a tree, plunge a cardboard box into an excavated hole backfilled with good soil. The box will take a year to rot down but in the meantime the clematis will have ascended into the light. Plant on the shady side so they head towards the light. 'Tetrarose' is one of the finest pinks, and *C. montana wilsonii* is a later-flowering white, with a powerful chocolate perfume and late enough to be in flower at the end of this season, as the leaves break on the trees.

18 April, *Peckham*
THE FIRST TASTE OF SPRING

———

Rain stopped play in the gardens we were building this winter, and the guys were plodding around knee-deep in mud for what seemed to be weeks. The hollies and the yews that were supposed to be in the ground in February were still frozen in at the nursery in Scotland, and we didn't take delivery until the end of March. By then the spring was gathering around us like a tidal wave in the making and we had to throw ourselves at the planting to get things in the ground before they leafed up.

I love this time of year, despite the fact that it feels like everything is in fast-forward. It is more frenetic than usual this year, with winter having dragged its heels, and I feel like standing still and counting to ten to try to take in the changes. There have been unlikely collisions with unplanned-for things coming together – daffodils a month late, with forsythia and cherry – and I am sure we are in for more surprises.

I seized a window of cold, clear days that opened up in the middle of March. Sparkling blue skies and wind had dried the ground, so I set to and dug with a vengeance. The salad beds were the first to be turned over, with last year's compost trenched in. It is a pleasure to see the soil improving, like a cake mix, darker and more friable with each year that passes. I knocked it with a fork when I finished, levelled out a section to go under cloches and broadcast the first of the early salad and wild rocket. It was a risk, as there was still frost in the air, but I had had enough of waiting.

With the addition of a little heat from the cloches, it is amazing what you can put on your plate this early in the year, and I have set up the fortnight-to-three-weekly rotation to keep me in salad. I will be eating the thinnings of 'Little Gem' lettuce in no time and the frilly mustard are close. Between the rows I have 'White Icicle' radish, which is ready for pulling in just three weeks. The crunch and heat together are remarkable and they rarely make it back to the kitchen. They are washed in a bucket and eaten there and then.

The potatoes are in and already showing, and I am earthing up in case we get a frost. I doubt that this will happen here in London but it is best to be prepared with a protective layer of fleece, because frosts can persist well into May outside the capital. Fleece will help to keep the birds from pulling the onion sets, which should also be in the ground by now. Hardy vegetables, and sweet peas of course, can also be put in the ground. Broad beans will be up in days and it's safe now to sow beetroot and annual herbs such as dill and parsley, though coriander will need a little more heat to get it going and can wait until early May. If we get a dry spell, remember to water the young seedlings. It should also be safe to put dahlia tubers in, though cuttings should wait in frost-prone areas.

It is too early to think about planting out summer bedding, despite the nurseries flaunting it in ranks of unseasonal colour. It is still spring (and we have waited long enough to enjoy it), but in three weeks we should be able to think about the next season with frost safely behind us. In the meantime, and if you have the room, it is canny to prepare your half-hardy annuals by acclimatising them to being outside. I do this in the cold frame, chocking it open in the day and closing it down again at night. The process will harden off vulnerably soft foliage and get the plants used to the season ahead of them. For now though, count to ten and take in the here and now.

21 April, *Hillside*
HAPPY EPIMEDIUMS

————

I was about ten when I unearthed my first epimedium. My mother and I were clearing brambles in our long-overgrown family garden, and as we made our way through the thicket we uncovered a clump of something we didn't recognise. The leaves were leathery and brittle after the winter, but what caught our attention was the copper push of spring foliage. Rising just above the canopy of last year's leaves on impossibly fine stems was a series of overlapping hearts, netted with ruby-red veins and already sheltering a smattering of creamy flowers, like fairy columbines. It had probably survived the neglect of round about forty years.

Once the love affair kicked in, I identified our newfound

treasure as *Epimedium × versicolor* 'Sulphureum', a reliable and long-lived perennial known for its ability to deal with dry shade. You can depend upon the European forms, as they are happy to congregate into a weed-smothering groundcover that retains its foliage in winter. Part the low canopy in early March and you will see the tightly held clusters of flowers at ground level. If you take the shears to the foliage at this point, you will get to see the flowers rise alone, a process which captures the changeover between seasons perfectly. Once they rise, the naked flowers have just a week or so floating in space before the coppery rush of foliage follows them.

Epimedium × perralchicum 'Fröhnleiten' is one of the best selections and the toughest European *Epimedium*. The flowers are gold and a delight with dog's tooth violets and wood anemones. The foliage is a bright, glossy green that never seems to dim. There are other reliable species from this side of the world, but none quite as choice as those from China and Japan.

My car was like Noah's Ark when we moved here and my Asian epimediums made up the bulk of the contents. They are sitting here now in pots on the north side of the house. Although the Asian species do not come with the tough credentials of their European cousins, I have not found them to be difficult. Give them a little leaf mould and an assurance that they will not dry out in summer and they will reward you handsomely.

E. 'Amanogawa', which translates from the Japanese as Milky Way, is beautifully named, the pale white flowers hovering in space ahead of new foliage. The leaves are ruby red as they expand to fill the air around the flower and they gradually dim to green as spring ages. *E. myrianthum* is one of the best, the young leaves expanding into heavy ovals and crazed with shadowy patterns so that they appear to be dappled. *E. fargesii* has long-fingered foliage as jagged as the former is smooth.

Specialists have selected some fine forms that are proving to be completely reliable. One of the latest into flower and possibly the most exotic is *E. wushanense*. The leaves are long-fingered and heavily felted on the undersides. The flowers are widely spaced, on stems that sometimes reach to a metre. 'Caramel' is an aptly named form that I have found to be neater and still in flower in June. By then I am happy to leave spring behind, but I'm pleased for it to have lasted.

22 April, *Peckham*

PAINT THE TOWN PINK

———

Mention magnolias to most people and an image of suburbia springs to mind – the sugar-pink petticoats of *Magnolia × soulangeana* that appear on every street come March, and clash horribly with the forsythia.

But the plants can have another image entirely – that of dinosaurs breakfasting on scented, waxy blooms. They were one of the first flowering plants to appear, more than eighty million years ago. Their early relatives evolved in the late Jurassic period, before bees, and evolved to be pollinated by beetles, one of the oldest groups of insects. You can see the plants' primeval past in every detail: the paddle-shaped embryonic leaves as they first appear, the plump, rodent-like buds covered with silky fur, followed later in the season by the alien pods that burst open to reveal seeds of vibrant orange and fuchsia.

Nowadays magnolias like to live well. They prefer the moist atmosphere that comes with a woodland setting, but they also like heat, which, when combined with moisture in the growing season, can see them putting on muscle. As woodlanders, they also benefit from shelter from wind and frost. I have seen them growing wild in Japan, where the ancient-looking *M. obovata*, with its vast paddle-like foliage and exotic green-white flowers, is a distinctive layer in the Hokkaido forests. It reaches heights of over 30 m, but my strongest memory was not of the tree, but of a meal served in the forest on a plate which was a leaf, 45 cm long and half as much across.

I have never seen magnolias in China or the foothills of the Himalayas, but I can imagine them growing in the ferny gorges where the gullies fill with leaf mould and the branches ascend towards light through the cover of other trees. Their wide distribution, from east Asia to the north-east of the United States, means that the great majority are perfectly hardy – and happy to do their best in the damp British climate. In terms of soil, magnolias like it deep, humus-rich and free-draining. They also like it to be on the acid side of neutral, but the likes of *Magnolia* × *loebneri* 'Leonard Messel', with its strappy splay of candy-pink petals, are happy in alkaline conditions. Quite a few others can get away with it as long as the soil is deep.

Magnolias break winter early, with an opulent unfurling of flower. In the case of the *M. campbellii*, they do it recklessly with flowers wider than two outstretched hands. I couldn't believe it when I saw my first tree at Wisley, a spectacular 20 m growth lit up against a cold blue February sky. A few flowers were offered up on low-slung limbs, so we could dip our faces into them and marvel that such things might be possible in winter.

Magnolias also relay onwards, with a great crescendo at the end of March and early April, and continue into the summer. Pure white *M. denudata* is one of the earliest, with goblet-shaped blooms; the *M. stellata* follows, with flowers like Chinese fireworks, but there is a feast of others, stretching out to the sun-loving August-flowering *M. grandiflora*, which hails from the deep south of America and is the reason Mississippi is known as the Magnolia State.

Over the past few years I've been experimenting with magnolias in a series of different situations. We have them growing in limestone woodland in southern Italy and have spent hours on the Junker's Nursery website, imagining them becoming the high point of the garden in spring. Frost is long gone by the time they flower, but the soil is alkaline and the summers potentially lethal if there isn't enough water and shade. *Magnolia* × *loebneri* 'Merrill' has proved its adaptability there, putting on a metre a year in full sun. It has become one of my favourite dependable whites, blooming early to lighten the gloom.

'David Clulow', another of the best early whites, is doing well in the Italian garden, too. It has vast bowl-shaped blooms and it flowers well as a young plant, a demand our eighty-year-old client is impressing upon us as being increasingly important. We have the Jury hybrids there too, raised by the plantsman Felix Jury in New Zealand. He has been responsible for some magnificent young-flowering, large-flowered hybrids such as 'Iolanthe'. This, and also 'Atlas', has blooms as large and decadent as *M. campbellii*. It is worth checking out Jury's selections as he is obviously a man with a good eye and a lifetime's determination and devotion.

The farther north you go in the UK the more important it becomes to find shelter from frost. There is no point investing in trees that need time to mature if they are to be ruined every year in their moment of glory. A way around this is to work with the later-flowering magnolias such as the meaty pink *M. liliflora* 'Nigra', which is the colour of raw tuna. The tulip-shaped flowers of this plant smatter on well into summer.

'Elizabeth' is a fine, later-flowering variety and, if you can find a tree in the middle or third week of April, you will be spellbound. To describe them as yellow is maybe an exaggeration, but when their chocolate-coloured buds break, the expanding petals underneath are the richest clotted cream, tinged with green, and certainly not something you should put anywhere near a pink-blossom tree. It is a colour that needs more green around it, unfurling foliage and spring sunshine. As the flowers expand they fade to palest primrose, and on a still spring day the air under the tree is hung with a sweet perfume.

We have used 'Elizabeth' in a walled garden in North Yorkshire, planting it so that it is sheltered from early morning sunshine, as frost followed by a rapid thaw is lethal to the flowers. The young leaves are also chocolate-coloured. I have great hopes for it forming a scented arch over the door into the garden. But to be completely sure frost will not be an issue that far north, we have also planted *M. sieboldii* var. *sinensis*. This is the plant that I have chosen to be my magnolia at home in

London. It is shrubby by nature and likes a little shade to keep it cool, but it is remarkable for its exotic, pendulous flowers. These are produced in June and July, not in a mass, but in tantalising succession. The buds swell to the size and shape of a bantam's egg before opening into a down-turned bowl. Mine are placed by a path so I can look up into the pure, satin-white petals to see the boss of dark purple stamens within. Each flower is deliciously scented with a fresh incense-like perfume with hints of lemon and vanilla, and an unplaceable musky undercurrent.

Looking up into their translucent lanterns, I swear I can hear the buzz of giant beetles and the distant roar of the primeval forest.

26 April, *Hillside*
PRIMULA AND PROPER

———

The ditch which runs from a spring in the fields above us forms a wet crease between two of our fields. The land drains steeply into it from both sides and in places you can easily lose your wellies. The farmer before us did little with it other than spray out the brambles, which in our time here have seized their moment. This winter we made the big move to clear the length of it to reveal what lies underneath. Peeling back the undergrowth unearthed a series of cascades. They drop and gurgle from one level to the next and where the land falls more gently, the ditch runs in rubbly shallows. You couldn't have animated it more beautifully.

For a short while the water was visible, but it is closing over with the vegetation that was waiting in the wings. A giant primitive horsetail is already celebrating and so too is the deadly hemlock water dropwort that looks so much like parsnip or celery. We have ragged robin, campion, meadowsweet and angelica to look forward to, but the first plants to reveal themselves were the primroses.

They have obviously been more than happy under the cage of the brambles, but this spring they have revelled in the light. They're one of my favourite plants and since we have been here I have been dividing them to see if I can set off a number of colonies. They are easy plants if they have damp at the root and shade in the summer. In the garden they might be among summer perennials or beneath deciduous shrubs.

The primrose crosses readily – the parent may well be a cowslip or, in more gardened areas, a *Polyanthus*. Many *Polyanthus* have been bred to extremes with size of flower and strength of colour, but there are selections that retain an elegance. 'Gold Lace' is one of my favourites, with an almost black base and a piping of gold lining. The 'Cowichan' strain are like jewels, with dark coppery foliage and flowers that range from deep royal blue to ruby-red and burgundy. They were bred by Barnhaven, a wonderful primula nursery which is no longer in existence, but you can still seek them via the RHS Plant Finder (www.rhs.org.uk/plants).

As a child I had a Barnhaven catalogue, which in retrospect was written in thoroughly purple prose. The words had me lost in an exotic world where the plants were painted vividly in every detail. I will desist from such descriptions now, other than to say that as the primroses and polyanthus fade, the exotic bog primulas from Asia come into their own. *Primula florindae*, the giant Himalayan cowslip, is the most dramatic, rising to be more than 60 cm tall in early summer. The candelabra primula, so named for its ascending whirls of flower, which open in sequence up the length of silver-dusted stems, are perhaps at their sensational best when planted en masse in a damp position.

28 April, *Peckham*
FIRE AT WILL

———

For years I was rather reticent about tulips. It came from snobbishness about their use in park bedding. Standing tall, in regimented rows, they felt artificial and man-made, which is exactly what many of them are. Tulips have had long-standing attention from plant breeders and have been coerced into more otherworldly contortions than many other bulbs. But I have been slowly retraining myself never to judge a plant without giving it time, or at least trying to imagine how best it might be used.

Somewhere along the line I came to love the florists' tulips for their richness and flamboyance. It happened first when I was given a bunch of parrot tulips, slashed with orange and green and fuchsia pink. Did you know that tulips continue to grow if they are picked in bud? I was amazed as the bunch evolved over the week that it sat on the table: the stems sprawled out and down, seeming to sense each other so that space was left between the buds, and the flowers opened wide in the heat to reveal indigo anthers and glossy throats. They were just as incredible in their decadent death throes, casting off their withering petals like clothes on to the floor.

In the eighteenth century, tulip bulbs were exchanged for what would now be thousands of pounds a bulb when they developed the streaking, carried from one plant to the next by aphids. You can see these picked out in the Dutch Old Masters as a representation of wealth and decadence. As students at Kew, we were taken to Holland to see the bulb fields in April. It was an extraordinary sight, the land transformed into textile stripes of colour. Under the swollen buds of apple trees just about to blossom sat sheets of tulips, the spare bulbs thrown in among each other over decades in a melee of colour and form. There must have been hundreds of varieties splayed and basking in the watery sunshine, and it was a dramatic contrast to the order of the bulb fields. I saw there what the first bulb traders must have seen as they encountered tulips basking on Middle Eastern hillsides in the spring: rich treasure.

Today, I grow the hybrid tulips and love them for the flare of colour that they inject into a garden. I used them in the beds for several years, working the tall, lily-flowered *Tulipa* 'White Triumphator' among emerging *Thalictrum* and early-flowering *Pulmonaria*. They took over from the creamy *Narcissus* 'Jenny', and the *Allium aflatunense* followed through when they dropped their petals. I have a nasty feeling they have succumbed to tulip fire, a blight which lays around in the soil and causes the bulbs to dwindle rapidly or make a dramatic no-show. I am resting this ground and growing them in pots now, just in case, but it might be that because they originally come from the Middle East they hate our wet, slug-infested summers. Lifting them after they flower at least simulates the baking they need to flower again, and many varieties will live to come back for several years if you do this once the foliage has had time to feed the bulb for the next year.

Many of the hybrids are just too far removed from their parents to be reliable garden plants, so I forgive them for not coming back after the second or third year and replant with some new bulbs every autumn. In so doing I will stumble upon something unfamiliar and unexpected. Last year's replacements for 'White Triumphator' turned out to be the very similar 'Sapporo', which starts off primrose, and I think I've found a new favourite. Over the years I have grown to love 'Ballerina' for its sherbet-scented flowers in a punchy orange. 'West Point' is an incredible lily-flowered variety, too, quite the clearest, strongest yellow you can imagine and wonderful when opened out, as if to say 'feed me' in sunshine. 'Abu Hassan' is still my most loved rich mahogany red, enlivened with a saffron stripe.

If truth be told, my tulips are quite a carry-on, so I am keeping my options open with plants that are happy to stay in the ground and come back another year. Some, such as *T. acuminata*, will only last a couple of years, like the hybrids. You can forgive this species its short-lived nature, for the tapering, multicoloured flowers dance like flames through your borders. *T. turkestanica* is truly reliable. With strappy leaves and several cream flowers to a stem, the petals peel back in the sunshine to reveal yolky throats. I fancy some *T. saxatilis*, too, with lavender flowers opening to reveal petals cut low with bright yellow. *T. fosteriana*, with orange flowers, is another short-grower with wonderfully mottled foliage, and it is worth noting that any *fosteriana* hybrids are also pretty perennial. *T. kaufmanniana* is another good early, flowering low with eggy-orange flowers striped orange-red. It must be incredible to stumble upon them in the wild, like beacons among the rocks.

What unites tulips is a love of sunshine, and with this a free-draining soil that will allow them not to sit around with damp bottoms. I have them in only the brightest spots in my garden, and to keep them dry when they are dormant I'm planting them among deciduous shrubs that leaf-up late once they are over. My *Salix exigua* has proved perfect in this respect and I have quite a few species destined to join the *T. sprengeri* that are now happily self-seeding there among the 'Molly the Witch'. The *T. sprengeri* is one of the last tulips to flower, in the middle of May. It has seeded in masses for the first time, so it must be happy. I'm hoping for great things from this pure scarlet species.

T. sylvestris is the only tulip that grows wild in the UK. It is debatable if it is a real native or whether it was introduced, but it is a lovely thing for a sunny bank. Brilliant chrome-yellow, the flowers bowing their heads in sunshine, it looks out of place in an early April meadow. But I like to think of the meadow as a magic carpet where almost anything can happen. Tulips, you see, have a way of casting their spell over you.

29 April, *Hampshire*

NEW BEGINNINGS

———

I am writing this in suspension, in a week unlike any other. Outside the weather has broken, the rains replaced by brilliant clear skies, and the sun is streaming through the window. We are with my father in hospital, waiting for him to slip away after a long illness, and for the first time I can remember the spring has slowed.

The days have been filled with conversation and, with the luxury of time to think, I have taken myself up to the South Downs to taste the air. The route from the hospital runs along the base of the downs, where the blackthorn has already sprung in the sunshine. Where it has hopped and run and suckered its way along the verges the blackthorn has formed cages that protect an inner world of primroses. As you climb from South Harting through the fern-clad hangers that wrap the village the spring recedes, the air is still cold. The blackthorn that hunkers into the tufted grassland has been held in readiness, and over the week I have watched the buds swell in their leafless transition from dormancy.

Few things are more beautiful than spring blossom and, while I have felt the privilege of being here with my family, I have also had the pleasure of witnessing this change in blossom. The cherry plums (*Prunus cerasifera*) that had already broken bud at the start of the week are changed, their tiny petals now falling and caught on the breeze, as the first flush of leaf bud comes to replace them.

Observe a blossom season and you will see one tree handing over its moment of glory to the next, as the varieties follow on from each other. First the cherry plum to the blackthorn; next the balloon-shaped flowers of the pears; then the delicate sprays of *Amelanchier*, which cross over with the flurry of cherries. These are many and varied and range from the delicate and single to full-blown confections that are doubled and sugary. After several weeks the cherries finally give way to the crabs and the apples, which are dimmed only by leaves breaking on the trees as spring gives way to summer.

That moment, however, before the blossom breaks, is perhaps the most wondrous. On the news in Japan, the *hanami* season is charted in blossom maps that mark the movement of flower across the country. I urge you to get a blossom tree if you do not have one, for the chance of witnessing this window of spring. Slowed for a moment, you too can take in the miracle.

MAY

M

The pace continues now, with plants rearing up in every direction to a tipping point that happens in the third week of the month, somewhere around the Chelsea Flower Show. The show is brilliantly timed, with freshness and anticipation caught all in one week. The spectacle allows us a peek into the next season and, by the time the show is finished, you can be more or less sure that the last frost has bitten and the first chapter of summer has opened. In the city it is wisteria time, and the buildings in certain parts of town appear to open up to embrace the streets with blossom. Lilacs make their appearance in a cumulus of scented flower, and in the country, hedgerows push and narrow the lanes with a froth of cow parsley. Ferns unravel in a movement seemingly choreographed to capture the feeling of 'now'.

Despite the wealth of things to do at this time of year, I always try and take a little time to go out into nature to look.

A trip to a wild place to see where plants have found their niche is always inspirational and I return feeling as balanced as the very plant communities that I have borne witness to. Balance is key in a garden and to aim for it not only makes a garden feel more restful, it also goes towards making your life easier. Understand, for instance, where *Tulipa sprengeri* likes to live and they will seed themselves around, and there is nothing more rewarding than plants showing you they are happy by making themselves at home.

I spend the last week of the month busying in the garden. The half-hardy perennials can go in the ground, vegetables that like the promise of heat can be sown or planted out with confidence, and the annuals that until now have needed cosseting and protection can be moved outside with the summer ahead of them. Anticipation is found at every turn, with lupins and foxgloves racing skyward, but still with plenty of bud to come.

2 **May**, *London*

TREE OF LIFE

———

The London Maggie's Centre for cancer care stands on a sliver of land between the Fulham Palace Road and Charing Cross Hospital in Hammersmith. Already there are five centres in Scotland, designed by Page and Park, Richard Murphy, Frank Gehry and Zaha Hadid, but the London centre, designed by Richard Rogers's practice, is the first of six planned for England and Wales.

They are the vision of Maggie Keswick Jencks who, while being treated for cancer, identified the need for patients to access emotional and psychological support and practical information in an uplifting environment, since, in her words, 'Above all, what matters is not to lose the joy of living in the fear of dying.' The buildings are closely linked to NHS oncology departments, but they don't have corridors or hospital paraphernalia. Visitors feel they are entering an 'open house' where the informality of conversation around a kitchen table helps to create an atmosphere of ease and sanctuary.

I was particularly excited to be offered the opportunity to create a series of gardens for the new centre, as I am a believer in the healing power of gardens and gardening. The calming effect of green and the fact that a beautiful, sensual environment can transport you can affect anyone. For those of us who choose to garden, there is nothing quite like the feeling of freedom that comes when you combine the cerebral with the physical. Building in the 'feel-good' is something that is now second nature in the way that I approach garden-making, but this was an opportunity to do it in the knowledge that all the energy was going to those who need it most.

The centre is based on the embrace of an arm that gradually envelops visitors as they move towards the kitchen at the heart of the building. A tall tomato-orange wall wraps around the building, providing protection from the busy road and the hubbub of the hospital. My brief from Laura Lee and Marcia Blakenham, chief executive and vice chairman respectively of Maggie's, was that the building should be protected and cushioned by the green of a garden. The centre has been designed with three internal winter gardens and sun-filled roof terraces so that you are never more than a step away from the healing power of vegetation.

When I visited the site it was a delight to find that there was already a group of established London planes there. They have textured trunks that lean at angles and immediately suggested a leafy woodland approach meandering between them. The entrance to the centre was key, as we knew that the biggest obstacle for many people scared by their situation was going to be getting over the threshold. The woodland walk has been planted with winter box (*Sarcococca*) for perfume and a soft undercurrent of leafy evergreen perennials, which will form a foil for a series of sensual ceramic sculptures by Hannah Bennett.

Hannah matched the glaze colours to the bark on the plane trees, and they lead your eye to the arrival courtyard, which is surrounded by a group of white *Magnolia* × *loebneri* 'Merrill'. There is a long bench here which connects the arrival courtyard through an opening in the front wall to the safety of the main inner courtyard. The last of the seven sculptures sits at the end of a leafy corridor by the front door, and is dished to hold a small pool of water to reflect the sky.

We surrounded the building with more than a hundred *Betula albosinensis* var. *septentrionalis* to filter noise and pollution. They are already showing the dark pink and mahogany patterning on the bark which, in time, will complement the warmth of the coloured walls. To play further with colour, a coppery layer of *Luzula sylvatica* 'Marginata' and orange-berried *Iris foetidissima* is massed beneath. The trees are concentrated in front of two frosted windows, which lets shadow patterns play on the glass and gives visitors a shielded connection to the outside world.

Visitors are encouraged to find their own space inside the building, so there is a choice of courtyards to sit in. The north-facing courtyard is filled with the lush greenery of *Tetrapanax*, scented *Nicotiana* and the exotically perfumed climber *Holboellia*. The east courtyard has an outdoor fireplace, *Sparrmannia* and *Iris japonica* 'Ledger's Variety'. The focal point of the southern courtyard is a huge table under the shade of a feathery *Albizia julibrissin*, the Chinese tree of happiness, the bark and flowers of which are used as a calming sedative in Chinese medicine. There is perfume here, too, with *Trachelospermum*, honey spurge and scented pelargoniums. There will be grapes to eat from the vines that will cover the pergola, and at Cath Knox's suggestion we have planted some giant pots with peppermint and lemon verbena so that visitors will be able to pick their own herbs for a cup of tea and a chat.

Cath has been living with cancer for twelve years, and getting to know her has made the project very real for me. 'When you are told you have cancer, every moment counts,' she told me. 'To have those moments captured in the blossom of a magnolia that you may not see the following year, to stumble across perfume caught on the breeze or the scent of mint crushed between your fingers becomes incredibly meaningful.' I have always intuitively known that intimacy, sensuality and sanctuary in a garden are key to creating a sense of wellbeing, but it has been made so much more vivid seeing it through the eyes of someone who is seizing life with a new intensity. That intense connection with nature is something from which we can all benefit, and I feel privileged to have been able to create an environment which will offer that experience to those who may need it most.

4 May, *Peckham*

GRACE AND FAVOUR

———

Four years ago, I was given a tray of *Tulipa sprengeri* by Chris and Toby Marchant, friends who run a wholesale nursery near Henley. It was a coincidence, for just the year before I had stumbled upon them at Great Dixter during Chelsea week and marvelled at their scarlet flowers thrown open and shining in the sunshine. Although I love a new conquest, I always fret when I am given plants, as the garden is already bursting at the seams. I am strict about introductions, as I am at pains to avoid that spotty complexion that collectors' gardens so often have. I trust the Marchants, though, so I duly did my research.

Firstly, I found that the bulbs are expensive and rarely offered in bulk by wholesale bulb specialists. Like the named forms of snowdrop, you don't have the option of buying by the hundred and splashing the garden with a drift. Yet there is an in-built contradiction, for in all the books *T. sprengeri* is heralded for its ability to seed and naturalise in a garden setting, even, it was rumoured, in grass. This is rare in a tulip, for most of the species are too picky to last long in ground that lies wet in winter, as it does here. The egg-yolk yellow *T. sylvestris* has naturalised in part of the UK, but most tulips like it dry. In their homelands of north Africa and central Asia they do their growing when winter wet is available, but on rocky hillsides that drain and bake during hot summers.

I have dabbled with the species tulips before, growing them in pots to see if I like them and then liberating them into the beds to test their ability to cope in the ground. I like this way of getting to know a plant because you can bring it up close, live with it and become familiar with its ways. The little *T. tarda* with its yellow centre and white petals made the garden sparkle in April, and the multi-headed ivory *T. turkestanica* was worth exploring for sheer curiosity value. These tulips are like the spark that ignited their blowsy cousins, but there is nothing lost to their often delicate stature, for they gain everything in intensity.

The lipstick pinks of *T. clusiana* are my experiment in the pots this year. They are as good in bud as they are in flower, with petals stained with layers of cherry and fuchsia over orange, yellow or cream. I have two: the blood-red and saffron *T. clusiana* var. *chrysantha* and the cherry-pink and cream *T. clusiana* 'Lady Jane'. They have proved their worth with tapers of candle-like flowers and will be worked into the beds to see if they have what it takes to make it in the long run. I hear that, of the many species of tulips that were trialled over the last three years at Wisley, these proved themselves as potential long-term garden plants, which is a serious bonus when planting tulips in beds. In my own little trial, I am only interested if they like me as much as I like them and they prove it with endurance. This is exactly what I wanted from my *T. sprengeri*.

They were not yet in flower when I planted a dozen pots, one bulb in each with glossy green foliage. The tapered buds were half the size of a florist's tulip, but already had twice the elegance, and I could see that the colour and timing would be perfect with my dusky-leaved peony, 'Molly the Witch'. I had learned that they were happy in a little shade, and the peony and the tulips could be left where they were to settle in in the dappled light beneath the coyote willows. The willow also seemed like it would suit the combination, for it came into leaf late, giving the tulips plenty of time to feast upon early sunshine. They first flowered at the end of May, and were out for more than a fortnight, straddling the spring/summer boundary of June. That summer, to add to my delight, they produced a crop of rattle-shaped seedheads that shook free their satiny circular seed in the heat of August.

I all but forgot about them until the next April, when I came upon a rash of grass-like seedlings, each holding the seed-case high, like a banner to show that they had made it. The parent plants had increased in size, too, but not by as much as the seedlings, and now, three years on, I am looking at a cluster of three generations and hoping for the first of the seedlings to flower next year.

I like a plant that proves its congeniality by seeding and I like the way a garden feels when plants are allowed to roam. The primrose sets a good example when it is happy in a bank, and there is nothing like the satisfaction of seeing snakeshead fritillaries take off. If you wait long enough, you can see where they like to be, where the ground lies damp enough for them or where the competition is right for the seedlings to make it.

This is what I am hoping the harvested seed from my *T. sprengeri* will be up for next year, for I am collecting it now they are establishing themselves. I will ferry them to my most patient clients and give them the chance to make their own colonies. In one garden, after the meadows are cut in summer, I am going to rake an area until it exposes enough bare earth upon which to throw the seed. In another, I will work the seed into a colony of violets that occupy a sunny bank under eglantine roses. The sun is important, for the full joy of the flower is in the opening. It is the last tulip of the season, the herald of summer, and I'm so pleased it seems to be here to stay.

6 May, *The Gower Peninsula*

FROND MEMORIES

———

During Easter week, I took a few days off to set my feet on the ground again after a busy start to the year. I had the loan of a friend's cabin on the Gower peninsula in South Wales and the simplicity of the place had been haunting my dreams for quite some time. There is no electricity, mains water, bathroom or loo; firewood for the little iron stove must be gathered from the beach and water from a spring in the woods. The luxury of this trip was time – which I spent watching the spring unravelling at close quarters.

The drive down saw the motorway embankments a froth of creamy blackthorn with sheets of primroses nestling beneath in the shade. Brilliant clouds of *Prunus avium* illuminated the skyline and were at their very moment of perfection – some bud, yet with flower to come. At points, the wild gean (as it is also known) were laced through the acid-green growth of *Acer platanoides*. It was a moment captured, but soon to be lost for another year because the week was hot and quite out of kilter with the season.

Soon we were stumbling through the steep field to the sand dunes where the cabins lie. The field, which becomes a muddy slide on a wet day, gives way to low woodland of ancient hazel coppice. Lining the stream that runs down into the dunes were the very last of the pussy willow caught in the evening sunshine. Beneath them were yet more primroses, set among violets so thick that the still spring air hung with the perfume. It was ridiculously pretty, so much so that I swear that, if I were ever to see a unicorn, it would have to be in one of those perfectly proportioned clearings where the grass sparkles in sunshine and the forest flowers skirt the dappled margins. Over the few days we were there I managed to do what I do so rarely: to slow the spring down to the point where you can feel the sap rising.

The Gower peninsula is justly famed for its landscape: for such a small piece of land, it changes dramatically as you pass along the many trails that lace its contours. On the high ground there are windswept moors with bracken, gorse, wild ponies and standing stones. Dipping down into the hollows the land gathers in folds of sheltered ancient woodland, full of moss, lichen and the twisted trunks of anthropomorphic trees. In the warm, south-facing sand dunes are birch colonies interspersed with giant pincushions created by the ants. The fuzz of the finest fescue grasses that cover these anthills is grazed to a texture like velvet by the wild rabbits. Further into the dunes, the birches give way to tall pine groves which must have been planted to stabilise the dunes. There is an old Chinese saying that if you plant pines you invite the wind. I was struck by the truth of this, as there was a distinctive whisper here that stopped you in your tracks.

I always question why I bother to go to the lengths to create gardens when I see such fine-tuned balance, everything in its place and just getting on with it, out in the wild. Further into the hollows, the hart's tongue ferns, so particular to the limestone of the west, had formed huge colonies which, just weeks before, would have been glinting, their evergreen fronds still good until the end of March. But I had caught the ferns just as the new growth starts, and the perfect leaf-green scrolls were unrolling and expanding daily. The embodiment of spring.

Back home, the ferns at the bottom of the garden were my first port of call. They thrive in what would be very much a second choice of home, if they had been given one. But the fact that they do so well is one of the reasons why I can make do with my garden in London, because they bring some of the feeling of those delicate woodlands and impart magic to an otherwise potentially dreary corner. Overhung by a neighbour's tree and sandwiched between council garages and the compost heap, it is the ferns that have made this part of the garden delightful, and as they have thrived I have added to the collection: feathery maidenhairs, *Adiantum venustum*, so delicate you cannot believe they are hardy, and the spooky, black-stemmed *Dryopteris wallichiana* with the arisaemas.

Being brought up in woodland has predisposed me to one of the most successful shade dwellers there is. I have always kept my eyes open for a good plant. If I have a wet, shady area it will be the shuttlecock fern, *Matteuccia struthiopteris*, that is top of the list. 'You've got to watch that one,' was Beth Chatto's comment as we wandered past hers last time I was down there admiring her garden in late April. It was at its best, growing among the roots of the swamp cypress where the mud is wet and clingy. Pure, perfect cones of green had just unrolled and were caught in low sunshine.

Though it is only really *Matteuccia*, the sensitive fern *Onoclea sensibilis*, and the giant royal fern *Osmunda regalis* that need this level of moisture to thrive, the one thing that unites all ferns is their liking for a damp atmosphere. They evolved in woodland and in truth prefer to be there still – or at least in the shade. Many, the *Dryopteris* in particular, will thrive in quite dry conditions as long as there is moisture when the fronds unroll in the spring, and they are kept free of sun in the middle of the day. Ferns also love shelter, for this brings with it an ambient moisture which protects their foliage from desiccation.

Where foliage texture is needed, ferns are one of the best fallbacks. *Polystichum setiferum*, with fronds that spiral out from the centre of the plant, is one of my favourites for dry shade. It is a perfect companion to *Cyclamen hederifolium* foliage in the winter, as it keeps its leaves and is low enough to let *Galanthus* and *Erythronium* rise through it. There are countless selections with unbelievably complicated names, but 'Herrenhausen' is reliably lovely. Variation is one of the fern's greatest strengths and the reason that the Victorians had continually to lengthen their names was that they are always throwing up sports. The female fern, *Dryopteris felix-femina*, shows a whole range in quite a short area, and at some points the leaf is so finely divided it resembles lace.

In the light well at the front of my house is a small pot-bound fern collection that is thriving. Right now, the first scrolls of *Osmunda regalis* are unfurling in a pot that sits permanently wet in a tray of water; I like to feel that I am fooling it into thinking it is in an Irish peat bog, to make it feel at home. Lighter and more flamboyant is the Japanese painted fern, *Athyrium niponicum* 'Pictum'. Deep purple, red and silver slash the foliage and the red is picked up in the new foliage of *Dryopteris erythrosora*. I love the glossiness against the giant leathery *Blechnum chilense* nearby. New to this little gathering last year was *Athyrium* 'Ghost', which is as pale and silvery as its name implies. Although the woods feel unreachable, there is magic enough here to bring the best of this season to within inches of my window.

8 May, *Hillside*

LAST LEAP TO SUMMER

———

The lanes down at the farm are narrowing daily as the verges are fattening. The primroses, violets and celandine have already been eclipsed, cast into shade by the stingers, the racing cleavers and the froth of cow parsley. This ubiquitous perennial is one of the first to stir in spring, the finely divided foliage pushing through ahead of the rest; but it will be over in a flash, spring breaking head on into summer.

A fleet of wild umbellifers is coming through now to join the cow parsley. There are Alexanders, a plant usually encountered in coastal hedgerows and thought to have been brought in by the Romans as an early salad crop, along with the dreaded ground elder. I grew up with ground elder and its sure but steady progress through our woodland garden, and consequently harbour a fear of it. Sure enough, the young foliage will cut-and-come-again like no other salad crop I know, but despite its aromatic, lemony taste it would be madness to introduce it actively. Luckily, there is none up by the house and I am assuming it must have been rejected, as it appears in the tangle of wire and unwanted things dumped down by the stream.

When you look closely at this elegant family, several members are noteworthy for their culinary usefulness. I have yet to candy the stems of the angelica, but I use the plant as a vertical accent in gardens where there is room. You have to be careful with angelica, as its early growth and biennial habits mean it catches you by surprise, springing up to eclipse a more reticent neighbour. I liked the way the great gardener Margery Fish grew it along a barn wall, boxed in with *Buxus* hedging.

The bulbous vegetable of the fennel is a nightmare to grow without bolting, but the perennial *Foeniculum vulgare* is a delightful addition to the garden. I grow a dark selected form called 'Giant Bronze' in the borders where it appears in the spring, rising up in several smoky guises before filling out in high summer with hotly aromatic flowers. Few things are better for bees and hoverflies. Coriander, dill, lovage and parsley are also mainstays of our kitchen gardens but there are dangers in the family, too. Hemlock has yet to show itself here, but hemlock water dropwort is tracing the wet loam in the ditch. *The Forager Handbook* (Ebury Press) says this deadly poisonous lofty perennial is easily confused with wild celery, so I will enjoy its outline only as I get to know the land.

Halfway down the ditch are the upwardly mobile stems

of *Angelica sylvestris*, our native angelica. Most are green, but several are stained a dark plum red and remind me of the 'Vicar's Mead' selection I first saw growing at Heronswood Nursery in Seattle. They were 1.5 m tall in the Pacific climate, and I struggled to grow them in London without the water they obviously needed. I am happy to be the observer of these wildings while I am kitchen gardening.

Their elegant outline and gently sculptural form lend the umbellifers a quietly aristocratic air while retaining a wildness when used in the garden. To reference the softness of the hedgerow cow parsley I often use *Chaerophyllum hirsutum* 'Roseum', which is better behaved and arguably as graceful. It is also a reliable perennial in a dappled corner, with deeply divided foliage that gives way to an eruption of lavender-pink flowers. Cut back to the base at the end of the month when it is over, it provides low-down greenery for the rest of the season.

9 May, *Peckham*
KEEP YOUR EYE ON THE BALL

———

The alliums are up early, spearing ground while most things are still asleep. I have several here, but it is 'Purple Sensation' that is the first to make itself felt. By April, when the hornbeam is full of catkin, their foliage is lush and blue-green, pushing up vigorously and consuming the hellebores as they wane. They like this early time, feeding their bulbs while there is little around to compete.

The foliage has reached its climax when the tulips are showing their first flower, and there is a wonderful moment late in April when the buds of the tulips are at their most opulent and are lolling in sunshine. The allium buds are pushing through absolutely vertically as the next wave. Held aloft and rising up to 90 cm or so before they break, the buds are like a conurbation of Turkish domes. By the time the papery tunic on the alliums has broken, the garden is in full swing and caught between spring and summer. The Banksia roses are in full flower, as are the *Gladiolus byzantinus*, and there is a riot of fresh green foliage as far as you can see.

When I was gardening at Home Farm, I grew *Allium hollandicum* 'Purple Sensation' through the old roses with *Papaver orientale* 'Perry's White', and they held the show for a month before the roses started to bloom in early June. 'Purple Sensation' is a darker, richer purple than the mauve of its parent, *A. hollandicum*, and occasionally the self-sown reversions would weave back into the mix. I let the seedheads run their course at Home Farm, and they seeded freely on the sunny bank, but I remove the seedheads here before the seed is scattered to keep them in check. The seedlings only take three years to flower and they have a lust for life that you have to watch, in case they consume neighbours that are slower to get off the blocks.

I grow *A. stipitatum* 'Mount Everest' at the end of the garden. As the name suggests, it is big and white, but it still retains elegance. I have to watch that the foliage doesn't overwhelm the *Aquilegia* 'Yellow Star' but they make a perfect combination with the single-flowered 'Cooper's Burmese' rose behind them. 'Mount Everest' is creamy white and very similar to 'Mont Blanc'.

I would grow a larger range of alliums if I could, but the *Nectaroscordum siculum* have dictated the way things are running in the sunny part of the garden. The green-flowered Sicilian honey garlic has curiously coloured flowers, which in the subspecies *bulgaricum* is overlaid with a dusky grey-mauve. They are full of bees when the heads of pendulous bells first open, but the flowers rise up to form distinctive seed cases as soon as they have been pollinated. These are every bit as good as the flower and I leave them in place well after the foliage has withered away below ground in June.

If you have a hot spot, *A. christophii* is a must. It is considerably shorter than those mentioned, at about 60 cm, but the flowers are spectacular, forming a sphere 30 cm across of metallic mauve stars. Alliums are happy on quite heavy soils as long as they are not waterlogged in winter, but *A. schubertii* is very particular about heat and sharp drainage. This is an extraordinary plant, with a constellation of flowers up to 30 cm in diameter held in several orbits, as the spokes to each flower vary in length. I marvel at their construction, and also at the fact that this damp old country of ours allows us to play with so many treasures.

SPRING PERENNIALS

––––––

The growth is a remarkable thing during these weeks between spring and summer. If you could hear it, there would be a tangible hum, made from a million buds breaking and stems flexing. The tide of green sweeps up and over bare earth, cloaking it as fast as the leaves fill out above us. Blink and you miss the soft marbling on the new leaves of the *Epimedium* and the dusty bloom overlaying the ruby young growth on the 'Molly the Witch'. Blink again and this first of the peonies will be open – primrose cups filled with bees.

The flurry of spring perennials starts the summer garden. One layer takes over from the next, replacing and adding like an increasingly complex textile. Many of the first to rise are wood-landers, happy to take the early light, then dwell in the shade as the summer canopy closes over. *Epimedium* is a good example, flowering in a mass of tiny columbines and in combination with coppery foliage. Most are tough enough to live in dry shade once they are established, making them great contenders for running under the skirts of deciduous shrubs. You cannot go wrong with *Epimedium perralchicum* or *E. × versicolor* 'Sulphureum' as long as you give them a good start.

Though the lungworts can be prone to mildew if they get dry at the root, *Pulmonaria* are a mainstay of spring planting. Neat by nature, they rarely rise to more than 30 cm and will gently spread when happy, to make weed-proof groundcover. This winter, my *Pulmonaria rubra* was in flower in February and providing a feeding ground to the first lone bees through March and April. The foliage of this humble plant is simply green but most have the spots and some have silver marbling. In some this is spectacular, the foliage lighting up shady areas in summer.

Pulmonaria 'Blue Ensign' is plain-leaved but it makes up for it with a carpet of gentian-blue flowers. I use these under *Rosa glauca* as a groundcover and love that moment when the smoky-pink foliage on the rose comes to life. There are a wealth of marbled cultivars. *P. saccharata* 'Leopard' is a good one, with flowers colouring pink and mauve as they age. 'Opal' is well named and a cool companion among unfurling ferns. I am fond of 'Sissinghurst White' for a similar position or as a companion to early-flowering *Viola riviniana* 'Purpurea'. With its purple foliage and copious flush of early flower, 'Purpurea' likes to find itself on the edge of things, in cracks where nothing else will grow.

The common-or-garden *Valeriana officinalis*, with its sleep-inducing roots and animal attraction for cats, is a plant I would miss if it wasn't there in spring. Tall and wiry like an umbellifer, it has sweetly perfumed flowers that foam just-pink. As with many of the early-flowering perennials, cut them to the base, leaves and all, immediately after flowering and they will return later in summer with a fresh crop of foliage.

TENDER IS THE LIGHT

———

Be it little more than a large Tupperware container, the box that holds my seed collection is a veritable cornucopia. This is the third time it has been opened this year. The first was inside, in February, and the half-hardy annuals that were sown shortly afterwards are now ready to be planted. The second time, on a bright day on the terrace, was to pull out the hardy vegetables. I now have several rows of salad, some rocket and radishes sown in the warm Easter week. I am thinning for baby leaves and crunching on radishes. The white Japanese ones make your eyes smart, and you have to be vigilant and get to them quickly. Radishes live fast and need to be eaten young, and you must sow every fortnight to keep a good supply on your plate. Most of mine never make it from the end of the garden. They are eaten seconds after pulling.

The third time the box was opened was to select the tender vegetable seeds that need the certainty of warm ground to thrive. I like to wait until mid-May or Chelsea week to be completely sure that anything tender will not come to harm. The tender South American vegetables, like maize and gourds and many beans, are a long way from home and need the heat. Warm soil, warm nights and long sunlit days are what these vegetables thrive upon and why it is worth waiting until summer is with us before committing them to their growing positions. With warmth they will race away and you will be pushed to keep up with them after the first twist of runner beans has been trained on to the poles. Plant too early when there isn't enough warmth and these hothouse flowers will sit and sulk, or worse still, rot before they have had a chance.

Several of the vegetables that were brought back from the Americas were grown as ornamentals until we in Europe discovered how delicious they were. The runner beans and tomatoes were given pride of place, and I still like to play to their strengths and work them into plantings to give edible height on wigwams in the borders. Be sure that you can get to them – a well-positioned slab to get from a path to a harvesting position will keep your relationship with them practical. A sturdy tripod also goes a long way, and I will save my best black canes from the bamboo or source handsome hazel branches out in the countryside. Seek out the hot spots for these vegetables to do well and prepare the soil under the tripod with a barrowload of compost or muck dug in under the roots. Because they grow fast and furious, and their main aim in life is to reproduce, they like to live well, and the organic matter will help by also holding water deep down in the soil.

Tomatoes are incredibly easy and fast from seed but they are better put in as young plants now, if you don't have a glasshouse, to make the most of the summer. Seek out those that are earmarked for outdoor use, and keep to the cherry tomatoes for the sweetest, most easily ripened fruit. 'Gardener's Delight' is a classic, and I have grown the equally sweet 'Sungold' for several years without fail. It is a delicious thing handling tomatoes, their musky green smell making your mouth water. I hear some supermarkets spray the fruit with an artificial perfume to make their tomatoes more delectable when the packet is opened –

even more reason to grow them close to home and organically. The bush varieties like 'Masokota' and 'Tiny Tim' make great pot plants: a deep window box on a sunny sill makes a good home for them. (Simpson's does the best range of seed and plug plants in season.)

Beans, courgettes and pumpkins like to get their feet deep in the ground and thrive when soil conditions are rich and stable. They do better when sown directly so that they can get their tap-roots down without interruption. I have great hopes for some old Italian seed of a flat yellow French climbing bean that I found deep down in my box and have set a few on damp tissue paper to test their viability. I have confidence that the old seed will germinate and am trusting in the experience of a friend's mother who lived in a twelfth-century house in Suffolk. She had an internal wall replaced and, as it was wattle and daub – no more than woven willow and a mixture of mud and manure – it was thrown in a heap at the bottom of the garden. It was early summer, and after rain the heap started to grow thick with field beans that had been sitting dormant in the mud since the wall was erected. They were 800 years old and grew into a new century without flinching.

The gourds – the courgettes, squashes and pumpkins – are best sown directly, too. With warmth they will race away, and this is one reason why you often see them planted as a topping to compost heaps. When I was at Kew the heaps were legendary. They were more than 5 m high and steamed on cool mornings, and the man who looked after them grew all manner of things – some legal, some not – in this hinterland on the top. By the end of summer the gourds came spewing over the edges, and I have never seen anything quite like it. They travelled several metres in days because they loved the good living, the moist but free-draining growing medium and as much sun as they could get. If you are growing them at ground level, dig in a good trench of muck or compost. They need moisture and goodness to produce their spectacle of fruit. I like yellow and green courgettes and always go for the bush varieties if space is limited. The flowers are delicious stuffed with ricotta and deep-fried in a light batter like tempura.

If you have the room, grow trailing gourds: 'Uchiki Kuri' is a smallish, orange-skinned pumpkin variety that has a nutty flavour, and 'Crown Prince' is a curious emerald-green squash with saffron-yellow skin. Delicious. They can be trained up arches or cover ground where you might be letting a piece of veggie patch lie fallow. You can grow them at 1 m intervals through quite a thick mulch if you are improving the soil, or a covering of carpet or newspaper if you are smothering out perennial weeds. Sink an upturned plastic bottle (with its base cut off and top removed) close to the plant to make watering through the mulch easy.

From this point on, it is important to keep an eye on the greater picture. Weeding, watering, earthing up potatoes so that they don't grow green, pinching out your tomatoes and keeping up with successional sowing every two to three weeks will mean you avoid glut or famine. Sow small amounts and short rows of salad and leaf crops like spinach. Stagger the French beans, perhaps six weeks between three sowings, and eat the tops to the broad beans when you pinch them out to avoid the black fly. A good vegetable patch is a bit like an old friend that likes a fortnightly visit. You will get more from the relationship if you keep up the regular contact.

13 May, *Greece*

A GARDENER'S ODYSSEY

———

About a month ago, we packed our walking boots and set off on a Greek adventure. The aim was to steal a march on spring, and our timing couldn't have been more perfect.

I have travelled many times to look at flowers in the wild – there is nothing like seeing them in context to teach you how they grow – but nothing had prepared me for anything quite so magical. Looking back at the photos, I feel like we were walking in a dream – our days were spent scaling the mountainsides, following goat tracks into disused olive groves and boulder-strewn hillsides.

The sea was a constant companion, glinting silvery blue in the corner of my eye, and we were ahead of the crowds, which rendered the landscape timeless. I began to understand why the gods were created here. An inky oak tree with a dark pool of shade drew us in from time to time and we would sit amid a carpet of flowering camomile broken only by bee and spider orchids. Out in the sunshine, just a stone's throw away, *Cistus* were blooming, their papery flowers of carmine pink fluttering in the breeze.

Our journeys were broken by exclamation of the next discovery as we ambled, with friends, through a landscape of gently shifting treasures. In the hollows, protected from the drying wind, a downy-leaved lupin bloomed azure blue against saffron *Calendula*, and a tall wild barley marked where a farmer had once cultivated ground. The awns were tilting over in readiness for pollination, capturing every breath of wind, while amber and brick-red peas scrambled through a little quaking grass at their feet.

Getting to know why plants live the way they do and what they choose to live alongside is good education, but the natural combinations were more than half the delight. A purple vetch reaching up into buttercup-yellow broom jostled with acid-green *Smyrnium* and buttery *Oxalis*. A bolt of giant fennel pushed through a night-scented stock. These were partnerships you wish you could have dreamed up for yourself. Filigree umbellifers of ivory white, the perfect complement to the jagged outline of a silvery thistle. The punchy pink of a tiny campion, with a velvet-purple *Anchusa* as a partner.

One day, inevitably, we ended up on a beach of hot black sand which burned the soles of your feet when you threw your boots aside. Darkened dunes were hunkered down with mastic bush and, pushing through a gap in the still-bare branches of colonising *Vitex agnus-castus*, I found a bowl-shaped valley giving way to oaks with juniper clinging to the cliff faces. The dark shadows at their base were lit by a surf of moon daisies, and a hush descended for a moment as my ears adjusted from the waves to a roar of bees feeding in a sea of *Lavandula stoechas*. It was a scene of unforgettable beauty; a moment of perfection, with life going about its business as it has done for millennia.

I have had this epiphany several times before when nature shows me it simply does it better. It is good to be reminded that there is beauty in the balance and that it is important to let it have the upper hand whenever we can allow it. It is also important to take the time to look, because the unfamiliar always gives cause for reflection.

I returned to my carved-out plot, happy in the knowledge that it has boundaries and that the rows of tulips and regimentation required to grow my vegetables are simply a device to help me find a little corner of order. It was never more clear, with the contrast of such delights still fresh, that real gardening comes when we have the confidence to let go a little; for it is good to walk around the self-sown poppy in the path or to enjoy a tangle in the corner. Look into the tangle and you'll see another order – one that we can learn from to get a little closer to things being perfect.

15 May, *Hillside*
FRUITS OF OUR LABOUR

———

In the first or second week of March and shortly after the hazel catkins browned, an extraordinary thing happened as the fields came to life, and the grass on the hillsides glowed a shimmering, luminous green. A friend who was staying at the time said he felt like he was in an altered reality; you could almost hear the grass growing, the soft, sappy blades bending and glinting in the first of the spring sunshine.

The farmer who is using our fields to graze his sheep had not long before taken them away for lambing and he looked on lustfully at the feeding opportunity. I had asked him by to see if he could help me extend my vegetable garden and I needed to tie him down as the spring was upon us. The following week, in a window of bright, dry weather, he arrived with a load of glorious muck and his smallest tractor and plough.

I can't quite convey the excitement in seeing the pasture turned to newly ploughed soil. Though I have told myself I am waiting a year to see what the land will tell me, I have been busily acquiring plants in the name of gauging what will and won't do well on the slopes. The experiments lie mostly in seed-raised vegetables, dahlias for cutting and the beginnings of a fruit garden, as these first years will be about production. Before they were turned over to grazing for cattle, the slopes of the valley were market gardens and my neighbour remembers the fields from when she was a girl. There were cobnuts by the ditch, an extensive orchard and vegetables in rows up the slopes. There is a shed, still standing, that was used for forcing the early rhubarb so it feels right to follow suit before planning anything more.

I have always wanted a mulberry tree and have planted one to christen the newly extended plot. Unless you train *Morus nigra* on a wall, the black mulberry likes to sprawl, rather like an elderly gentleman, hunched, with legs and arms akimbo. You might think it takes a lifetime, or indeed several, to acquire such character, but the black mulberry is surprisingly fast and can easily grow more than 30 cm a year in the right conditions.

Though mulberry is reputed to root from a branch pushed into the ground in winter, I have opted for a young, pot-grown specimen of the form called 'Chelsea', as it will grow quickly. I've had bad luck when I've tried planting the black mulberry as a larger tree – they sulk for the time it takes a youngster to catch up.

I expect my tree to be fruiting in three or four years and the fruit, which comes late in August, is about the size and shape of a loganberry and deliciously tart and juicy, enough to stain paving where it might fall and your hands and arms as the juice runs to your elbows when picking.

As it seems the rhubarb was good here, I have re-introduced three varieties to stagger the cropping season. 'Timperley Early' is the first and has slender stems, forming a delicate plant for a rhubarb. 'Champagne' and 'Victoria' will follow on with chunkier growth.

I have put them at the bottom of the slope where the soil will be damper, and heaped the young crowns with manure. The plants won't be cropped for a couple of years so that they can build up strength in their crowns.

Because I don't want to erect a fruit cage until I have a better idea of the plot, I am planting a fruit hedge along the fences that keep the sheep in their place. There are black, white, red and pink currants and autumn-fruiting raspberries – easier to look after than summer varieties that fruit on the previous year's canes. Autumn types fruit on this year's wood and simply need cutting to the base in the spring and mulching to retain the moisture. I have a 'Ben More' blackcurrant and 'Autumn Bliss' raspberry, and will throw netting over the fence when they are large enough for cropping. If the summer is kind, I should be in the fine position of having to compete with the blackbirds for my breakfast.

16 May, *London*
SCENTS AND THE CITY

———

Recently I cycled home late after a birthday dinner. I had to make my way from north-west London to Peckham, in the south-east, and I followed a route that I have put together over the years. It takes in the parks and the streets where I know favourite things grow. It was one of those rare still evenings, the first of the summer, and I took my time.

The plane trees were sage green in the street lights and the air was heady with the almondy smell of cumulative blossom and bud break. Hyde Park was cut with the smell of newly mown grass and there was a feeling of expectancy in new leaf and flower. I found favourite trees on my route home. A *Davidia involucrata* was just coming into bloom in Kensington and I stood on the pavement and marvelled at the papery bracts dangling above me. The handkerchief tree must be an extraordinary thing to see in Chinese woodland, where it is native.

I have planted several davidias for clients in the past few years, and promised them that the wait will be worth it: fifteen years after planting is often mentioned in the books, but I have flowered several in five where the conditions are right. They like a hearty soil and plenty of sun, but above all they need shelter from the wind, so that the bracts are not torn to shreds when in season.

A *Magnolia* 'Elizabeth' was my next objective and the waxy flowers illuminated a side street in Chelsea. Our odd spring, pushed back so that everything came together, has meant that many plants have been flowering alongside unlikely neighbours, and the magnolia was a good two weeks late. 'Elizabeth' is one of the most elegant yellow-flowered magnolias and the flowers are a primrose, creamy green. They twist like tulips, and when there are enough together the tree will muster a sweet and delicious perfume.

The wisterias, such a mainstay of Chelsea, were beginning to furnish the hot sunny walls, but I passed them by to head for a house in Westminster where there is the best *Wisteria sinensis* I have ever seen. It is a good, true blue and flowering from top to bottom over four floors. I grow the Japanese *Wisteria floribunda*, as I prefer the greater length of the racemes, but the Chinese *W. sinensis* is good for this slightly earlier awakening. It was fingering the street as I approached.

Drifts of cherry blossom whirled on the pavements as I made my way towards my favourite *Prunus avium* 'Plena', which overhangs the railings of Kennington Park. The double gean is one of the latest cherries and, being double, it hangs on to its flowers longer than most. I stood underneath the whirls of blossom and stared up into the branches, where thousands upon thousands of perfect buttons reached up as far as I could crane my neck.

As I made my way through the side streets of south London, I marvelled at the way the parks and the streets and the gardens had come together in a collective awakening. As I pulled my bike up the steps at the front of the house, the first Banksian rose had burst. The first of many buds to break – and my last of an evening lived vicariously.

22 May, *Hillside*
THEY MIGHT BE GIANTS

————

I have been waiting for this moment for quite some time, probably the best part of thirty years. It came, of course, with moving to the farm, and more specifically the fold in the land where the ditch runs down to meet the stream. The cattle that are grazing the steeper of the two fields can get down to water on the far side, but a girdle of thorn and bramble prevents them from reaching our side, where we are currently grazing the sheep. The sheep don't like to cross the water, so for now there is an unchecked island of growth there. If you stray across to inspect the growth on the yellow flag iris, you sink deep into mud, which squelches suggestively beneath you.

I have had my eye on this piece of ground since we moved here, for I have never had somewhere of my own that is properly suited to gunnera. When I was a teenager I cycled regularly to visit one in the coomb where a beast of a plant lurked on the muddy banks of a pond. In winter, when dismembered by frost, it would slump into the water, a ghastly skeleton stripped of life and volume. Just a few weeks before, you'd been able to crawl among it and shelter from the rain, which would patter on the vast parasol of foliage. The giant rhizomes from which the rasping leafage erupted twisted and interlocked and the inner world smelled fecund and primordial.

Eventually I plucked up the courage to approach the owners, who lived up a long drive that plunged into rhododendrons. I offered them a hard-earned fiver in exchange for a knuckle of potential. They accepted my money and offered me a spade to help with the amputation and I cycled away, never happier. I dug a pit for it, lined with plastic and backfilled with compost, but in truth my offshoot was never happy until we came up with the idea of growing it in the overflow to the cesspit. It thrived there, but by then I had left home and once again had to enjoy it vicariously.

It was a strange feeling to revisit the experience when I went down to spend a day with my parents in March. The plant is a shadow of itself now, as its life source has been terminated, but its roots must be deep enough to draw upon the moisture in the ground.

Gunnera manicata is called the 'giant rhubarb' with good reason, and though it isn't related, its growth habits are similar. The woody rhizomes are arguably tender, and best practice, traditionally, is to fold the foliage over the crown to protect it in winter. In truth I suspect that once the plants are established they are hardier than you might think.

It will take a couple of years for my rooted cuttings to settle in. I planted them with their roots in the mud but their crowns above the constantly wet ground. I have never been afraid of using large foliage in a small space, but damp ground really is a necessity if you get the gunnera bug. I have grown them in oil barrels in the past, with the drainage holes made halfway up the barrel so they have a soupy mud to draw from in the base.

For those of us with drier conditions but the desire for dramatic leafage, *Rheum palmatum* is a fine choice. This rhubarb is related to the culinary form and it starts life early, like its cousin, breaking ground from dramatic buds of sealing-wax red. *Rheum palmatum* 'Atrosanguineum' is infused with red through its foliage, its stems and in the lofty sprays of flower. 'Ace of Hearts' is an altogether smaller plant with a less-divided leaf that is suitable for a smaller garden. The disadvantage of *Rheum* as a resting point for the eye is that it is a first half of summer plant. Once its flowers soar to the sky, it loses its foliage at the base to leave a hole that isn't easily plugged, but the drama while it lasts is worth the effort. They like good living, so they should be mulched heavily with cow muck every spring. I think it was Beth Chatto who said: 'Feed the brute', and it goes a long way to promote the spectacular foliage.

24 May, *Peckham*
LILAC SEASON

———

Our lightest months in early summer are also the season of some of our most flamboyant flowering shrubs, many of which eclipse their companions for a glorious flurry. Once-flowering roses and sweetly scented *Philadelphus* may only be with us for a moment, but they are worth it for that feeling of time slowing down.

In Russia, lilac grows wild on the fringes of woodland to spill into the sunshine. They can be a hungry neighbour in a mixed planting, but if you have the right place you will be happy you have planted one. This year I have promised myself that I will get to see a national collection, to pick a couple with just the right tone of lilac and grace in the branches.

Once it has had its moment, the common lilac is a scruff for the second half of summer, but in season there is nothing else like it. The foliage is pristine as the clustered buds swell. The best lilac is delightful for being made up of several tones, with a dark reverse to each bud and a paler interior so that the colour appears to lighten as the flowers bud, open and age. I prefer the single-flowered varieties, which retain a lightness in the panicles. The doubles are physically weighty and hardly seem necessary in a plant that is not shy of flowering.

Of the common lilac varieties, *Syringa vulgaris* 'Maud Notcutt' is a good pure white. I'd like to find 'Massena', which I once grew among creamy tree lupins at Home Farm. It has ruby buds and the flowers open a thundery purple. I have plans to combine it with a lilac, such as 'Firmament', and let them go together near the compost heaps. They will be planted in rough grass and the cow parsley allowed to seed among them. When they are grown I'll bring whole branches in bud into the house to extend their season.

You should never be worried about plants that have a short season. But it is a good idea to invite only the best and then to know that you can live with them for the rest of the year after their flowers are long gone. For those of us with smaller spaces and where a good companion is an important criterion in a shrub, there are lilacs that are more light-footed. *S. microphylla* 'Superba' is a delightful shrub of a metre or so with well-mannered branches and roots. The flowers are like those of a larger lilac in miniature.

I've also been planting *Syringa* × *josiflexa* 'Bellicent' in clients' gardens and found this to be a very superior thing, forming an open, arching shrub with plenty of air in it. The rose-pink flowers are in elongated sprays, each individual flower appearing to be dripping from the branches.

You cannot begrudge such a flower for only being with us briefly. Plant a clematis at its base to cover for the late summer and let yourself enjoy the moment.

25 May, *Peckham*
RESTLESS NATIVES

———

I have just come in from an early-morning inspection of the garden.

The fresh new foliage of summer is beaded with moisture and when I look back there is a meandering trail in the silvery dew where I have been tracking back and forth.

The garden is filling out daily, the soil in retreat and growth ballooning. Having to watch where you put your feet is a good thing in a garden and after a couple of years all new plantings should be protecting the ground in which they are growing. Keeping the ground covered is an art because a garden is always in flux.

A favourite mainstay in the balancing act is the perennial *Geranium*. Not to be confused with the brilliance of the South

African *Pelargonium*, which confusingly has geranium as the common name, the hardy cranesbills are a wide-ranging and adaptable tribe. They are happy in quite deep shade and dry shade at that, but also adaptable to sun. Cranesbill refers to the dispersal mechanism for the seed, which forms the bill and the projectile to the seeds that sit waiting until ripe. At the right moment, they are shot several metres to new territory where, if conditions are good, they will take hold.

I have the white form of *Geranium robertianum* growing in the studio garden. The woodsy smell of Herb Robert takes me back to my childhood and I shall always love it for the tiny mauve flowers suspended in air and its combination of delicacy and tenacity. The white form is delightful for its ephemeral quality.

G. macrorrhizum has the same particular perfume to its foliage, which is furry to the touch and almost evergreen. This is an excellent plant and one that I can rely upon. Forming a slowly spreading weave of woody above-ground stems, it is happy to live under the skirts of shrubs or out in the sunshine. 'Bevan's Variety' is the largest, at about 45 cm, with May-flowering dark mauve flowers. 'White Ness' is smaller and pure white whereas 'Alba' is tinged with pink and has good autumn colour.

Right now the mourning widow is at its best. *G. phaeum* 'Samobor' is my favourite. The flower is small and darkest grey-purple. Cut the whole plant back after it has flowered and it will come back with renewed foliage.

Our native bloody cranesbill, *G. sanguineum*, will be happy in a dry site as it grows in coastal sand dunes. 'Tiny Monster' has the largest and brightest flowers, but for drama you might find a place for *G. psilostemon*. This will rise to over a metre, pushing up magenta dark-eyed flowers among the shrub roses.

The lime-leaved 'Ann Folkard' strikes a punchy contrast to the deep magenta flowers and I love using it in dappled places to scramble through at low level and illuminate a dappled corner. It is very long-flowering, as is 'Rozanne', whose blue and white flowers start in May and are still going with the asters in autumn.

JUNE

J

The meadows are at their best in June, eclipsing the failing foliage of spring bulbs and fraying the edges of the fields. I'll mow a path for contrast and ease of access and, for a while, I feel that this is all I ever want of a garden. An environment gently steered, but a place that has a will of its own and infinite complexity. Moon daisies are allowed to mingle so that it is hard to see where the hand of the gardener begins and nature ends. I like to strike this balance and, for this month at least, you can let things have free rein.

The June garden is still full of promise and greens remain fresh and foliage pristine. There is a quiet rush to the longest day of the year with everything reaching towards this moment. The roses are never better than with the first flowers out and the promise of bud to come. Their duration is long, starting in early April with the delicate Banksian roses, but June is a month known for rain, and the once-blooming varieties can be dashed for a year after only one downpour. One of the joys of gardening is learning that for every disaster there is always a solution, and although I wouldn't be without the ephemeral roses, it is good to get to know and grow those that repeat flower. With timely deadheading, there are weeks left in them yet.

The summer solstice sees the first evening primroses opening and with it the feeling changes subtly, but with sure significance. The change in hours of light between night and day triggers a reaction in the late-summer bloomers, and very quickly you see buds on the asters and the first flowers on the dahlias. These are the plants that will keep you going, for the season's zenith, once passed, gives rise to an ensuing slump. The first of the perennial geraniums are finished and paths disappear beneath the resulting sprawl. It is time for a liberating cut-back, leaves and all, to encourage a fresh flush for the second half of summer.

8 June, *London*

PLEASURE GARDEN

———

After finishing my studies at Kew in 1986, I spent about five years moving around: a year at Jerusalem Botanic Garden, a year a mile up a dirt track on Miriam Rothschild's wild and woolly estate at Ashton Wold, and time out on the Norfolk Fens. I had plans with my partner at the time to buy a field on the Milford Haven estuary, where we intended to live on our houseboat and make a garden, but when my garden design business started to take off, I found myself inching back to London. I was twenty-seven and in love again, which is how I came to live on Bonnington Square, in south London.

The first time I saw the square I knew I wanted to live there. There was a party house with no floors, children running barefoot in the street, a cast of local characters who were the definition of bohemian, and the Bonnington Square Cafe, which is still run on a vegetarian co-operative basis. Friends dropped in with no notice and frequently stayed until dawn, and the boundaries between where you lived and where you spent your time were constantly blurred. One summer morning I awoke to find the outside of the house opposite had been papered from top to bottom in newspaper. Visitors often said it was like stepping back in time.

Although the Harleyford Road Community Garden on the other side of the square existed when I arrived, the greening of the square had now started. Cracks in the pavements had been dug out and planted up by the local guerrilla gardeners, and odd corners were already colonised. I had just been for the first time to New York, where I was inspired by the Operation Green Thumb community gardens on the Lower East Side. The same sense of a community working to improve its surroundings set the square apart from the roaring traffic of Vauxhall Cross, and that community has gone on to develop as one of my favourite gardens in central London.

My roof garden overlooked the site where this garden was created, on an area seven houses long that was bombed during the war. A chain-link fence surrounded the site, which had been turned into a children's playground in the seventies, with a broken slide and dilapidated swing sitting on a pad of dog-soiled concrete. Although someone had planted a lone walnut tree, bindweed and buddleia had won the day.

In 1990 a builder asked the council for permission to store equipment on the waste ground, which alerted locals to the potential for development interest in this area of open land. Fast as lightning, Evan English, one of my neighbours, proposed that the site should be turned into a community garden. With a core group of residents behind him, he struck lucky with a local councillor who had one of the last GLC grants to give out to such a project. So, with just over £20,000 in our pockets and a team of council-appointed landscape architects, we put in the bones of the new garden.

The chain-link fence was replaced with railings, the tarmac and concrete with hoggin, and a series of raised beds created with topsoil spread over the basements of the old houses. A giant slip wheel, salvaged from the defunct local marble works, was partially reassembled to add a dramatic sculptural element. Another resident, the New Zealand garden designer James Frazer, and I put together the planting scheme and had a lot of fun mixing architectural New Zealand natives and English garden staples. A massive planting day that first autumn was followed by another party. None of this could have happened without Evan's single-mindedness, and once the momentum was up, so was the support of the community. There was an annual street fair to raise additional funds for plants and furniture, and monthly workdays to keep the garden looking its best.

The square was given an entirely new focus with a garden at its core and created a renewed sense of pride among the residents. It was then given its official name, the Bonnington

Square Pleasure Garden, partly a reference to the notorious seventeenth-century Vauxhall Pleasure Gardens, partly because it had been a pleasure to create and was intended to be a pleasure to use. Life on the square had changed. The picnic lawn was busy every weekend, and we saw people who had never ventured from their houses using the park as an extension of their homes.

The following year came the Paradise Project, a plan to green the streets around the square. We were given more help with funds for trees, and soon catalpas, Judas trees, mimosa and arbutus took to the pavements – and climbers to the walls of anyone who wanted to green their building. People quickly started to plant up the pavements in front of their houses. Window boxes of herbs and flowers appeared, old telegraph poles were colonised by morning glory and vines, and a rash of roof gardens appeared, so I was no longer alone in my green eyrie.

It is more than ten years since I left the square to make a garden of my own, but the Pleasure Garden has continued to evolve with the community, which is still very much behind it. A new generation of gardeners – many of whom had never gardened before moving there – keep it feeling vital. It is an object lesson in what can be achieved when people join forces to stop so-called 'wasteland' being lost to yet more bricks and mortar.

CALIFORNIA DREAMING

———

This year I am making a garden for a client in California. We are down on the flat, one valley inland from the Pacific. In theory you can grow just about anything here, but we are being careful about our plant choices, because water is in short supply. We are having to plant up the garden at the height of summer because the hardscape has taken longer than we thought. Key trees and shrubs that are already 'boxed' (the American equivalent of a large pot) will not be a problem to source, but our choice of perennial material by that time will be limited and we'll have to rely on annuals until the perennials become available again in the autumn.

Cue a trip to Annie's Annuals, a nursery that is the Californian equivalent of the Beth Chatto Gardens. It is situated in Richmond on the rough-and-ready industrial outskirts of San Francisco, with chain-link fences dividing off part of a car park. A series of rubble-edged raised beds bursts at the seams with plants that I have never seen before. Beyond, on a sea of raised benches, lies a cornucopia of delights. Nothing is sold in anything more than a 9 cm pot and every group of plants has a jaunty label with a photo and a description in Annie's own words. When you meet her you see where the enthusiastic text came from. She is a total delight and I could have talked with her for hours about her very particular and eclectic tastes.

A good portion of the plants are perennial, but the main interest lies in the power of the annual and its ability to inject new life into a garden. There's *Eriogonum nudum* 'Ella Nelson's Yellow', a buckwheat with flowers the colour of clotted cream, and *Viola* 'Tiger Eyes', with its little gold faces striped with black. There's also *Linaria reticulata* 'Flamenco', with its crimson lip and golden standard, and a host of opium poppies – at least two dozen varieties that had me scrawling in my notebook. As a self-obsessed plantaholic, it was extremely difficult for me not to be able to bring treasure home to the UK.

Now that it is summer here, our UK nurseries are offering young plants for bedding, and many of them are annual or half-hardy perennials. Petunia, tobacco plant, pelargonium and a handful of other staples are available for pumping up the volume and adding long-lasting colour.

Still, I wish we had a nursery such as Annie's to enthuse us about 'unusual' annuals from seed. In the main they are far from difficult: they are often pioneers, the first plants to colonise open ground. Unlike the traditional bedding plants that are grown on so that they are ready at the start of our growing season, many annuals prefer to be sown direct and come quickly to fruition. Cosmos, sunflowers, lacy *Orlaya grandiflora* and the lacier *Ammi majus* can all be sown direct, even this far into summer. So if you have a gap, plug it with something fast and ready to please.

17 June, *Peckham*

THE GAME OF THE ROSE

———

By the first week in May, the Banksian rose, *Rosa banksiae* 'Lutea', that I have festooning the front of the house, was at its absolute best. Those who see such things would stop on the pavement with smiles on their faces, marvelling at it, while house-callers, from gas man to courier, would ask me what it was. I love this rose without question, because it is like the blossom tree that I don't have room for in the garden. It straddles the season, starting in mid-April and running on for the best part of four weeks, by which time you can safely call it early summer. It is a vigorous plant by nature, throwing out thornless wands of arching growth as much as 4 m long in a season. Ripened by summer heat, these bear what can only be described as garlands of flowers, the exact colour of Wall's vanilla ice cream. They are scentless (or with the ephemeral scent of fresh air at close quarters) – I forgive them this because they are so ridiculously pretty and there is enough blossom for the prettiness not to be saccharine.

I had planned to grow its double-white cousin, *R. banksiae* 'Alba Plena', but the plant I was supplied with was misnamed and I didn't have the heart to take it out after it started to flower a few years later. I first met the white form one Easter when I was walking through the Trastevere district of Rome. I was already rather swept away by the slightly surreal mood of the city, strewn as it is with the relics of antiquity, but the scent of violets drew me to it from the other end of the street. Sweet, warm spring air carried the perfume from a plant that tumbled over a wall from a private courtyard within. It was unforgettable, the sort of experience that surely contributed to the decadent mood of *La Dolce Vita* and drew Anita Ekberg into the Fontana di Trevi.

R. banksiae is out with wisteria and they make a wonderful combination, as long as you can keep the two apart. Both like heat and sunshine to ripen wood to flowering, and on the back of my house, on a west wall that gets all the sun there is going, I have the white single *R. banksiae* var. *normalis*. This is the more fleeting counterpart to the double form I found in Rome, and its simple off-white flowers are the perfect companion to the pure clean white of the wisteria I also have there. Single roses, like cherries, are shorter-flowered than their double counterparts, and var. *normalis* tests my devotion by flowering for not much more than two weeks. I open the doors to the room below to let the perfume into the house when it is in bloom even if the weather turns chilly. Moments such as these help you to slow the season.

Longevity can breed complacency, so I learn to make time for my short-flowering roses. Strictly speaking, you need to have room for such ephemera. Room enough to set the pale-yellow 'Frühlingsgold' or its burnt-caramel sister 'Frühlings-morgen' among cow parsley, for nothing could be more of the moment than the arching limbs hung with huge, loose dog roses, hovering above a froth of Queen Anne's lace. But the moment is there only as long as the cow parsley and then it is over. For those of us without land, I think that a rose really needs to offer something a little more. It needs to earn its keep without making you work too hard for it, and by that I mean I want good disease-resistant foliage, remontant (repeat flowering) if possible, and if not, fruit for certain. In an ideal world I want all three.

There will always be back-up with old dependables such as 'Mme Alfred Carrière' to keep you in creamy bloom if you have the room, but on the whole I like to keep as close to the species as possible, for there you often find both health and grace. I have written many times about my favourite *R. primula*. I love it as much for the smell of its foliage – as powerful as a Catholic church in full swing – as for the pale-yellow dog roses in earliest summer. The foliage can be relied upon to perfume the garden on damp mornings as long as it is in leaf. The same can be said of the eglantine roses, which also come with scented foliage. It is a British native that you will detect in a hedgerow more from the sweet smell of apples than its simple flowers – I like to plant them as part of deciduous hawthorn hedges or treat them as a hedge in themselves, for they can be run over two or three times in the summer with the clippers. The Lord Penzance's briars are selections that have been singled out for cream and apricot-pink flowers and, come the autumn, where they have not had their flowers removed by trimming, they will provide further with fruit.

Tough rugosas such as the dusky-purple 'Roseraie de l'Hay' or 'Blanc Double de Coubert' are perfect plants for the low-maintenance gardener, and always in bloom. They can also take a little shade. Recurrent flowering has blessed the double shell-pink 'Stanwell Perpetual', too, an arching Scotch briar, and something of a tomboy with its rather shambolic but delightful semi-double blooms. You can go for it with a rose like this, and plant it with clove-scented border pinks and perennial peas. These informal shrub roses can be worked into a mixed planting. They look better with companions and nothing like their demanding cousins, restricted and regimented in sterile island beds of dirt.

In my own garden, where any shrub has to earn its keep for more than just one moment, I have committed to *Rosa odorata* 'Mutabilis' (formally *R. chinensis* 'Mutabilis'). Badly named, this is another rose you can forgive for being a rose with no scent because it compensates with myriad changeable flowers. Twisting open from tiny buds with just five petals each, the flowers turn from apricot to hot pink over the days that they are out. It is in flower from Easter until Christmas, having the *R. chinensis* gene that gave many of the modern-day roses their ability to keep on coming.

I have also set aside room for *R. chinensis* 'Bengal Crimson' (or 'Bengal Rose' or 'Bengal Beauty', depending where you read about it). I first saw it at the Chelsea Physic Garden years ago and was smitten, but forgot all about it. Last year I was made a present of a plant for opening their summer fair. I like the way plants that you are meant to have come back to find you.

It is a delightful, informal shrub and all the names describe it well – its single cherry-red flowers splayed wide and recoiled on themselves as if they were stretching are like sweet wrappers scattered over the bush. They also change as the flowers age to soft rose red, so there is a breadth of colour across the bright green foliage. The *chinensis* roses are distinctive in their twigginess and soft habit and, as they like to loll, you need to give them room. 'Louis IV' is the smallest, the deepest plum red, and 'Old

Blush China' a neat and well-behaved mauve pink. Delightful.

Right now, at the height of rose season, it is worth indulging yourself in a rose garden such as Mottisfont Abbey in Hampshire, for there you will be able to enjoy all the once-blooming, 'old-fashioned' roses without having any of the hassle associated with growing them. A wet June can ruin their crumpled blooms, blackspot, mildew and rust their foliage, but they are the most decadent of flowers to experience vicariously. Saturated colour so rich and velvety you can see why people put up with forty-nine weeks of dysfunctional behaviour for three of complete opulence. Gallicas such as 'Charles de Mills' quartered and full, petals fading from crimson and deep purple through to lavender as they age; 'Rosa Mundi' striped like candy; 'Mme Hardy' like double cream; 'Fantin Latour', heavy in your hand and sweetly scented – the rose, there is no denying it, is what makes this month a month like no other.

June 20, *Peckham*

MY LITTLE PEONY

———

When my family acquired my childhood garden in the mid-1970s, it had already been in a serious state of neglect for the best part of forty years. We came upon several treasures in the undergrowth, but few things were quite as unbothered as a stand of peony that marked the site of a long-forgotten border. They seemed oblivious to shade from advancing saplings, the swell of bramble and metre-high nettles, and they dealt with the insidious creep of ground elder as if it was nothing. They were the old-timers, there to mark the incarnation of a previous garden, and they were staying put.

The *Paeonia officinalis* 'Rubra Plena' are nothing special as far as peonies go, but the beetroot spring growth and exotic frill of petals inspired a love of the group that has endured and continues to do so. My 'Molly the Witch' are already over in the garden here, but for the week that they were out in May I was out there every morning to make the most of their fleeting presence. This is one of the first to flower, but the blooms are only the culmination of a fascinating awakening. The show is over before the longest day of the year, but it starts in March, with scarlet-tipped shoots which break to reveal smoky-purple foliage. The dark infusion fades to green as the buds swell and start to show yellow. Seedlings will take four years to flower, but you won't have to do any more than mulch and defend your clumps from inadvertent footfall when they are dormant and you are working the beds. They don't mind a little summer shade and will be happy to drop into the shadows for the second half of the summer.

I have several peonies here that I like as much for their early foliage as I do their flower. Beth Chatto gave me 'Late Windflower' and it has taken to the dappled shade under the *Hydrangea aspera*. The early foliage emerges like an insect, shining and meaty red-brown, but by the time the elegantly poised flowers are with us late in May it has greened up and handed the mantle over to the flowers. They are cherubic in bud, pointed like a lip kissing, but open flat to reveal a boss of yellow stamens. The flowers are a soapy white and unbelievably elegant, and several buds will relay to keep you in flower for more than a fortnight.

The shrubby *P. delavayi* is also wonderful in leaf. It is a variable species, and I have three here that I raised from seed. The darkest has flowers the colour of dried blood, and the palest is apricot. *P. delavayi* var. *ludlowii* is the largest-growing of them all, with golden king cups and pale green leaves that are architectural for the duration of the summer. Several peonies also produce fine autumn foliage, and I have woven a drift of the herbaceous 'White Wings' into one garden for this purpose.

The single flowers are aptly named and emerge with white foxgloves in the dappled shade of a nuttery, but the foliage colours crimson and tomato red and is as wonderful at the other end of the season.

This year I am seeking out some of the best herbaceous peonies to get to know them better, to extend a cutting garden for a client. They will be flamboyant varieties, luxuriant and as delicate as tissue paper, and many will be scented. The Chinese and the Japanese revered the peony in whole gardens dedicated to their cultivation, and for a month we will be able to savour their blooms up close in a jar. It will take three years before they are strong enough to pick, and there will be a range of forms and colours so that you can change the mood according to what is cut. I will have 'Bowl of Beauty', sugary and almost single but with an inner crest of petals like an exotic bird, and scented 'Duchesse de Nemours' to name just two, but there will be more in deep, bloody red and coral and cream. It will be nice to think that in fifty years' time they will hopefully still be going strong and inspiring another generation of gardeners.

22 June, *London*

TENDER IS THE NIGHT

———

After a slightly boozy reception at the Chelsea Flower Show last month, a couple of colleagues and I found ourselves wandering the show after dark. We had the grounds almost to ourselves, save for the maintenance teams and the stragglers still clutching tilted champagne glasses.

Once we had walked the darkening gardens the tent drew us into its brightly lit interior. As we moved from stand to stand the atmosphere shifted distinctly and I soon came to realise it was as much to do with the perfume as it was the intensively huddled plant collections. Clouds of rose, lily or strawberry hovered in the vicinity of their host exhibit and the smell of turf provided the interlude to this surreal experience.

We all know that smell is one of the most evocative of the senses. In a garden it can also be transporting, taking you back in time or better still putting you right in the moment.

Night-scented plants release their perfume in an effort to attract nocturnal insects and I like them particularly for that extra layer that they bring to a garden after nightfall.

Arriving home after Chelsea, we were greeted by the smell of a stock as the car doors swung open. We think the plant came here on the boot of a friend, trodden from their garden to ours. A solitary plant has provided such riches: indeed the perfume is powerful enough to jump the hedge or to sweeten a room as a posy. The headiness is reminiscent of talc and grandmothers' bedrooms as I remember them, but despite its strength it is never overpowering.

Matthiola perennis 'Alba' is a biennial or a short-lived perennial. Grow it from seed in spring or early summer and you will have a flowering plant the following spring. Though it is special, it is not hard to grow as long as it has a sunny, free-draining position.

It will start to flower in April and by the time it has peaked, in late May, it will be covered in ripening seedpods. Save a few for scattering in a suitable new position on the edge of things where there is light and air, and rip out the parent plant at the end of the second season. You will find it has seeded itself if it likes you and seedlings can be lifted and grown in a pot so you can give them to friends or bring them into the house.

Matthiola perennis 'Alba' is a far better plant than night-scented stock because it is perfumed in the day as well as by night, but a packet of *Matthiola longipetala* is always worth having in the drawer to sow at the base of pots close by the house.

Sow night-scented stock at three-weekly intervals throughout the summer, as flowering plants are in season for about three weeks before they go to seed. Seed to flower is usually about six to eight weeks, so sow now for the summer holidays and the expectation that night-time will bring magic.

24 June, *Peckham*
RAISING THE FLAGS

———

Early in the year, when every tiny shift in growth is a relief, the iris start to score their vertical, cutting us boldly off from one season and taking us into the next. In the marshy ground of ditches and in a distinctive line at the margins of ponds and lakes, it is our native flag iris, *Iris pseudacorus*, that makes this mark. Pushing away from ground that is so cold it is hard to believe it will ever be able to muster growth, its spears need just a glimpse of April sunshine to move, and before long they are already standing 30 cm proud. Backlit by low sun, the envelopes of foliage are at their best, full of expectation, one layer of leaf folded over the next; dark green where the leaves are overlapping, pale and luminous where only one thick. This is just the beginning.

The iris is a good metaphor for the flood of energy that leads up to Midsummer's Day, and it is no coincidence that the Japanese choose to plant whole gardens with moisture-loving *I. ensata* and *I. kaempferi* for precisely this moment. Although you often see images of these gardens apparently floating in water, part of the event when they flower is that the gardens are flooded to create the reflections, a double dose to mark a zenith in the season. A rush that in Britain will see meadows filling and softening contours, verges hung heavy and hedges fat with fresh extension growth. At no other point in the year are the greens so vibrant, the garden so full with expectation as right here and now, when dawn breaks at four and you can sit out until eleven.

Although most of the iris are past their best by Midsummer's Day, this is no reason not to draw them to attention, for their foliage continues to be wonderful in the garden and their seed pods are just getting going and will be good for months. Although I grow the sun-loving *I. germanica* where there is a hot spot and a need for flamboyance in May, I have no place for them now in my garden as it becomes progressively fuller. But, if truth were told, I prefer those that like to live on the damp side as these, on the whole, are happier in company and modest enough for even quite small gardens. The aforementioned *I. pseudacorus* is a wonderful thing if you have the room, but this is a plant that can easily overwhelm its neighbours, and I only ever plant it with burly aquatics and on a big scale. It is so strong it even competes with bulrush and outstrips many of its companions where there is livestock, since herbivores choose to ignore its poisonous growth. It is a plant for the larger garden and, all too often, I have seen it sitting fat in a domestic pond, displacing almost everything around it like a big baby in a sink.

Although variegation is rarely restful, one of the best is *I. pseudacorus* 'Variegata', with its flash of cream and green. This colouring is most evident early in the year but, by the time summer kicks in, it fades to green, assuming a more modest air and competing less with its neighbours. Its growth is also moderated slightly by having just that bit less chlorophyll coursing through its veins. Although I don't have sufficient water in my garden – no more than a small copper with a solitary water lily – I do grow a close relative of the yellow flag, a cross from American parentage of the equivalent species. In the ground with neither bog nor an endless supply of water, my *I.* × *robusta*

'Gerald Darby' is a manageable size, no more than hip height when it is in leaf, a little taller when in flower.

As it emerges, the dark staining in the young foliage is what singles this plant out – a deep blue, the blades looking like they have drawn up Quink ink. The colouring travels into the young foliage from the heart of the plant and then up into the flowering stems, as they rise out of the arch of the now heavy leaf. This darkness is insistent and it only stops where the green sheath protects the dark buds. These teeter for a few days as if standing on tiptoe, until one day (the first of June for me this year) they break. Pure washed-out, denim-blue standards, falls streaked with violet, a white throat on which sits a smudge of saturated egg-yolk yellow. There are several flowers to a spike and they last for a good three weeks – up until the solstice if we don't get a hot blast of weather. I am also growing this plant with muskily scented *Primula florindae* in the mud of a pond in the Cotswolds and here, with all the moisture it desires, it is almost double the size.

I am currently growing it in preference to *I. sibirica*, which was a hard decision, but in the end one that was made for me as the plants began to dwindle. I have grown Siberian irises since I was a child, as much for their foliage as their flower, which in truth is as brief as a dog rose. But I love their verticality and the fact that they stay where they are put, and I have played with several over the years to get to know the best. I had a deep blue form laced with gold on the falls called 'Emperor', but it came unstuck in the garden here, as things rose up over the years to shade it out. Although they can cope with a little ambient shade, the thing they seem to like least is close competition. Iris are designed to have their head and shoulders above the crowd. This is how they like to live and how they look their best.

I. sibirica is pure china blue in the true form, but there are several that stand aside as highly desirable. In one garden I have teamed up the dark royal purple *I. sibirica* 'Shirley Pope' with white *Thalictrum aquilegifolium* 'Album'. They are staggered through a low undercurrent of *Geranium* 'Ann Folkard', which has a bright lemony leaf and forms good company in that it prefers to live low and give the iris its head. *I.* 'White Swirl' is the clean lemony white that they grow in the white garden at Sissinghurst, which is pure and unadulterated. Although I have not tried it yet, I couldn't help but admire 'Butter and Sugar' in Beth Chatto's garden last time I was there in June – a creamy yellow fall teamed with a white standard. When I move on from 'Gerald Darby' to continue this wonderful journey of getting to know the *Iris*, it will be to the *I. ensata*. There is a wonderful collection at Wakehurst Place in Sussex, towering at almost 2 m, but taking up not much more than standing room on the ground. This is quite something to see. Real loftiness.

Altogether smaller in scale, so that you have to stoop rather than crane your neck, is *Iris chrysographes*. The species is variable; some flowers are veined with green like a snake, over a velvety brown base, but my favourite is the 'Black Form'. This is arguably as dark as any flower can be and the delicate flowers absorb light like coals suspended on wire-thin stems. When I have the space to enjoy it (for it is an iris I will come back to again and again as a favourite), I plant it through a veil of Bowles's golden grass, *Milium effusum* 'Aureum'. The pitch-dark velvety flowers are all the better for being suspended among the seedheads of the pale primrose grass and, though they last just a moment, it is one that perfectly closes this glorious prelude to high summer.

25 June, *Hampshire and the West Country*
THE LIFE AQUATIC

————

It was the pond that my father made in our orchard when I was five or six that really opened up my eyes to the possibilities of growth and evolution. It was 2 m by 2.4 m, with a marginal shelf to the back and 60 cm deep in the centre, where we would have the deep-water aquatics. A hose snaked down from the house to fill the pond and, during the seemingly interminable time it took for the mail-order plants to arrive, the water turned an opaque and unwelcoming green.

The novelty of this aquatic world was captivating and I pored over the plant descriptions of the aquatic order in bed, dreaming of what the plants would look like and how they would grow. Two water lilies – one white, one pink – three oxygenating plants, five marginals, a clutch of water snails and two goldfish was the extent of it.

I can still remember, when the box arrived, the smell of stagnant mud that filled the seemingly inert bagfuls of plants. They were potted up by the book, with hessian lining the perforated plastic baskets and gravel on the tops to prevent fish from stirring up the soil.

I carefully lowered the baskets into the murk with the lilies on blocks so that their young foliage could easily make its way up to the top. These blocks were removed once the first leaves had made their way to the surface and the plants dropped to their correct level.

I spent that whole summer lying on the grassy edge, my face down and just above the surface of the watery lens. Within days, once the oxygenating weeds started to rebalance the water, the pond cleared, revealing the already contented water snails doing their bit to help control the algae. Fingers of growth emerged from the water lily baskets and an embryonic bud made its way towards the surface. Water boatmen scudded through the extending tendrils of waterweed, and pond skaters occupied the surface. Dragonflies darted in aggressively to protect their new territory. The following spring, when rootling around on the muddy bottom, I would be horrified by their scorpionic larvae, then amazed to see one crawl on to a stem above the water to rupture and reveal the adult.

How did the wildlife know the pond had arrived in this garden? We were miles from natural water at the top of a hill, but – I now know – no distance at all for wildlife to travel from other neighbours' ponds. By August, *Mimulus*, aromatic water mint and flowering rush were fraying the edge of the water and making a union between the new pond and the long grass of the old orchard.

Today, wherever it is appropriate, I will angle for an expanse of wildlife water. Newts, tadpoles, fish and the accompanying insect life are magical things for kids to witness, and even the tiniest pond or a well-stocked water butt will tempt these into the garden.

There is nothing quite like the restfulness summoned while watching reflections on water, and still water's ability to bring the sky down to the earth has lost none of its potent symbolism. For this reason, if I am creating bodies of water, I will always try to make them as large as they can be. Look at any Japanese garden that revolves around water – often, as much as half the garden is devoted to it. A good rule of thumb is to mark out what you think might feel right in a space and then, if you can, double it. Water plants will rapidly reclaim the margins and shrink the water's surface and, for a pond to be ecologically balanced, at least a third of the water surface should be covered with floating aquatics to provide shade, thus preventing algal bloom.

Wildlife ponds are very different things from architectural reflecting pools, and you need to think about how wildlife can access the water and how to get as wide a range of plants growing side by side. To do well, a pond must have sun to warm the water. Sloping sides at some point are also essential, so that birds can come to bathe and amphibians can move freely between water and land. A marginal shelf sloping down to no more than 30 cm deep will allow you to grow damp-lovers such as purple loosestrife and ragged robin on the edges, the likes of water buttercup, water mint and water forget-me-not in the warm shallows, and reeds and flag iris with their roots properly in the water. Sides that slope more steeply can be employed elsewhere to prevent marginal growth so the water can be more easily seen.

Ideally, a pond should be puddled so that putting a butyl or PVC liner in the ground can be avoided. However, puddling is dependent upon there being clay present locally. In the old days, puddling was carried out by driving livestock over a depression in the clay in wet weather, compressing it into a watertight surface. Today, we puddle by driving a digger over the base and sloping sides of a pool to do the same thing on a bigger scale. Trees and puddled ponds are not good together, however, and are the reason that you will often see a dry pond near a self-sown willow or alder. Tree roots rupture a clay lining and fallen leaves stagnate water, so they are best kept apart.

When we tested the soil to create the pond at Home Farm, we found that the clay had seams of silt and stones running through it, which would give a porosity that would make the puddle lining fail. It would have been nice to be a purist, but the benefits of creating a pond there using a PVC liner far outweighed the fact that we were putting plastic in the ground. The heavy gauge 4 mm liner also came with a fifty-year guarantee, and with ponds disappearing across the country at an alarming rate, it was not a hard decision.

If you don't have a natural source of water in your garden, it is best to construct a pool in the later summer while conditions are dry, but with winter rains at hand to fill the pond. The lake we excavated last winter for a new garden in the West Country was constructed in the winter so that the pond could be filled from drains collecting winter run-off. By May it was full enough to plant. Aquatic plants should never be moved when dormant and, ideally, they should go in once the water warms, with a season ahead to get away.

We are planting this area in two phases, being very careful to introduce only native species – because invasive alien water-weeds, such as *Azolla caroliniana*, that like the warmer winters we are now encountering are becoming an increasing problem in waterways. *Phragmites*, flag iris and flowering rush were planted in the margins; these will grow away in no time and provide cover for wildlife in the first season. Small plants of water mint and meadowsweet were pushed into shallow mud to bind the steepest banks, and a wetland seed mix supplied by Emorsgate Wild Seeds was then sown around the edges where the ground is wet. This mix will establish over the next few months to green up the margins. If I could, I would be there this summer, lying on the edge, watching this world evolve.

26 June, *Peckham*
SOCIABLE CLIMBERS

———

No summer border is complete without the sweet scent of honey-suckle. But how do you pick the right one? Honeysuckles, like roses and jasmine, are plants that will weave romance into a garden. Perhaps it is the subliminal nature of the unseen, the sweet perfume caught on air that adds to the potency, for you will often sense one before you see it, clambering somewhere above your head.

The flowers that so often mark the early summer are having their moment and I will seek them out to bury my nose in them. In terms of perfume, honeysuckle is one of our most exotic natives, but it is a toughie, the seedlings springing up against the odds at the foot of a hedge or the edge of woodland. Their scarlet berries will have provided a welcome feast at the end of the previous summer and the seed will have found its way to the next habitat by a mixture of order and chance. A perfect spot, if you were a honeysuckle seedling, would be in the damp shade of overhanging branches, but with the opportunity of light to reach into as soon as you had your feet down. The combination of cool feet and sunshine to heat up the perfume and ripen fruit is made possible by a suitable host that can take the twine and reach of limbs.

The range of a mature honeysuckle is considerable and it will only settle and relax its reach once the plant has established a domain. This is why, if you have the room, the best way to grow them is to let them loose and enjoy the informality. But you have to choose a compatible host as the reality is that honeysuckle and roses are at odds with each other unless you choose a rose that you have no intention of pruning. Ramblers such as 'Wedding Day' or 'Rambling Rector' sent up into a tree are ideal, but a climbing rose that needs more regular maintenance will simply become inoperable come the time of untangling the nest.

Pruning the summer-flowering honeysuckles is best carried out after they have flowered, by shortening the long extension growths to a couple of leaves from the main stem. This is where they will produce the first flowers for next year. Of the once-blooming forms, *Lonicera periclymenum* 'Belgica' is the first, with a brick-red exterior and a rich spicy perfume. 'Serotina', known as Late Dutch, has a darker reverse, the interior of the flowers opening cream and darkening to butter. Between the two varieties you can relive the moment as one fades and the other takes over. My favourite form of our native woodbine is 'Graham Thomas'. The flowers are green on the exterior, opening cream and darkening as they age. Several flushes will follow a June high, so that there is always a sprig to pick for the house.

Lonicera × *tellmanniana* and the larger flowering *L. tragophylla* are spectacular, with yolky flowers that are distinctly orange. I grew them both when I was a teenager and haven't since because they are without perfume, but they do have the advantage of actively preferring shade. The majority of honeysuckle prefer full sun, so remember to plant so that by the time they have moved to the sunny side of their support, they are facing you and not providing the show for your neighbours.

Lonicera japonica 'Halliana' is widely available, but I have rarely grown it successfully without it succumbing to mildew. It is also a terrible runner, moving on from the root to slowly colonise ground. It is a notifiable weed in parts of America and though it is billed as semi-evergreen, it retains its foliage with the mildew and can easily look forlorn. In search for evergreen, I picked up *L. similis* var. *delavayi* a couple of years ago and have it growing at the studio garden on a north-facing wall. So far so good, but it looks like it has an appetite and could conquer some territory. It's deliciously perfumed, sharp and zesty, and the flowers are fine and filamentous. Dark, inky-green foliage has been a delight in the winter, but watch this space as I may become entangled in the wrong way if it gets the better of me. It is a risk that is certainly worth taking.

27 June, *Peckham*

WHITE MISCHIEF

―――――

At the end of the Chelsea Flower Show week, I caught a flight to Japan. The purpose of my trip was to plant a 'wild' garden at the base of a mountain in Hokkaido. I was going away for no more than a week, but it was a wrench to leave my garden. As though risen from the ashes of a late spring, it was brimful and as fresh as it ever would be. The *Iris* 'Gypsy Beauty' were newly burst – I knew I would miss the best of them – the *Nectaroscordum* would be fertilised by the bees by the time I returned, their dusky bells lifting upwards to prove it. I had sown what I could in the salad beds, earthed up the potatoes and staked what I thought might lean by the time I returned, but nothing made up for the fact that I would miss the fleeting change from spring to summer.

What epitomised this moment, and what had me standing at the base of the house drinking in the last minutes before leaving, was my white wisteria. It has been flowering for about seven of the eleven years it has been in, and until a couple of years ago we were able to count the number of racemes that increased year on year. This year it would have been impossible, for it has now reached the upper bedroom windows, and from top to meticulously trained bottom it was festooned with flower. They came out during a hot weekend in early May, in a flurry. Cooler weather then slowed their progress, and by the time I was leaving they were at their zenith, a great cascade that had me standing open-mouthed and marvelling. On my return, this pristine moment had passed for another year, the fresh purity replaced with something else, late spring dimmed to summer.

A client in southern Italy introduced me to the purity of white. She had been gardening in the heat for many years and knew the benefits of planting to make you feel cool. We played with white *Agapanthus* and *Plumbago* in the sun and *Philadelphus coronarius* and *Rosa* 'White Wings', setting them against the froth of white sweet rocket and *Aquilegia* 'Kristall'. We went for whites that were clear of pink to retain the clarity. If they were to contain another colour, the *Wisteria floribunda* 'Alba' provided the lead, with the palest hint of yellow on the keel of each flower. We used the green-white *Cobaea scandens* f. *alba* and even *Nicotiana* 'Lime Green' to push the mood, but we were purists to the core and the garden appeared to keep its cool despite the heat.

The garden took on a wonderful mood at either end of the day, and particularly at dusk when the flowers glowed. *Nicotiana affinis* seized this moment, its nocturnal flowers opening in the evening to attract moths. We used them as wayfinders on moonlit nights.

I came to the idea of white flowers rather slowly, as I had always found the perfection of the White Garden at Sissinghurst rather too much. It was too pristine and there was too much of it, like a luxury bedroom furnished for absolute comfort with white shag pile. I much preferred the cow parsley in the hedgerow because its white is just a smattering, a touch of sparkle, and this is how I like to use white in the garden. The *Rosa* 'Cooper's Burmese' on the back fence is the complement to the white wisteria and it keeps the planting around it feeling fresh and lively as long as it is out. It is a wonderful chalky bloom, single and with little perfume, but with a presence that is pure and unadulterated. Although it blooms only once, I can forgive its brevity as I do a blossom tree, because it marks the month so strikingly. At its feet I have the white form of *Thalictrum aquilegifolium*, *Allium* 'Mount Everest' and the lemon-peel-yellow poppy, *Stylophorum lasiocarpum*.

Nearby there are white arum lilies set against the dark, constant green of the bamboo. The arums make the white of *Persicaria polymorpha* a very definite cream and highlight the problem I had with Sissinghurst of putting too many whites together in one space. White flowers always have something else in them, be it blue, pink, mauve or even brown, and these off-whites soon look grubby when they are shown up by the purity of something like *Zantedeschia aethiopica*. A cream rose such as *Rosa* 'Nevada' needs to be with the right partners, and, since it fades to pink, it is a shame for this ageing process to feel muddied by wrongly placed companions. Something light and airy like *Anthriscus* 'Ravenswing' is ideal.

Out in the sun, *Gaura lindheimeri* is one of my absolute favourites for a hot, free-draining position, and its smattering of flower can be used among plants that might appear to be blocky or brash. Jasmine is good in the sun, too, as is *Hosta plantaginea*, which I plant in pots to keep the slugs at bay. This is a plant that encapsulates the best of what I like in my whites: purity and elegance. *Lilium regale* has it, and so do the wood anemones and *Dicentra* 'Langtrees' that are yet to make a show in the shade. This year I have also replaced the medley of fiesta-coloured dahlias at the end of the garden with a group of the cactus-flowered 'White Star'. Final, incontrovertible proof of my full conversion.

29 June, *Hampshire and Peckham*
ODE TO MISS JOY

———

I have been gardening since about the age of five or six, but I was luckier than most because I grew up with people around me who were fascinated by growth and growing things. My mother has always had a vegetable patch – she was brought up in vicarages with big gardens and her father always grew vegetables for the family. My father grew the colour in the garden and he was always brave and uninhibited with it.

I was also lucky to meet my great friend Geraldine at about the age of seven. Geraldine was a passionate naturalist and so her garden was full of life. Every plant had a story to it and had to battle it out with the weeds; bearded iris nestling among the self-sown *Eschscholtzia* and fumitory, or larkspur and a sting of nettles in with the gooseberries. She would part tall tassels of grass and tangled scarlet pimpernel and invite me to look at her thriving *Fritillaria pyrenaica*.

The *Fritillaria* and other treasures were smuggled back from her annual trips to the mountains of Europe. She would arrive home tanned, interested to see how I had looked after the morning glory and the plumbago, and the tomatoes in the greenhouse, and from the boot of her Morris Minor unwrap her muddy treasures. She would tell me about the alpine meadows and rock faces where these plants had grown, and describe what she had seen them growing with. It was Geraldine who championed my annual entries in the village flower show at the end of the summer holidays, and every year we would trundle down the hill, the car sloshing with vases destined for the display benches.

In our road, opposite Geraldine, there was a house called Hill Cottage. All you could see of it behind the vast hedge that had crept out across the verge was a chimney sprouting a solitary birch tree. Miss Joy, the old lady who lived there with, as legend had it, an army of rats, emerged from a hole in the hedge each autumn to distribute windfalls on people's doorsteps. A neighbour who had cleared the apples from their step to the compost heap found Miss Joy picking over the heap and returning the best apples to the step. As children we found her frightening, wire-thin and bent double with heavy baskets of bruised apples; you could never see her face under home-made hats of faded chiffon. At that point I had no idea how influential Miss Joy's legacy would also be.

One autumn in the mid-seventies, Miss Joy failed to emerge from the hole in the hedge and, after she died, the house came up for sale. My mother went in with another neighbour and me to help clear it. I had never been so frightened and excited in the same moment, and I shall never forget the weight and tangle and gloom of the mood that lay behind the hedge. The garden had overwhelmed the old lady, and laurel and rhododendrons pressed against the windows, filling the house with an eerie submarine-green light. *Akebia quinata* had got in under the skirting boards and wrapped itself around furniture shrouded in mouldering dustsheets. The curtains had rotted from the floor up and there really was a rat hole at the bottom of every door. In those few days my mother fell in love with the house and, in a huge leap of faith, my parents bought it.

The garden at Hill Cottage extended to half a hectare and its gentle restoration became my world for the next seven years, until I left home. It took the best part of three years to clear it and there were huge bonfires every weekend. It was six months before we even got around to the far side of the house, where a rotting balcony was supported by a vast *Rosa multiflora*, the rootstock of a long-overwhelmed rose that must once have been there. The grounds had returned to woodland but, at the end of a little track to the orchard, where Miss Joy had made her way to stoke a small boiler, there was a shattered greenhouse containing a camellia that died that first winter. The lawn had been taken over by bamboo and Japanese knotweed. One day, we cut a tree to find a fetid pond; another day, a felled laurel opened up two long borders choked with 3 m high nettles and brambles. Underneath the thicket, old double peonies and hemerocallis were miraculously blooming in the half-light.

An old picture revealed that the vast Turkey oak in the centre of the garden had been planted by Miss Joy herself, from an acorn brought back from her years as a nurse in the First World War. Twisted amelanchier among majestic Scots pines and gaunt apple trees in the orchard gave us a huge head-start and, as we cleared, the treasures emerged: a wintersweet, overwhelmed by bramble, revealed itself through scent alone; epimedium had proven its worth as a long-lived ground cover, its veined foliage like a miracle among the undergrowth to untrained eyes;

bluebells and curiously coloured pink and grey-pink primroses that must have crossed with polyanthus years beforehand. And one spring, a pure white trillium emerged, reminding us that the passions of this old lady lived on in this wild garden.

I learnt an enormous amount there – most importantly that, if you disturb the balance, nature will compensate. A spangled dell of speedwell, chickweed and primroses was lost to lurking ground elder and nettles in a season as soon as too much light was allowed to fall to the floor. I also learnt that, try as I might to grow plants that loved sun in this wooded space, nature simply wouldn't allow it.

In 1976, my dad took me to the Chelsea Flower Show, and it was there that I first saw Beth Chatto's stand, which, at that point, was light years ahead of the pack. Here were wild plants, or the best selections of them, grouped in associations inspired by nature. Wet plants were growing with other damp-lovers, while the dry-loving silver plants were woven among each other in monochromatic associations that years later I would understand when I went to the Mediterranean and saw wild lavenders and thyme and silvered thistles in combination. I became a fan instantly and still draw upon her ethos of putting the right plant in the right place, and gardening with wild plants rather than overworked cultivars.

The gardens I design aim to capture a mood or a feeling, and I try hard for them to sit comfortably in the land. I want to be able to walk in a space and to be affected and consumed by the atmosphere, like you might as a child without having to question your reaction. I want people to be able to experience the seasons and the change and the bigger picture, and I want them to be able to access the minutiae, too. I am lucky to be able to garden where I never dreamed of being able to do so – in the north of Japan and in southern Italy – and to be able to share some of the best places here in the British Isles through my vocation. I guess I am trying to capture a little of Hill Cottage in each of these places, achieving a delicate balance between steering nature and being part of it rather than trying to dominate it. Let's face it, it has a lot to teach us.

JULY

J

If we have them at all, those still, balmy nights of summer will probably happen in July. And it is then that a rare thing happens, as perfume weaves its way through open windows. I have many memories that will be sparked by a particular scent, which takes me to an exact time or place: the *Lilium regale* that ignited my childhood passion, jasmine taking me immediately to a garden in Italy, or the essence of the garden making its way into Vita Sackville-West's bedroom at Sissinghurst. I was lucky enough to stay there once and, by the end of the night, having hardly slept a wink for the excitement, I understood how she had planned for these evenings when the garden overwhelms your senses.

The July garden is fulsome, with strength in colour and heat in the sun to push growth. Vegetables are cropping now: first-formed courgettes, ripening tomatoes, and beans twining their way fast up their poles. You have to continue picking the sweet peas if they are not to exhaust themselves, keeping an eye on the bigger picture to maintain such profusion. Deadheading, and keeping unruly plants in check, are the keys to retaining the promise of the season and avoiding a slump in August.

As the garden ripens, a high-summer layer replaces the freshness of last month. Meadows and verges turn from green to buff and thistles come through hard and sharp, pushing head and shoulders above their neighbours. Greens darken and, as wood starts to ripen, it is time to take cuttings, to summer-prune the fruit trees and harvest the lavender. I can never bring myself to do this when the first flowers are opening and the essential oils are at their most plentiful, for it seems counterintuitive to curtail the drone of bees and the movement of butterflies that speak of summer at its finest.

6 July, *Israel and London*
SHADOW PLAY

———

I spent a year at the Jerusalem Botanical Gardens in the mid-eighties and frequently travelled out to the flatlands of the Negev Desert. The sun packed a punch by seven in the morning and the white-out light hurt the eyes, but it was a place that I found both deeply beautiful and alarmingly hostile at the same time. It was a dramatic contrast to my early years of living in cool Hampshire woodland. If it had not been for the shimmering black pools of shade beneath the horizontal acacias, I would never have entertained the possibility of enjoying this place.

The contrast I experienced there made a strong impression and informed how I feel today about light and shadow.

Even in our cool climate, where the sunny days have to be savoured, a garden without shade lacks depth and a sense of the unknown. Imagine walking from bright light into a cool and dappled tunnel of greenery with its sense of mystery and intrigue and the feeling of safety and protection. Shade provides contrast and punctuation in a space and animates the ground plane, which alters from moment to moment. You also limit the range of what you can grow if your garden is relentlessly open and exposed to the light. A whole palette of plants which provide a cool mood are lost and, consequently, the depth of experience that comes with them. At its most basic I simply cannot imagine not being able to choose to sit either in the sun or the shade.

At the garden I have been creating in Italy I have learnt that, without shade, there is no other choice than to stay inside. The southern Italian heat is already as intense by early summer as it ever gets in Britain and continues for several months without letting up. In the Mediterranean there is a tradition of providing shade and we have tapped into that vernacular to ensure the outside spaces are usable all summer. On one terrace close to the dining room there is an outdoor eating area covered by a high pergola. The mood is cool and sophisticated and we have grown *Wisteria floribunda* 'Alba' over it. The metal structure is three metres high to give the head space needed when the long racemes of blossom cascade nearly a metre long towards earth. It is a breathtakingly beautiful sight in early summer and, when the heat kicks in and the foliage increases in weight, the dappled light here provides a pool of much-needed coolness.

Further into the garden, where the mood is more informal, the pergolas are constructed from rustic chestnut poles like those in the nearby orchards which provide support for climbing vines. In the small cutting garden that is crammed with flowers and vegetables, the arbour is clothed in grapes. At the garden's boundary, where two seats are positioned to take in the view of the landscape, another arbour is planted with roses, 'Wedding Day' and 'Mme Alfred Carrière'. They are chosen for the informal atmosphere they bring with them and for the fact that this shady, protected place will also be perfumed.

In Britain, I am more cautious about introducing shade. In a climate that may or may not have a summer I never completely cover a seating area, but always leave a section open to the sky. My London garden is unusual for a city garden since it is not, in the main, overshadowed by neighbouring buildings or trees. It faces west, so in the morning the terrace by the kitchen is cool in the shade of the house, and we have to make our way to the end of the garden to have breakfast in the early sunshine. By lunchtime the sun is full on the terrace, which is when the bamboo hedge that runs its length comes into its own. Without it we would be completely unprotected, and eating alfresco in dappled light is one of the most pleasurable summer activities.

Further into the garden, shade on the wooden terrace is provided by planting, as I did not want to have structure in the garden. London is hard enough as it is, so this space was designed around the broken shade of the old *Cytisus battandieri*. When it died of honey fungus this area lost its magic and so I replaced it with a multi-stemmed hornbeam, which casts a heavy shade at the hottest time of the morning. Of course, this heavier shade meant that I had to adjust the neighbouring planting to have a more woodland feel, but I have hardly complained about the opportunity to try more plants.

Planting that provides shade is a wonderful thing to play with and it is important that the surfaces that you are using beneath are simple enough to capture the shadow patterns that fall upon them. Distinctive leaves such as maple cast a good pattern, but it is also worth choosing plants that are mobile and shift in breeze. The dark limestone terrace is wonderful with the shimmering shadows of the bamboo on it and the skirt of shade under the *Cercis canadensis* 'Forest Pansy' nearby animates the area directly outside the kitchen. Shadow patterns are also one of the chief reasons why, in certain circumstances, I will consent to including the simplicity of cut grass in a garden.

The shade that a tree casts can vary immensely, so choosing your canopy well is very important. You only have to look at what grows beneath a conifer plantation to feel the onset of a small depression – the shade is opaque and unforgiving. Shade trees need to be open and changeable so that in the spring, when light is weaker, the cover is less and in the height of summer it is still open enough to allow some light to fall to the ground.

A plant such as *Gleditsia triacanthos* is ideal. The honeylocust is an open, leguminous tree that has become well used as a street tree in recent years for its ability to cope with drought. The limbs reach out and curve down like arms and are innately graceful. Late into leaf, the foliage is typical of many leguminous trees, being small and delicate. There are many forms now available but the thornless *G. triacanthos* 'Sunburst' is one of the best, with a flare of acid-yellow that comes with the young growth. This is the tree that I will always plant instead of the overused *Robinia pseudoacacia* 'Frisia' which, although undeniably bright, overwhelms the tree line with the sheer quantity of gold in the leaf.

If you have a hot spot that needs cooling, the golden rain tree, *Koelreuteria paniculata*, is a magical thing. It forms a low dome not much more than 6 m in height, but spreads wider, allowing ample opportunity for seating underneath. Its lacy foliage is also late to emerge in spring, but in the heat of August it produces a froth of yellow panicles that appear for a couple of weeks like a halo over the frame of the tree.

Trees like fig and catalpa provide well for heavy shade because of their wide umbrella-like canopies and large leaves, which is why they are so often used in the scorching Mediterranean. In our climate, where we treat each sunny day as if it were the last, smaller leaves produce a more welcome, spangled light. Birch, planted in groups, create exquisite shade and shadow as their branches are always shifting. Willows fall into the same camp, and I have a vivid recollection of sitting under willows by the River Dan on the Lebanese border during my year in Israel. We were fed fresh trout on that day with salty olives, pita and sun-sweet tomatoes. I swear the food was better for being in this dappled shade. The memories certainly were.

8 July, *Italy*
PARADISE REGAINED

————

At the 1994 Chelsea Flower Show I was introduced to an Italian woman by Rosie Atkins, a friend and the founding editor of *Gardens Illustrated*. 'This is Violante Visconti. She has an incredible garden near Ninfa.' I didn't know of Ninfa then but, when she returned the next day especially to have another look at my garden, I began to take note. She loved the near-black bearded iris and the velvety 'Tuscany Superb' roses and said, in a gravelly and commanding tone: 'You must come to my garden. Soon!'

By the end of the week, an envelope with an airline ticket had dropped through the letter box. Somewhat seduced by the confidence and glamour of this gesture, I accepted the invitation. Violante was waiting, with partner Carlo, at Rome airport the following Friday, and we set off at a fearful pace, hurtling south in a blue cube of smoke, the windows closed so we could talk. Between drawing on a constant supply of cigarettes and craning around perilously while she was driving, Violante explained they had bought an organic 500-hectare estate from a friend. They had fallen in love with it and decided to make a garden there. She also added, with some urgency: 'We are in our late sixties and we want the garden quickly!' Night fell, I closed my eyes to divert my attention from the speedometer, and the next thing I knew we were bumping down a rough drive.

It was a drive I have come to love. Two-and-a-half kilometres long and lined, at first, with walnut trees. I was given the job of leaping out into the pitch dark to open the three gates that took us into a valley, through meadows strewn with long-horned cattle and the scurry of wild boar in the headlights. The valley closed tighter as we proceeded, huge trees looming over us as we moved into woodland. Eventually we stopped at an old farmhouse at the base of a volcanic plug that was backlit by the night sky. 'That is where we will be tomorrow,' said Violante as we retired.

The next day I was awoken by a cacophony of birds. Above me, as I opened the shutters, lay the medieval ruin of Torrecchia Vecchia, its walls emerging from a tangle of bay and evergreen oak. There were troglodyte caves on the hill opposite and above them ancient cork oaks. The trunks glowed rust red and a skirt of black shade made them appear to hover on the hillside. In the little valley below there was a Roman bridge, once part of the Roman way that ran from Rome to Naples, along the stream in the nut woods. Come the autumn these woods, primitive and rough, were pink with *Cyclamen hederifolium*, and in the spring, blue with *Anemone apennina*.

The ruin itself had been deserted 800 years previously, possibly due to malaria or an earthquake, which seemed to show itself through rents in some of the buildings. Violante and Carlo had made a start on the site and found indications of a Roman settlement under the medieval village. A limb from a statue and beautiful terracotta drain tiles had haphazardly come to the surface, so they decided to tread lightly to avoid unnecessary disturbance. The walls were being cleared of ivy and bramble and painstakingly stabilised to prevent further decay, and architect Gae Aulenti (of Musée d'Orsay fame) had been appointed to make a series of apartments within the ruins of the castle and a home in the eighteenth-century granary. The rest of the six hectares that lay within the walls were to be garden.

Lauro Marchetti, the curator of Ninfa, the nearby garden from which we were to draw inspiration, had already started to put in the irrigation and the first of the trees. Ninfa is perhaps one of the most romantic gardens in Italy. Work on the garden in the ruins of the derelict village was initiated in the twenties by the English-born Ada Caetani, whose husband's family had occupied it since the Middle Ages. The walls are festooned with ancient wisteria, and roses trail into an icy river that slips through the site from the hill. It was there that Violante explained that she was after an Englishman's eye. She wanted a garden that looked as if it were just about to be reclaimed by nature. It was to grow out of the ruin of Torrecchia and be part of it.

She had made a start already. Passionflowers and wisterias had been sent up the trees and the walls of the ruins, scaling ten or a dozen metres in a season and, once I had her confidence, we started to work together to make a garden. A garden that at one moment was all about restraint, and the next, a fecund, rustic romance, not unlike a Poussin painting. The terraces, for shade, were essential and always sensual, perfumed wherever possible, but progressively more rustic as you moved from the house. White wisteria and jasmine sat close to the living areas, while wild rambling roses over simple bowers in the heart of the garden made them distinct destinations.

There was no natural water on the hill itself, but we made a rill that snaked through the garden down a ravine planted with white *Iris ensata*, *Zantedeschia* and *Gunnera*. We planted a river of *Iris japonica* that spilled down an old track to envelop a pond surrounded by weeping cherries. In order to buy the time Violante was so short of, twenty ancient pomegranates were chosen to frame the entrance courtyards, and huge camphor trees to close over the approach as you entered through the castle walls. Everything was chosen so that it felt right in the place, never overly ornamental, and close to nature. A white Judas tree walk was underplanted with blue lacecap hydrangeas, scented *Viburnum carlesii* and *V. × burkwoodii* planted close to the wild *V. tinus* in the margins. Wild Banksian roses, smelling of violets in April, were allowed to festoon the castle walls, clambering 20 m to cascade back down again.

Sadly, Violante died of cancer four years after my first visit, but not before we had appointed Stuart Barfoot, a talented young gardener from England, to keep this wild vision on the right side of neglect. It is a fine tuning that Carlo has supported, and I return twice a year to build upon Violante's vision. Stuart started a magnolia collection, and we have battled with the savagely hot summers to keep the garden feeling cool. A new fountain in the old chapel brings the sky down to ground level. Surrounded with pots of lemons, the ground strewn with self-sown larkspur, poppies and clary sage, it is a scented retreat with just the sound of water and views over the hills from the crumbling windows.

Carlo insisted on planting *Davidia* five years ago, even though he knows they take fifteen years to flower. He has just turned eighty. I have a feeling that Violante, who is in every shadow and around every corner, is rooting for him.

13 July, *Hillside*
CUTTING REMARKS

———

Last year, on a memorable evening, a friend took us to see a house in the woods. She said the place was worth visiting for the atmosphere. It was high summer and the grass was tall in the middle of a rough track across the fields, so we ditched the car and walked the last kilometre. At the end of the track the gate to the property opened into woodland. We continued into the cool, where saplings and ferns were advancing upon the way.

As your eye adjusted, you came to see the intended moments in this garden. A sculpture among the nettles, a bench made from a fallen log placed to take in a pool of warming sunshine and, on the skirts of the woodland, the spill of the Wickwar rose. Its limbs stretched out and down from voluminous mounds of growth and the limbs hung with sprays of creamy dog roses. They glowed in the shadow.

I had read about *Rosa soulieana* and its ranginess, and the bittersweet experience of being taken over by it. But when you see a plant in the right place, with room to become itself, bad press is cast aside. We left with a handful of cuttings and the scars of trying to get them without the necessary implements. Christopher Lloyd wrote that you should always carry a moistened plastic bag in your pocket when visiting a garden, but we wrapped the cuttings in damp grass and dock leaves and they were planted before nightfall.

Midsummer is the perfect time to take semi-ripe cuttings. Extension growth has ripened just enough and there is time for roots to strike to enable independence before the end of the growing season. Though I aspire to a greenhouse and mist bench, conditions are still makeshift and my propagation unit is a bucket with bubble wrap stretched over the top to keep the atmosphere moist.

The most important thing when taking summer cuttings is to keep them stable and for their leaves not to desiccate. I use a 50:50 mix of sharp grit and loam to ensure free drainage.

Heel cuttings are best for evergreens such as box, rosemary and lavender. A heel is a lateral growth pulled free with a small section of bark from where it joins the stem. Tip cuttings are just as easy, though they need a little more atmospheric moisture. Take up to 15 cm with a sharp pair of secateurs or a knife and cut just below a leaf. Pull the bottom foliage and plunge the lower third into compost.

I loosen the plastic cover on my makeshift unit to let in some air after a couple of weeks and then remove it entirely once I can see the cuttings making headway on their own roots. Summer cuttings of pelargonium and half-hardy perennials that you intend to overwinter can be potted up a month or so after rooting, but I like to leave the hardy woodies to overwinter in the frame before potting up in the spring. My Wickwar roses from a year ago are already straining to get into the ground. The cuttings were easy; finding a home for the beast is a little more tricky.

14 July, *Hillside*
CORDIALLY YOURS

———

It is a beautiful day; there are skylarks, high puffs of cloud and broken sunshine. It is too cool for shirt-sleeves when the pools of sunshine are out of reach but warm enough to bask when a brisk wind pushes the clouds aside. The meadows are up, the grasses playing tall and not yet pushed about by wet and squall, and I am writing today with the sound of bumblebees busying themselves in the linaria.

The garden is still late and although the elderflower is blooming sweetly in London and on the motorway verges on the first hour out of town, it is a couple of weeks behind in Somerset. Growing fast and lushly, they dominate at this time of year, elbowing their neighbours aside and making sure they get the light they need for their harvest of berries. Having lived fast, they do get old before their neighbours, splitting at the base after a decade or so to leave a broken tooth in the hedge line. Bad behaviour aside, the deadwood makes the best of kindling and a year without elderflower syrup is a year without summer captured in a jar.

I would never volunteer to plant a common *Sambucus nigra* in a garden setting. The likelihood is that they will arrive on their own from seed carried in by songbirds that have feasted on the glut of berries. These are some of the first to ripen in the autumn, hanging shiny and black in heavy trusses, and they are gone in a minute once the weather cools.

Elder will grow anywhere, and this is why, in the selected

varieties, they make a useful garden plant. They will grow as happily on chalk as they will on thin acidic sand, and give them heavy, wet clay and they will put on more than a metre a year. They are adaptable to sun or to shade, growing tighter and flowering more heavily in sun and more lushly in shade, where flowering will also be lighter. Though the foliage might burn in salt-laden winds, it will regenerate and they make good front-liners for this reason.

Their speed of growth and willingness to settle in fast is useful behaviour and I will often use them to provide height and volume when it's needed. *Sambucus* race upwards when they are happy, and this makes them useful as a 'nurse' plant for slower-growing shrubs that need some initial shelter. I used them in my garden in London, to provide height and volume in the early years, and removed them later, seeing their contribution as easy come, easy go.

Sambucus nigra 'Laciniata' is the closest you can get to the wild elder without the thuggish behaviour. The flowers are cream and held flat, like balancing plates among netted foliage. Growth is light and airy, each leaf netted like a delicate seaweed, and they make a delightful foil for ascending foxgloves and wilding roses. They are also good for growing in grass and I'll use them to feather a garden out into more natural places.

Sambucus nigra 'Black Lace' is in many ways similar to look at but it is altogether more ornamental for its colouring. The foliage is as dark as damsons and glossy when it emerges. The flowers are the colour of blackberry fool and make a wonderful complement to moody perennials such as *Astrantia* 'Roma' and *Lilium martagon*. Once the plants establish, you can also use them as a frame for *Clematis viticella*, their tiny flowers adding a myriad of later-summer interest. Cut the plants back to a tight framework in the winter to encourage a wonderful crop of lush foliage.

'Black Beauty' is another dark-leaved variety with uncut foliage, dark-coloured stems and the same pink in the flower. It is quieter than 'Black Lace' and perhaps less of a talking point. Of the yellow-leaved varieties the American elder, *Sambucus racemosa* 'Sutherland Gold', is the best. Find it a cooler corner to keep it in good condition and team it with *Digitalis purpurea* 'Apricot' to amplify its early salmon colouring. It will not flower as profusely, or provide you with cordial, but as it dims to a soft gold you will be happy to have the continued freshness of a summer solstice.

15 July, *Japan*
THE GARDEN OF 1,000 YEARS

———

This summer I have been taking part in the Millennium Forest Garden Show in Hokkaido. The island is the northernmost landmass of the Japanese archipelago, and equivalent in size to Ireland. An hour's flight from Tokyo, the 400-hectare park is the brainchild of entrepreneur Mitsushige Hayashi, who acquired the land with a view to offsetting the carbon footprint of his newspaper, *Tokachi Mainichi*.

The vision for the garden, to which I was asked to contribute along with the landscape designer Fumiaki Takano, is to create something that is sustainable for the next 1,000 years – a big ambition, and one that hopes to preserve this section of the island. In reality, none of us have much control over climate change or economy, but we believe education is the key. In a country where the greater part of the population is urbanised and far removed from landscape and nature, the idea is to re-engage people with the environment.

I have been working at the park since 2000 and in that time we have been coaxing visitors from their comfort zone. Delicate wooden walkways float over managed woodland flora and lead to a rolling landform of five hectares. I designed the Earth Garden to merge a flat, arable field into the foothills of the mountain and encourage people to move out into the landscape. We used ornamental gardens, too, and a kitchen garden with vegetables and fruit from East and West.

Although winter is the dominant season in Hokkaido and it arrives early – at its coldest, it reaches −25 °C and the landscape becomes a white-out – the island has become a focus of contemporary Japanese gardening. Cool summer nights allow a whole range of plants to thrive which would succumb to the heat and humidity of the other islands, and the park is part of a garden trail connecting the seven major gardens flourishing here.

The Garden Show is this year's contribution to the future of the park and it is unlike any other in that it is set within the forest and deliberately influenced by this context. The theme for the show explores 'a crush with nature' and the contestants have been encouraged to see the gardens as an access point into the natural world, rather than creating a space unrelated to its environment.

The show could not be more different from Chelsea. There are no prizes and each of the gardens is given the same small budget. Most importantly, the gardens will be able to evolve within the forest context for the three-month duration of the show. The gardens nestle into the woods along a watercourse that is fed from the mountains. They are reached by soft bark paths that meander quietly between the dappled glades.

My own garden takes the form of an arcing bridge that links the woodland with the meadows and mountains beyond. But everyone had their own particular angle on the 'crush' with the forest. A particular favourite caught the angling light in a grid of Perspex verticals that you walked through and became lost in as a child might be lost in a forest. Another had a series of bells attached to the branches in the tree canopy, which rang in the breeze.

There were subtleties in the garden by Haruki Shirai that made people think about living close to nature. The designer integrated horses, which came to a watering hole, and there were vegetables in a clearing. The dress garden, by flamboyant contrast, became an emblem for the show.

If the gardens can be used to encourage people to think about planting for the longer term – rather than just for the year ahead of them – I have a feeling that this show is on to something.

22 July, *Peckham*

THE ROYAL FAMILY

———

Just about the middle of June, the first buds popped on the *Lilium regale*. This is always a very particular moment, made stronger by the powerful addition of perfume. Dad used to grow an oak barrel full of them when we were kids. I can see them now pushing up through the leaf mould and remember charting their ascent quite clearly. Once they had broken ground, there'd be a frill of coppery growth like a sea anemone and the excitement of parting the foliage to count the embryonic buds. The buds swelled fast but imperceptibly, because they were under regular scrutiny, until one day, just like they did in my garden a month ago, they peeled open. A wine-coloured reverse gave few clues of the pearly-white interior, the throat infused with gold. The anthers, a hot orange, dust the interior of the flower with freckles of pollen in rain – and the smell . . . well, there are few things quite as delicious on warm summer air.

When I got the bug more seriously, aged about ten, I blew my pocket money one autumn on quite a large order of several different lilies, and these first plants paved the way for my ongoing love affair. The descriptions in the catalogue were not much more than a few sentences each, but they furnished my imagination with images of dappled glades hung with the delicate flowers. I bought three *L. canadense* only, but everything about them was a delight. The plump, pale-orange bulbs had just a few scales each and were so very different from the heavy, burgundy bulbs of the *L. regale*. The whirls of foliage forming tiers up the wiry stems, the way that flowers hovered like a mobile delicately balanced at the very tip of the plant – I pined for damp ground in which to introduce the North American *L. pardalinum* var. *giganteum*, and winced at the thought of Native Americans eating the bulbs as they once did. I saw it towering way over head height in the bog garden at Wakehurst Place one July, with its fiery red colouring and leopard-spotted throat. Our acid sand wasn't ideal, but most loved the cool conditions of our dappled woodland.

I played with the hybrids, too. The rich gold *L.* 'Shuksan' introduced me to a love of spotting. *L.* 'Citronella' proved to be trustworthy and long-lived in my yellow border. I had it in quite a large group around the *Ligularia* 'The Rocket'. *L.* 'Enchantment' was far less naturalistic in feel, so it was put into pots so that its soft orange, upturned flowers could lighten up the back door. I liked the hybrids as long as they had some grace in them and, after a while, became less enchanted with 'Enchantment'. The wine-red *L.* 'Pink Perfection' and 'African Queen' kept the relay going, coming into flower just after the *L. regale* were tipping over their prime. The *L. speciosum* followed on, quite late in August, a sugary pink with *L. auratum* marking the end of the summer holidays. The spectacular golden-rayed lily of Japan did well for us. It was extensively collected in the nineteenth century from the slopes of extinct volcanoes, where it grew in volcanic ash, and consequently it liked our free-draining ground. It is a great pity that this lily has now been replaced by poor impersonations bred as floristry hybrids, and one day I hope to seek it out in the wild again in Japan to complete the circle.

It is not just my rose-tinted memory of those first experiences, but lilies were easier before the scarlet lily beetle made itself the menace it is today. When I was at Wisley, in the early eighties, it was localised in Surrey and we sprayed it with malathion. I hated this job and vowed never to use spray myself, so now that the menace has spread up and down the country I have to restrict myself to growing only as many lilies as I can hand-pick to keep them free of the beetles and the revolting leaf-eating grubs. The beetles appear in several waves from early spring to late summer. They freefall to the ground if you disturb them, and lie on their backs, their black undersides making them all but invisible against the soil. You need to keep on top of the adults, for a fortnight's holiday is all it takes once you have the grubs feeding to find stems stripped of foliage on your return. This may only weaken the lilies in the first year, but repeated attacks will be their end.

Other than that, the main enemies of the lily are slugs, which can attack certain species in the winter when the bulbs lie dormant, so plant the bulbs in the autumn in a layer of sharp grit as a protection. The grit also helps with drainage. Nearly all lilies like moisture, but they like it to pass through rather than to lie wet. A heavy soil should be lightened with leaf mould, a sandy soil improved in its water-holding abilities with the same or compost. I have not met a lily yet that likes farmyard manure. They are mostly woodlanders by nature, and you do best to emulate those conditions. Cool and moist at the root, with heads in the light. The Madonna lily, *L. candidum*, is one of the few exceptions, preferring shallow planting, limestone soil and plenty of sunshine.

Pot culture is ideal for many lilies, as it allows you to control their environment, but many are quite happy naturalised in the ground. *L. pardalinum* is a good example, and an exception among lilies for its ability to tolerate damper conditions. *L. martagon* is also easy and will self-seed happily if it likes you. The first time I saw this beautiful, soft-pink Turk's cap in a garden was among *Astrantia* in a corner at Sissinghurst. The first time I saw it in the wild was in a nut wood in the Pyrenees, growing in exactly the same combination. Vita Sackville-West must have come across it too on one of her travels and recognised a good thing when she saw it.

I have learned with lilies to be happy when they like you and to give in to defeat when they don't, because there are so many to try. The soft-tangerine *L. henryi* has been a star in my garden over the years. Happy in the ground and producing so many flowers it needs support, it blooms mid-season when many from the first wave in June are over. Their steadiness allows me room to experiment, and this year I have a few bulbs of *L. nepalense*. This is a lily that I first saw growing well in the Edinburgh Botanic Gardens, where the cool climate and rain suit it well. I have an idea it will not do well with me in the south, but at least this year it will have the rain it needs to thrive. One lime-green flower only per stem, but one that is quite unlike any other with its dark maroon throat. The excitement at the thought of succeeding with it is every bit as good as it was more than thirty years ago with that first bulb order.

24 July, *Hillside*
DREAMING SPIRES

———

As spring turned to summer, I scoured our Somerset hedges for signs of foxglove. Not far away in the next county down, the Devonshire hedges were speared with mauve, but they have eluded us here and I entered summer for the first time in many years without them. As a child – equal in height, I suppose, and drawn to the detail at that level – I would spend hours watching bees working the spires. The buzz of their wings would amplify as they plunged inside the trumpets and when they moved on I would slide my finger inside to feel the velvety softness. We had them growing freely on our thin, acidic sand and they would appear as a pioneer ahead of the brambles wherever we cleared new ground.

When I realised their potential as border plants I took to growing the 'apricot strain', which had to be kept apart from the pinks if they were not to be cross-pollinated. I would feed them up with leaf mould and revel in the sense of achievement that I could grow them to 2 m at least. Foxgloves were the next step on from the quick fix of sunflowers – you had to wait a year while they formed a hearty rosette and then they rose fast to mark the first half of summer, followed by an almost certain death. I grew the white forms of *Digitalis purpurea*, too, and became adept at telling the difference between the seedlings that were going to be mauve when there was self-seeding. They gave the telltale signals of colour in their blood with a purple stain on the underside of the mid-rib. The purples were weeded out to keep the lines pure and the whites filtered through the shady borders to illuminate the darkness with a slash of light.

D. purpurea are pioneers, happy to lie dormant when woodland becomes too dense or shady, but they are one of the first to seize a window when a fallen tree floods light to the forest floor. They appear in coppiced woodland as a colourful aftermath, but they are far from shy if given a position in open ground. I have never understood why foxgloves and bluebells are often found striding out into the open beyond their comfort zone. Coastline walks and moorland will spawn them freely, their rosette of foliage presumably protected by the competition around them. In a garden setting, this adaptability can be used to advantage, for they are just as happy to seed about under the shrub roses as they are to find a crack in the edge of a path out in the open.

I like the way that the vertical lines of foxglove draw the eye like an exclamation mark. They are delicate, using only as much ground as they need, but providing plenty of bang for your buck with the upward motion. 'Pam's Choice' is a darkly spotted white form, while 'Primrose Carousel' is a delight at only 90 cm and useful seeding away at the edge of a border.

Though our native foxglove is a biennial, several European species are short-lived perennials or perennial given the right conditions. *D. ferruginea* likes a bright, dry position and quickly lets you know if it isn't happy by seeding into drier, open ground, or a crack in the paving. Tapering spires rise from a rosette of finely pointed leaves, a city of slender skyscrapers humming with bees when the rust-coloured flowers are opening. This is a plant that likes to move about and prefers life on the tough side, so it is great for a droughty garden as long as you establish the first plants carefully. *D. grandiflora* and *D. lutea* are more perennial. Both have creamy yellow flowers and are delightful standing clear of lower perennials such as *Origanum* or *Potentilla nepalensis*.

This year I am growing *D.* × *mertonensis* for the first time in a while. It is moody looking, with felty foliage and a temperamental habit that rules it out from being thoroughly perennial. That said, it is worth the effort of finding it a cool position but with plenty of light, as the flowers are the colour of crushed summer fruits. I am already pining for more than the odd foxglove in the hedgerows.

25 July, *Hawaii and Peckham*
FRAGRANT, ELEGANT AND RADIANT

———

I have just returned from a new commission on the Hawaiian Islands. It was a shock arriving to such fecundity, impenetrable greenery taking every centimetre that had not been claimed by a chainsaw or mower. Monstera and other recognisable houseplants more usually associated with gathering dust in 1970s front rooms scaled trees to the very tops and the mountains were clothed in all their parts. Heavy clouds dumped tepid rain as they collided with the hillsides and rainbows glinted sometimes four or five at a time. There was an energy in the growth that you could feel in the air.

After two days of travel and as the car came to a halt at our final destination, a glorious sweet smell filled the air as the doors were thrown open. I searched to find the source, but the perfume was omnipresent, an amalgamation of many flowers doing their best to attract their pollinators. Later that night, as the weight of perfume drifted in through the mosquito screens, I lay in bed and tried to recognise what was what. For moments, heady datura was clear in the mix. Night or day, the moist warm air carried the scent of flowers. Frangipani planted by almost every front door and hedges of a pale, finely turned native hibiscus meant your senses were constantly teased as you moved from cloud to fragrant cloud.

I returned to a wet English summer, where the smells were crisp and clean. Cut grass and wet foliage were chanced upon rather than constant, and it was strange for a few days, while I got used to having to find the perfume, to seek it out on the cooler air. There are just a handful of humid evenings in an English summer when perfume carries freely and I have learned to place those plants that offer it to best effect. They are planted so that the prevailing breeze blows through them towards you rather than away. The sheltered corners are also ideal as scent can linger there on still air. Daphne and roses, wisteria and honeysuckle are used by doors so you pass them daily and climbers encouraged to frame windows so their scent is carried into the house. Warm walls are particularly useful as the heat held in the wall helps to dissipate the perfume after the sun goes down. It is an art getting the best of it here, but one worth cultivating.

In our garden I have grown scented climbers on the fences so that I am surrounded. The curious green bells of *Holboellia latifolia* start the season in April and fill the place with an exotic perfume that feels quite out of place in a British spring but welcome nonetheless. This is a surprisingly easy plant for a sheltered corner and it will cope with sun or shade, its evergreen foliage slowly covering distance if you let it. Right now, it is the *Trachelospermum jasminoides* that is wafting through the windows and hanging in the still air of the terrace.

Many of my scented plants are grown in pots so that they can be brought to where I need them. The regal lily, *Lilium regale*, and then apricot 'African Queen' claim the crossover from June to July as their own. Then it's night-scented stock, which is sown on rotation every three weeks in shallow pans so that it can be brought up close to the windows. The flowers are discreet, but at dusk they come into their own and are as easy as cress. *Nicotiana affinis* and *N. suaveolens* perfume the garden for three to four months at a stretch, and scented-leaved pelargoniums are placed on stations along the path so that I never have to go far without the opportunity of crushing a leaf or two. *Pelargonium* 'Purple Unique' is a favourite just now, the leaf sticky to the touch and smelling of churches and incense. There are peppermint and rose pelargoniums, too, and a pan of *Mentha requienii*, a prostrate mint that covers the surface like moss and keeps you cool if you lie your hand flat upon it and bring it to your nose. These delights are perhaps more memorable for the very fact that you have to find them. Unseen treasures to tease the senses.

26 July, *Sissinghurst and Great Dixter*
DOWN THE GARDEN PATH

———

In the middle of June I took a two-day trip to Kent and East Sussex to visit Sissinghurst and Great Dixter. It was a journey I made with my father on several memorable expeditions. We would drive over from Hampshire, often returning in silence, talked out, inspired and overwhelmed in equal measure. Retracing my steps several decades later I found myself in the privileged position of overnighting in both gardens. The two stays were pinch-yourself experiences that made me wonder how a gardening-obsessed boy came to be such a lucky man.

I spent the first day with Troy Scott Smith, head gardener of Sissinghurst, and by evening thunder was threatening. The rose garden hung heavy with first-opened blooms on our way to Vita Sackville-West's house in the cottage garden. We huddled under the eaves at the castle gates as the thunder started and the poplars on the plain whipped in a storm that lasted just minutes.

The storm moved on, the rain subsiding as fast as it had started, to leave us alone in a dripping, still silence. The castle sat in soft focus, the smell of eglantine and *Rhododendron luteum* lingering in the hollows. Bees droned in the gutters and bats worked the meadows. As the colour dimmed and the hedges darkened, night fell to throw a solitary shadow of the tower across the lawn in the moonlight.

I slept that night in a bed covered with an ancient pair of embroidered curtains with the windows wide open and the garden all around sweeping up and over the walls, and understanding as fully as I ever would what Vita and Harold Nicolson were trying to do here.

Next day I made the journey cross-country to Dixter, where my bed for the night would be the one Christopher Lloyd was born in. It was quite a weekend of treading in the wake of two writer-gardeners who shaped the way we see gardens today.

Dixter was looking spectacular, the meadows breaking the boundaries and nestling the cars in the car park. I have never seen the meadows in the garden at quite such a pitch, with swathes of common spotted orchid sitting proud and in their thousands. A tide of oxeye daisies swept up and out of the long grassland. *Ferula communis* 'Glauca' tapered from a froth of filigree foliage and darkly stemmed *Peucedanum verticillare* bolted skyward in the High Garden, an aptly named place that left me intoxicated.

A new magenta *Viscaria* caught my eye, *Lychnis coronaria* blinked crimson through a froth of *Orlaya grandiflora*, and *Papaver* 'Ladybird' burned so brightly it appeared to have a halo. This is a garden that has moved as Christopher Lloyd would have wanted, shifting bravely forward and full of spirit. It bursts with energy and exuberance and the gardeners who work here live that energy. Go if you can. It is as good as ever, and is probably getting better.

27 July, *Hillside*
ORDER OF THE THISTLE

––––––

We cut the meadows in the middle of July, soon after the yellow rattle had seeded and before the creeping thistle set in. The rattle is a semi-parasitic annual and was sown three years ago to sap the strength of the grasses it uses as hosts. I was worried that colonies of thistle might take advantage of the empty space, but the rattle appears to be holding them back, too. I had been told this was the case and though it is too early to say because it might simply not be a thistle year, it will be nice to aspire to a miracle.

Although I try to be open to all plant life, I am happy to see the thistles' vigour diminished. Yes, they provide nectar for the bees and host the Red Admiral butterfly. But they take advantage of bare ground, sending deep and far-reaching roots. They make the meadows less easy to wander through and they are a nightmare if they get into the garden.

My prejudice ends there, however, because thistles in flower bring the feeling of high summer. I have started a collection because the plants feel right on our windy hillside, where they like the light and the dry soil.

I love all the sea thistles and *Eryngium* is hard to beat for its architecture and metallic iridescence. But there are a host of thistles that remain prickle-free. *Cirsium rivulare* 'Atropurpureum' is the first to flower. A tall, wiry stem rises 1–1.5 m from a clump of soft, green foliage. The flowers are unusual this early in the summer for being a glowing ruby red. Team it with the translucence of plum-red *Cotinus* 'Royal Purple' or among the golden awns of *Stipa gigantea* and let it hover. Cut it to the base when the rush of flowers stops and the stems start to topple. This will replenish the foliage and often provide a second crop of flowers.

Also thornless are the *Centaurea*, which I like for their architecture and repeat flowering. Our native knapweed, *C. nigra*, is too strong for the borders, but *C. orientalis* is perfect, flowering for months with a host of lemon blooms. Each comes with a papery golden sheath that protects the bud before it opens. Growing to about knee height, they are good in a small garden.

C. 'Jordy' is as dark as flowers get, with a wiry crown of finely spun petals. The flowers have a medieval quality and are wonderful with the pale lace of *Orlaya grandiflora*. *C.* 'Lady Flora Hastings' has a larger flower, a few centimetres across. It is perhaps the best white and good for the front of the border where it will sprawl over a path to make a good companion to *Alchemilla mollis* or bloody cranesbill.

If you have the room to let the cardoon soar in the borders, there is nothing quite like *Cynara cardunculus*. It has a spectacular eruption of foliage which comes to life early, taking the floor in March. The foliage climbs the stems as it bolts skyward, branching at 2 m to flower at 2.2–2.5 m. The flowers are an electric mauve. On a sunny day they will be festooned with butterflies and bumblebees.

30 July, *Peckham*

A TURN FOR THE BEST

———

Not long after the summer solstice, I found myself cycling quite unexpectedly across Richmond Park. It was early evening and I was already late for my appointment, but I was drawn through Richmond Gate without taking a breath to consider the diversion. The light from the west was sliding through the trees, and as I cycled I realised I had a grin fixed on my face that was entirely involuntary. It was there because I was lost in the moment, racing through pockets of air scented by bracken that had been heated in the sun and plunging into hollows made cool by the shade of ancient oaks. As I looked up and around, people going about their evening business were lost in the tall grass like grazing animals. Dead trees, the lightning bolts among the fat oaks, added to the untamed feeling of this vast expanse of park, and glimpses of the river below were shot with silver.

It was a half-hour of revelation, when everything seemed to be as beautiful as it ever could be and at the very point it had always been heading for in the first half of summer. The meadows were standing tall, still green and only showing colour where the duskiness of the flowering heads threw a maroon cast and the trees were heavily laden and untarnished. It was the summer at its most luxuriant, the high season teetering on the equinox.

A couple of days later, the garden at home started to express the slide into full-blown summer. Initially it was with the first-popped *Lilium regale*, and then luminous evening primrose joined them as dusk fell. Then the first of the rusty day lilies sounded off, kick-starting a mini riot at the end of the garden. It has been like that ever since, the *Crocosmia* turning up the volume, the indigo salvias, magenta *Lychnis* and tangerine of the *Alstroemeria* adding to the colour cacophony.

A month on, and things have begun to shift. Gone is the freshness and expectation of June, and you can see this in the brown that is creeping in with the seedpods. The poppy heads are already rattling seed free, the honey spurge spitting theirs far and wide on a hot afternoon. In tandem with the fading of the first half of summer, there is a fattening and a filling out. The buds are plump on the dahlias and the tomatoes beginning to colour. In a good year and on a hot day, you might be lucky enough to taste the first of the figs.

These are productive times, and the garden is in full swing. That said, there are holes in the salad beds where we have over-picked the cut-and-come-again greens and never let the Little Gem grow into adults. We are already munching our way through a third sowing of mizuna and purple-leaved pak choi. New salad leaves have to be re-sown to keep the succession going, and this can happen at fortnightly to three-week intervals until the beginning of September. Sow lettuce on cool evenings, as it germinates erratically when soil temperatures are higher than 25 °C. Cool days are also the best for planting out the leeks and the winter greens where the potatoes have been dug. A handful of seaweed meal and blood, fish and bone is all that should be needed if you dug in muck or compost when you planted the spuds.

The herb beds can also be kept lively, so that you keep

yourself in good supply. The sorrel, chives and mint benefit from being cut to the base to promote a fresh new crop of foliage. The sage and thyme are better for a summer trim to keep young leaves going and mildew at bay. If you have a cool corner it is also worth setting out a cluster of heel cuttings. The shrubby herbs from the Mediterranean are better as young bushes, and no time is better than now to root a new generation.

Though these are the days to loll in the grass, if you let things slide when the garden feels at its fullest you will get half as much as summer has to give. There are also holes developing in the beds where those plants that come in the first part of summer have been and gone. Lupins, the early geraniums and the oriental poppies should have been cut back to the base as soon as they were over to encourage replacement foliage, but it is a mistake to wade in too soon. This is a moment that has to be handled carefully and I have learned to exercise restraint to let the freshness fade into handsome maturity. I'll wait until the last minute and cut the meadows only once the seed has dropped, and I'll take a lead from these environments and leave the seedheads in the beds standing where they are offering me something.

Your energies are best kept for the plants that are designed to keep us in colour and benefit from the removal of the flowers to fool them into thinking that they have to keep going to reproduce themselves. Fifteen minutes is all it takes to keep the pelargoniums in trim, and the repeat-flowering roses never look better than when given a working over to remove spent flowers and make way for the next generation. Keeping this up until the autumn can extend the season a way yet.

A little smartness goes a long way in the right places, but it is also worth letting the garden run its course. Where would we be without the hips come September, but why go hungry when a little effort will furnish us well for what summer has yet to offer?

AUGUST

The light in August is very particular to the month. Is it the land that makes the light feel golden, with hedges and trees as dark and full as they ever will be and fields bleached blonde? Lawns are browned if it has been dry, for this is often one of our parched months. No matter, they will recover in no time as soon as there is rain, and then you feel that curious combination of relief and sadness for you sense the summer is ebbing.

I always have a plan for the August garden, because it is a month that can easily fall between summer and autumn. The energy has gone out of plants that have peaked and a little pause, or at worst a slump, is palpable. Roses are between flushes and there are gaps in the kitchen garden where you have got your timing wrong and failed with successional sowing. This is easily done, but if you have got it right, there will be a new flush of growth on the early flowering perennials that were cut back in July. Action now clears a little of the heaviness, and after you have given the wisteria its summer prune, you will have light again through previously shaded windows.

August is also a month when you can realign your focus and take from the garden rather than put into it. The weeds are in abeyance if you have got on top of them in dry weather and the lawn is between cuts and slowed by lower rainfall. There is seed to harvest, with poppies and calendula to scatter for next year, or special treasures to be sown fresh in the cold frame for the pleasure of raising your own plants. Figs and plums are ripening and it is a race to get to them before the wasps do. In times of glut you simply have to accept that you only need enough for yourself, and the birds can take the rest. In a good year, the August garden is the land of plenty and you want for nothing more.

5 August, *Hampshire*

PLAYING FOR TIME

———

I distinctly remember a red dahlia in my mum's strawberry patch when I was a child. We had to pass by it every day on the way through the garden to school. It was never more than a lush mound of foliage before the end of the summer term but, some time over the holidays, it would rear up commandingly and explode in colour. I loved its fleshy flamboyance, and the fact that it wasn't there one minute and then way above my head the next.

There is something about being small with access to a world that adults can no longer reach that, as a child, I recognised as my territory. I had hiding places beneath bushes in warm, dry nests of foliage and eyries in the forks of trees that grown-ups didn't know existed. There was a hollow in the roots of our beech tree that filled with water and, although no larger than a side plate, the life within it was a world in itself. Twitching mosquito larvae, rotting beech mast and bloated snails that had 'fallen in' held my attention for days.

At five I was propagating primrose seed in yogurt pots and making gardens on the roof of my self-styled mud and brick troll house. I liked the idea that I could fashion little worlds of my own from raw materials and, once I discovered the alchemy of growth, I was hooked. Soil, water and attention seemed to be all the ingredients required and, very soon, the roof garden of the troll house (and the trolls themselves) were usurped by beds of my own in the grown-ups' garden.

I suppose that I responded most readily to things that showed immediate results to attention given. The amaryllis that transformed itself from a dry bulb to a glistening cluster of trumpets, the beans that split within days when they were placed in a saucer on damp tissue paper. The young shoots were already there in miniature and once in the soil they just kept going, breaking ground in an eruption at the base of the bamboo tower and racing away in a vigorous action, just like they did in the fairytale.

The courgettes and the pumpkins were just as fascinating, their first leaves filling out like sails in the sunshine. In no time, and like magic, there were the very same fruit that I recognised from the greengrocer's nestling in the shade under the bristly foliage. So this is where they came from!

Things that moved fast and fruited were the most rewarding initially, and I quickly learned to enjoy the process of growing tomatoes. The musty smell that hung about the plant when you brushed it, the speed at which the seedlings grew and the excitement of the first truss of flowers. Soon, at the base of each flower, was a miniature fruit that grew and grew, and I still remember the day that the first blush of tomato red completed the final product. That is until I realised that there were yellow tomatoes too, and that they were just as easy.

The attention span of children may be short, but not so short that they can't start to see their efforts rewarded. A season is a long time to a child and, within a summer, there are several opportunities for them to witness the results. Vegetables allow them to see the whole process from scratch: how a bean grows into a pod, and how inside that silky pod there are more beans for the taking. A humble potato sprouted on a windowsill in February is in the ground over Easter and pushing through in a fortnight if the weather suits. The sprawl of foliage seems vast and endless to a child and the flowers come in no time. As an adult, forking out the first of the season's spuds is an incredible feeling, but as a child it is hard to believe that the wrinkled thing you put in the ground is responsible for the pale waxy tubers that have developed under the soil. Furthermore, it is hard to imagine that these are the very same things that chips and mash are made from.

Flowers also have their fascination, particularly those that show results in no time. The brighter the better seems to be the way to go, and there are few things easier than nasturtiums. Push a finger into the soil to make a hole just big enough to pop a seed into, pat the soil back into place and soon there will be a pair of perfectly circular leaves. On wet days, or after a dewy morning, each leaf holds a pristine jewel of water. There will be bees to pollinate the hooded flowers and ladybirds to eat the blackfly, and more seeds to collect if you lift up the foliage once summer is in full swing. Tagetes, calendula and morning glory are just as easy. You can count the flowers of ipomoea as they open every morning, and night-scented stock is worth trying simply because they produce perfume as well as fruit and flowers.

This summer my four-year-old niece started her first sunflowers, and when she returns from her summer holidays she will not believe how tall they have grown in her absence. I will also be planting some bulbs with her this autumn, after we have cut the flower heads off the sunflowers and hung them upside down outside the window for the birds. The wait might be a little longer, because a winter to a child is a lifetime, but before you know it the paperwhites and hyacinths will be fingering through the soil in readiness for the pots to be wrapped for the grandparents for Christmas.

6 August, *Peckham*
SNAP JUDGMENTS

———

August is a month when London suddenly empties out and the tempo changes. In the main, my clients are away, and professional garden-making, if it ever has a moment of quiet, is having it. In my own garden, too, the relaxed mood begins to assert itself. If I haven't prepared properly earlier while everything was growing at full pelt, it may well be too late. If I haven't got the succession working well in the veggie beds, I will just have to ignore the bare patches and try not to feel guilty about the missed crop of rocket. And if anything has been left unstaked, wading in now to try to remedy it merely guarantees fractiousness: it takes hours of fiddling in order not to break or bundle the unwieldy stems.

Of course, a gardener's work is never really finished, and what I love about this moment is the sense that if it is not right now, all you can do is make plans to get it right later. As for this summer, it is simply a case of maintaining things for another month or two.

The garden is now preparing itself for harvest. The first of the outdoor tomatoes are ripening, the courgettes are sneakily turning to marrows while my back is turned, and the spinach is bolting at the first sign of drought. The garden is doing its very best to ensure that the next generation is in place.

Quietly, and almost everywhere, seed is setting and hips are swelling and, rather than just watching this happen, I like to try to get in on the act so that nothing that I might need more of is missed. I like to have a good store of seed, if not for myself then to give to friends who have admired the mahogany nasturtiums or the single black opium poppies. It is great to feel that, within the little world of my garden, I am as autonomous and self-sufficient as I can be.

One of the first indicators that seed is ready to harvest can often be seen at the hottest point of the hottest day in July. It is then that the *Euphorbia mellifera* (honey spurge) start to explode. The seedheads have been swelling since late April, after the rust-coloured domes of flower were pollinated. During flowering, and for a good two weeks, the garden is filled with the most delicious smell of honey, but by high summer the plants are ready to distribute their progeny. They do this by design: the domed seedpods dry to a woody husk that twists and ruptures when it reaches a certain point of desiccation. The seed is flung a good 3–3.5 m away from the parent plant, expanding its territory. The snap of pods and the patter of seed falling on a hot afternoon are two sure signs of high summer.

This kind of engineering ingenuity makes seed collecting almost impossible, because you can never quite tell when the pod is ripe. Legumes do this too, the sides of the pod drying at slightly different rates when the seed inside is ripe, and then springing open to throw the seed. Geraniums and impatiens have also evolved kinetic seed-dispersal mechanisms. The cranes-bills do it by forming a structure like a medieval catapult, which hurls the seed away from the parent plant on a coiled spring. The design of the balsam-dispersal mechanism is so effective that they have managed to colonise great tracts of land along waterways in this country. Beating them at their own game, though, is quite simple, as long as you get the timing right. Watch until the seedpod starts to turn from green to brown and then tie a paper or muslin bag over the seed. (Plastic bags are not ideal as the seedheads will sweat, and seed needs to be dry to disperse.) When the pods rupture, they will do so in captivity and all you have to do then is filter the seed from the chaff.

Other methods of dispersal are slightly easier to deal with. One of my favourite grasses is *Stipa barbata*, which has its home in exposed positions in southern Europe and north Africa, where its low, tussocky growth is happiest in sparse growing conditions with plenty of air, light and free drainage. My original plant came from the garden of the late naturalist Karl Foerster in Potsdam, Berlin, where I saw the plants in June with their ethereal awns in full sail. At about 90 cm long, each flowering spike has up to a dozen seeds, and the seed, which is like a little fishing weight, is attached to a silver feather headdress almost 30 cm long. In their moment of glory they move languidly like seaweed shifting in the current. The magic continues when the seed ripens, as the long awn twists into a loose corkscrew before parting company with the flower spike. On the north African steppes, where there is a constant breeze, the wind takes the seeds a short way away from the parent and places them point-down in the dirt, like a dart. An extraordinary thing happens next: as the awn dries it twists still further, screwing the seed into the ground where it will germinate next spring. All the gardener has to do is intervene just before the seeds leave their parent and gather them up to store for next year.

When gathering almost anything, it is really important to harvest it at just the right moment. The seed must be ripe and just ready to scatter. If you are harvesting calendula, for instance, the spent head should be turning brown, and lightly rubbing it with your thumb should loosen the seed easily. Poppy seed is ready when the pod becomes woody and the pepper pot perforations at the top begin to open. Harvest too young and the seed inside will be unformed, wait too long and the seed will have already started to drop. You need to keep your eye in and catch them just before their moment of escape.

Once you have gathered the seed it is important to keep it dry, as anything stored wet will rot before it has a chance to ripen fully. This means gathering the seed or the seedpods and then laying them out on newspaper in a dry room for a week or so to allow any moisture to evaporate. It is only then that the chaff can be separated from the seed. The seed should be put into paper envelopes, labelled and dated to avoid any confusion. I like to store mine in a sealed Tupperware container in a cool room, or the fridge if there is space, as cool, dry conditions prolong the life of seed. If you are a perfectionist, a bag of silica gel also helps to maintain these conditions.

Some seed is best sown fresh, as it loses its viability more rapidly. The umbellifers (now reclassed as *Apiaceae*) are the best example, and any member of the cow parsley family should be sown fresh. Fennel, *Astrantia* and, my new favourite, *Bupleurum longifolium* should be shaken into a bowl and then scattered finely over a pot of sharp-draining compost. Scatter just enough sharp sand over the seed to cover it and protect it from slugs and desiccation, and water in.

Covered with a sheet of glass the pots can then be put in a cool corner, out of reach of squirrels and mice. Here, they will be subjected to the cold snaps in the winter and, all being well, should come through as planned as soon as the weather warms. You may well have forgotten about your August harvest by then, and the surprise will be all the sweeter for it.

THE INBETWEENERS

My drive down to Somerset takes me at least ten days back in time from London. In the capital, August buddleias are already more brown than mauve, and escapee asters are beginning to suffuse the embankments with the coming season. Greens are darkened, lawns showing wear. They have gone through their cycle already, seed dropped in readiness for autumn germination.

August is transitional. If you have weighted the garden too heavily with roses and the first half of summer perennials, you may be caught between one wave of flower and the next. The berries are ripening in hedgerows, and bindweed is lighting up whatever it has got the better of with its telltale pale trumpets. I must admit to never having the courage to grow it as an ornamental, as they do at Waltham Place in Berkshire. Where the bindweed can take the wilder places, I like to weave morning glory into the garden, 'Knowlian's Black' being a good dark form, or the morning glory blue where a lighter colour might freshen things up. As the month cools, the flowers will stay open until they are only just closing at tea time.

August is a month that you need to plan for so that the frayed edges are eclipsed by a little order, with restructured hedges. I have learned to plan the borders with reserves in mind for exactly this moment, with ornamental grasses where they are welcome. Tall *Molinia* 'Windspiel' will bolt up and above the gold of late-blooming *Rudbeckia*, dampening the blaze of yellow by casting its veil. *Panicum* are also good weavers, but if you are to use *Miscanthus*, remember that with its bold, clumping nature and plumes of flower it needs its own space if it is not to steal the limelight.

I have woven *Mina lobata*, another half-hardy relative of the bindweed, through the golden-flowered *Miscanthus nepalensis* for an August lift. With flaming claw-like flowers, it will twine to lick its host in orange, coral and red. I also grow the French marigold, *Tagetes patula*, rather than the named varieties, because I prefer its rangy growth, which might use a bronze fennel to lean into and rise up out of the border at waist height. The mainstay annuals can cover for a multitude of sins while the garden is readying itself for the autumn.

This year I misjudged the *Tagetes* and mingled it with nasturtiums and sweetcorn in the vegetable garden. They have got the better of the sweetcorn, and the nasturtiums are rioting. August was the month I first went to Monet's garden at Giverny and I saw them running up sunflowers and all but taking the breadth of the paths so that you had to tread carefully where they were not touching.

Once you have a few tricks up your sleeve, and the balance weighted in the right direction, August can be allowed to be a place between two seasons: a time of plenty, of plums weighting branches and the borders full.

14 August, *Hillside*
PASTORAL CARE

———

Years ago, when I was a student at Wisley, the last three months of my final summer were spent on the trials fields, where we worked under the guiding hand of Bertie Doe, the very gardener who posed for the black and white stills in the original version of that classic book *The Vegetable Garden Displayed*. It was here that we learned the importance of order, for it was vital that the plants were put to the test under the best possible conditions. They were grown with textbook spacing, weeds were never tolerated and excellence in horticulture was practised with an old-fashioned rigour. The trials field was nothing to do with my naturalist leanings, but I warmed to the results when things were done correctly.

I was pondering this the other day as I was looking over the virgin plot on our steeply sloping hillside. I said I'd take a year to get to know the land here and it is amusing to see that my plot is as much a trials field as it is the beginning of a garden. We have 8 varieties of potatoes and as many of courgettes and tomatoes, 10 new willows, 56 dahlias, neatly lined out and orderly, and 20 David Austin roses to compare and contrast.

One of the most exciting experiments is the Pictorial Meadows seed mixes, developed by Dr Nigel Dunnett at Sheffield University as a substitute for expensive park bedding. Traditional bedding is heavy on resources, demanding artificial heat to get it started, and then needing to be pricked out, potted on and planted out. The seed mixes have been developed to be sown direct, like a meadow. As long as the ground is well prepared and clear of weeds, the theory goes that a wave of colour is every bit as possible, using half the resources.

I have used Pictorial Meadows before in my clients' gardens, but nothing compares to growing something for yourself. I have four of the annual mixes on trial to witness their performance up close. The ground was freshly turned and manured when the seed was broadcast in the first weekend of April, but it wasn't long before I was cursing my impatience. The seed germinated fast, in a fortnight, but very soon it was clear the mixes were infested with annual seed that had lain dormant in the ground and come up among them.

Five weeks after germinating, it was impossible to get among the weave of seedlings and I stood back and let them take their chances. It was a delight identifying the things I knew and trying with the seedlings I didn't, for each mix is composed of a finely balanced selection designed to provide a long succession of flower. There are three plots on my trials field, in which I have the Candy, the Pastel and the Volcanic mixes; the Marmalade Mix is sown up by the house, in the beds that were set to the previous owners' pelargoniums.

By the middle of May, six weeks after sowing, we had our first Shirley poppies and two weeks later they were dancing over gypsophila and fairy toadflax. Cosmos and lacy *Ammi majus* have taken over now and though they have been flattened by the July rain and wind, they have plenty of life left in them yet. The Candy Mix is less sophisticated than the others but the cornflowers have been a terrific draw for bees and butterflies.

The Volcanic Mix is dramatic, with red clover, black cornflowers and towering red orach. Dark orange Californian poppies started the season and a tiny coreopsis is picking up now for later. The Marmalade Mix has been so bright we can see it from our neighbour's on the other side of the valley. This mix was over-sown because the beds were smaller than the quantity in the packet called for, and I took the risk. The Californian poppy was up fast and furious and I thinned it to allow the later annuals breathing space. The red flax is completely delightful, hovering among gold chrysanthemums, and rudbeckia and coreopsis are coming through now for autumn. Despite my initial reservations – down to my impatience rather than the mixes – I'd say the trial has been a triumph.

17 August, *Friar Park*
MAGICAL MYSTERY TOUR

———

One of the most thrilling aspects to what I do as a garden-maker is that I get to see behind the garden gate. There is nothing more exciting than being allowed into someone else's world, and these places are often the dream that my clients have lived for. Sometimes it is a building that makes the place particular, other times it is a view or a winding track to the sea or a section of river that gives the place its value, but it is rarely a ready-made and appropriately timeworn Gothic fantasy of fourteen hectares.

Friar Park is an extraordinary garden, perched on a hill high above Henley. There is an ornate gatehouse with wrought-iron gates down at the very bottom of the drive. It gives you a flavour of the Victorian mansion that lies hidden in the trees at the top, but nothing quite prepares you for the garden that gives the house its setting. Olivia Harrison, wife of the late George Harrison, is the current custodian and the person keeping it from being overwhelmed by its own eccentricity, and between them, they were responsible for bringing it back from the brink of dereliction.

George was just twenty-seven when he arrived at Friar Park. It was 1970 and not long after the Beatles had split. The garden had gone into a serious decline under the Catholic nuns who were previous owners. The lawns were grown over and torn at the edges by encroaching brambles and the lakes were dry. Its creator, Sir Frank Crisp, who had been there between 1875 and 1919, had made Friar Park his grand project. He had done so with typical Victorian confidence, carving out his fantasy with no fear for scale and doing so with wit and eccentricity. Plant collecting was a profession at the time and new introductions were being brought back by the crate-load. Many were plants that had never been seen before and Crisp joined in with the excitement, choosing to build the landscapes for his plants rather than visit them in their habitats.

He became a passionate Alpine gardener and to house his ever-growing collection, he decided to create a rock garden. They were fashionable at the time and I can think of several around the country that sought to capture the magic of these elevated landscapes. But few are quite as dramatic as Friar Park's. The Matterhorn had only recently been climbed so Crisp built a version of it in sandstone, which over the years grew to more than a hectare in size. Today, and restored to its former glory, there is an airy Alpine meadow at the top and cascades that drop dramatically or trickle from level to level. A tumbling scree gives way to the lower slopes, and on the cool, shady side there are ravines that tower over your head and completely immerse you in the illusion. Among the many treasures, Olivia has blue Himalayan poppy and *Podophyllum* thriving here.

There were also walled and productive gardens, an Elizabethan garden, a white garden, a Japanese garden and a spooky topiary dell in Crisp's heyday, but the high drama of this landscape, and the considerable efforts that go into maintaining an estate of such complexity, had been too much for the nuns who lived there during the quarter century before the Harrisons arrived. To keep some money coming in, the nuns had let local builders use the lakes as a tip and all that was visible at the start of the seventies – and Olivia described it as having a *Planet of the Apes* aesthetic – was the summit of the Matterhorn, poking through a net of undergrowth and seeding trees.

Though he loved architecture, George told Olivia he was happy to live in one room of the mansion and take on what he needed when he needed it. Originally, he intended to go about the garden in the same way, but gardens have a way of snagging you and not letting you go. By the time Olivia arrived in 1974, he had already developed what was the beginning of a life-long passion. He started by fixing the fountain up by the house, the lawns were mown, the ivy cleared and, fittingly, he put two goats on the Matterhorn to clear the brambles. One day he lowered himself on a rope into one of the subterranean caverns under the lakes only to find the incredible remains of the waterways and grotto that Crisp had created there. The grand project had found a new custodian.

'We never set out to make the garden a restoration, we were just doing it for the joy of it,' Olivia said of the process of unveiling the grounds. 'You don't have to know anything or everything to make a garden and George set out quite independently to do it his own way. "It's amateur hour" was a mantra, and clearing away the dark Victorian palette of laurel and yew and overgrown box was key to being able to move the garden forward.'

Beth Chatto's visit to the gardens proved key as a confidence-building exercise. With typical practicality she had said: 'You know, George, if you had an old sofa in your house that you didn't like you'd throw it out!' The comment was a liberation and that was how they began to lift the gloom to make way for a new layer.

Beth also introduced the Harrisons to grasses, and in the clearings that replaced the long-lost gardens, a new layer of planting began to unroll in confident swathes that are of considerable size. George became something of a plant collector himself, visiting the Hillier Arboretum and the gardens of Cornwall. They planted freely at Friar Park, preferring not to get bogged down in the history and not to be precious about working in the new layer. Olivia explained George's free approach to the garden as being a way of coping with the events in his life. 'He preferred not to think too much beyond the here and the now for fear of being overwhelmed by the scale of what lay around him. Gardening was the ideal antidote and the title of his song "Be Here Now" described that perfectly.'

He liked to be spontaneous and to get the plants in to keep

everything moving. In doing so he discovered the combination of maples and ferns, and the revelation that if you combined them with Japanese wind anemones you could pull off a look that worked well within the mood of the place. In the autumn, the lake is now ablaze with the colour of the maples, and tucked away throughout the grounds there is a new layer of whimsy that complements Crisp's irreverent approach to tradition. A boat, dry-docked in the trees, commemorates their son's twenty-first. It is just one of many touches that are in the spirit of the old stone crocodile in the lake that issues the water from the bore hole and Crisp's sign 'Herons will be prosecuted!' He was a lawyer.

In 1997, George was diagnosed with cancer and as soon as he returned from his first treatment he started the woodland walk. The garden continued to provide sanctuary until he died in 2001, and Olivia continues to move it forward. I helped her to plant a sun garden in a clearing in the wood and, since then, the walled garden has burgeoned. Clematis hangs in swags from the yew hedges – she describes them as her drapes – and a new herb garden is bursting at the seams. She has also started to edit the trees on the boundaries to reveal the views beyond. Once again, confident moves, the only ones that really work in such a setting.

Before I left, Olivia took me on a magical tour in the rowing boat. We entered a cleft in the rocks alongside the waterfall that splits the two levels and paddled our way behind the cascade. Light bounced off the stucco walls as we entered the tunnel, but before long we had left the roar and the light behind and were paddling through the pitch-black. I began to wonder how far we could feel our way into the darkness but on rounding a corner the shimmering grotto was revealed. Blue glass panels set into the garden above let an eerie light fall over the columns of spa stone that rise from the water. As we floated through this mysterious inner landscape, I had to pinch myself that I was really there and part of the fantasy.

19 August, *Peckham*
THE LAST HURRAH

Held between the profusion of high summer and the weight of autumn, August is a month that can slip between seasons. There are gaps in the borders where the poppies have come and gone, and empty rows in the vegetable garden where armies of slugs have been. In a typical year, as August is usually the driest month, the lawns are browning and tatty round the edges, but I enjoy the feeling that we can loosen the reins a little.

The garden is making a move to replenish itself, with the weight of seed pods toppling the hollyhocks from their vertical position and the hips arching the roses. I allowed the *Tragopogon* to seed last year in my stock beds, and the giant dandelion clocks are standing tall and golden brown with seed. The chives and the sorrel are on their second round of flower after earlier cutbacks to encourage new leafage, and the sweet peas are podding up where they have outflowered my ambitions to keep up with picking. I save seed where I can, taking enough for myself but leaving the lion's share for the garden.

The August garden is rich with layering, seedheads and berries rubbing shoulders with late-summer flower. The grasses are remarkable now, rising up high to cover for potential gappiness and capturing a yellowing light in their growth. Many are still coming into flower and they form nets in which their neighbours appear to have been held in suspension. A star this late into the summer is the *Molinia caerulea* 'Transparent', which arches out in a filamentous dome 2 m across.

The foliage sits low now beneath the flower stalks, which reach up and away like a thousand delicate fishing rods. I first saw 'Transparent' in the gardens of Mien Ruys in Holland, where it was growing in glorious isolation, but I like it equally in combination. Starry crimson dahlias, tapering wands of hot pink *Persicaria* and wandering nasturtium find their way up into their branches like coloured fish in seaweed.

I am planning a new planting with the North American *Panicum* as the veil. The switchgrass is a fine-limbed race of prairie grasses, and much underrated. Their delicacy of growth, lightness of leaf and clump-forming habit make them good companions, and they do better if grown a little 'hard'.

Thistly *Eryngium* like the same conditions and team up well with flowering cardoon and fiery *Crocosmia*. The *Panicum* are variable, too, with some revealing a silvery cast, but the majority lean to brown and rich mahogany-red. 'Cloud Nine' will ascend in a stretch that matches the tallest of the sunflowers, while 'Heavy Metal' will sit around shoulder height to shimmer grey through the *Verbena bonariensis*. 'Shenandoah', which is less than a metre high, is just beginning to colour up now and to darken from a deep rich green to brown and chestnut. Later, as summer gives way to autumn, you will see it glow with ruby red as if it is lit from within, and I make sure that there are bubblegum-pink *Nerine* in the vicinity to make the most of the show.

Miscanthus are a different animal and I use them as I might shrubs to create volume in a planting. There is a formality in the way they grow, and as their season begins in August you see their mounds of rustling foliage give way to spectacular plumage.

In Japan, where the *Miscanthus* are native, the fan of flower represents the autumn, but plant breeders have ensured that the season is as long as it can be, and a plant such as 'Ferner Osten' is at its best while summer is still with us. I love this variety, the tassels emerging a thunderous plum-purple and shimmering with the last of the bergamot. They age to a smoky brown and then buff as the season progresses. 'Silberfeder' and 'Haiku' are silvery white and incandescent with the light in their flower heads. They are perfect among autumnal black-eyed Susan and outlive the latest asters to bridge not two but the best of three seasons.

20 August, *The West Country*
THE FRUITS OF SUMMER

———

One hot, memorable day last summer I went to visit a new client in the West Country. The garden swept up and over a rounded hill, at the top of which perched the house. Fine views were to be had across the valley and a stream still trickled between ancient oaks. The grounds had been tended, not gardened, and here lies the difference between a space that feels loved and one that is 'kept up' as an obligation. Lawn reigned as an easy-to-look-after surface, the hedges were swollen and out of shape and the borders, what there were of them, repeated the same old toughies like a ditty that you can't get out of your head; sedum, aster, lady's mantle, sedum, aster, lady's mantle.

Behind the house, tilted at just the right angle to capture the sun, lay a Victorian walled garden. Through the garden gate lay the footprints of the old glasshouses and, up in the top corner in the V formed by a south and a west wall, was a fruit cage. Rickety, yet the only thing standing bar the walls of the garden itself, it was brimful of plants. You could see that from a distance and, as I pushed the wire door open, it became clear that the previous owners of the house had loved growing fruit. Peaches were fan-trained against the whitewashed south-facing wall, which had heated up during the day and the warm fruit was plump and downy. I tried not to touch. A contorted apricot had taken over the corner and had already been harvested. A vine, which scaled the wall above, was heavy with darkening grapes. The bunches hadn't been thinned and the weight of the crop had pulled one of the main limbs off its support on the wall where it sagged over the path.

Red and white currants hung like jewels from bushes so old that some were no more than a couple of cranky limbs. The remains of the blackcurrants that hadn't been picked were oozing sugary, sun-ripened juice, each handful providing enough vitamin C to keep you going for a whole day. Inevitable wasps hovered around the slightly alcoholic smell of the fallen fruit that was scattered amongst the chickweed where, just to complete the picture, grew strawberries. Battling it out but protected from the birds, they were my first stolen mouthful: sun in a berry and that wonderful mix of tartness and perfume.

My childhood neighbour Geraldine also kept a fruit garden, but it was a random affair that cropped up wherever there was space in her wild and woolly garden. She had the best, time-tested varieties, singled out for flavour over productivity, but her main incentive was hedonism and she usually had a giveaway stain in the corner of her mouth. The currants lived at the back of the rose bed and raspberries were planted to hide the compost heap. Both early, mid-season and autumn-fruiting varieties kept the birds happy, but she always had a summer bowlful for breakfast. They were netted at the last minute with an old green mesh that did little more than trap the odd blackbird. Fruit was on tap if you knew where to find it, and there was always enough for jam.

To harvest the rangy fig tree she had made a Heath Robinson contraption, which was a cross between a butterfly net and a jabbing stick. At the end of 1976, I remember having to refuse the offer of a wasp-scarred 'Brown Turkey'. 'Break them open for the best bit,' she'd say, her cheeks covered in the red, bitty flesh. They were too much for me then, far too decadent and strange, but I pine for them now and, so far, my fig tree has done nothing more than provide me with the image of a fruit garden. No fruit yet, just promise – but the tree is a reminder that, in the not-too-distant future, I want to be able to forage on sun-ripened goodies in my own garden.

Things are beginning to move in that direction for I have taken on an allotment myself. From home it is a short trundle away with the barrow, so I can squeeze it into already full gardening weekends without having to go far. It is unlovely now, but I do not see it that way in my mind's eye. The chain-link fence, entwined with bindweed, offers protection from the urban foxes and their bad behaviour; the exhausted, dusty soil offers opportunity. As the plot is not overhung by trees, this means I have options for fruit and veg which, in the main, love the light, and I will find a way round the fact that there isn't water on tap close by. Although water has not exactly been a problem this year, it will be a good discipline to do with less.

A clear bed in the middle, in which my neighbours were growing their broad beans, has been used as a test bed. I sowed it with wild rocket and cos lettuce to see how good the soil really is, but I will do little more than clear the weeds and start to plan so that I can shower it with attention in the autumn.

The rekindled experience of last summer's fruit cage will manifest itself thus: a bed of raspberries will be planted on the shady side, where I have no control over what the neighbours grow. Raspberries grow as edge-of-woodland plants in the wild and like a cool, moisture-retentive soil with some sun on their heads to ripen the fruit. I will dig in plenty of compost over the autumn and make sure the new canes are planted so that they can get their feet in before next year. I will mulch the whole allotment in the spring should there be another drought and get a good, summer-fruiting variety such as 'Glen Moy', with 'Autumn Bliss' to follow through later. Summer-fruiting varieties fruit on last year's canes so I will cut them back once the fruit has been harvested to make way for the next year's shoots. Autumn-fruiters can be cut to the base in the spring as they fruit the same year. I will keep them apart as the autumn-fruiters are prone to running and put a couple of loganberries alongside them. The chain-link will be used to tie in their rangy limbs.

The cool side of the allotment will also be used for currants, as they are surprisingly shade-tolerant. I will have one blackcurrant, 'Ben Sarek', as space is limited and this is a neat bush, and one 'Red Lake', as there is much to be said for things to brighten up the food that you eat. I love their tartness and the zing that they bring to a fruit salad. I will single out the best strawberries for the sunny side of the plot as it is increasingly hard to get strawberries in the shops that are flavoursome. Most varieties are grown for productivity and organic strawberries are expensive. A small plot of 'Cambridge Late Pine', perhaps the best flavour of all, and 'Royal Sovereign' will be used as edging in front of some espaliered pears. My task for the autumn will be to find a good buttery variety that can do well without the heat of a wall behind it. Not such a hardship methinks. My mouth is watering already.

21 August, *Hillside*

MAKE A BEELINE

The two sisters who keep the cows on the fields above us pulled up on the lane outside our gate in January. The back of their car is always full of feed and dogs, the front seats pushed forward to compensate, so it was a job for Josie to unwind the window so that we could talk. We passed the time of day, discussing local matters as she reached into the glove compartment to rummage for a jar of honey. 'You don't mind if we store some hay in your tin barn up at the top do you,' she said as the jar exchanged hands. 'I hear you are planting an orchard. The bees will be good for your fruit and your blossom will be good for my bees.'

We were delighted with the honey, which seemed fair exchange for a barn that is standing empty. I plan to keep bees one day, and it seems fitting that the new orchard might guide the time frame, but for now I am planning how to enrich the land to suit them. Our native flora has a relatively limited window of flower and that, coupled with the pressures of industrialised agriculture, has put stresses and strains on an already dwindling population. We still don't know the full story of why bees are failing, but it is interesting to note that they are healthier in our urban areas. Our 'gardened' gardens, with their exotic contents, offer a longer window of feeding opportunity and a more diverse one, and, with it, considerable hope.

On the wild side, the meadows will be allowed to grow long and the wild flowers encouraged through proper management. I will be planting trees and shrubs that extend the season in the hedgerows, too. There will be early blackthorn in March and a succession of blossoming natives. We will allow the ivy up into the trees and leave it to flower in the hedgerows because its October blooming is good for late-season nectar and the last feeding for the bees in a warm year before the frosts.

Roughly speaking, the life cycle of a bee is from March to

September, so the gardened gardens will be planted for continuity amid the flux of the wild plants. The season can afford to start early with pussy willows under-planted with cultivated dead-nettles and comfrey. The latter flowers for a good eight weeks and, when it is done, the foliage can be cut for liquid fertiliser or compost. Layering the garden with nectar-rich plants will see sunflowers and fennel in with the vegetables and a range of lavenders. *Lavandula stoechas* can be in flower in late April with a relay of varieties to follow through to the last week of the summer holidays, when it needs pruning.

There will never be fewer than two plants in flower so that the bees can move about the garden, with early-flowering pulmonarias under plum trees to encourage the bees to travel and pollinate, and dill planted in the vegetable garden to encourage a better set of runner beans. I will make sure that among the 'cultivated' plants there are plenty of flowers that are single. Plants with single flowers are always more accessible for feeding. You only have to witness the activity on the single dahlias and the stillness around the doubles to see this. The same can be said of calendula and the single-flowered roses, so I will make sure I have the 'Kew Gardens' rose or the Alexandra rose among the double varieties.

Almost anything growing in the rose family will attract bees, but there are a host of herbs and Mediterranean sun-lovers that the bees will move to when the scabious in the meadows and honeysuckle in the hedgerows are dwindling.

Thyme, sage and *Origanum* all have forms that have been cultivated for their ornamental value and for superior flowering – and nectar. A plant such as *Origanum laevigatum*

'Herrenhausen' will literally flower for weeks while echinacea, eryngium, phlomis and bronze fennel will not only keep the garden going until the autumn wave of asters, but will provide the bees with a sanctuary in increasingly difficult times.

22 August, *Peckham*

THE REGENERATION GAME

———

Despite the glorious summer, it has been a hard year in the garden. Fox cubs, now young adults, have made the garden their playground, careering through the beds and crapping knowingly on the table and chairs, the lettuces, the cold frame and even inside one of my shoes. They came into the kitchen to do so and took the other shoe and chewed it to pieces in a clearing they had made by flattening the cleome. They wilfully smashed all the hemerocallis when they were just coming to bud and have snapped off the rodgersia to clear what have now become dusty tracks. I have been on the verge of tears and, I might add, bloodiness more than once and thanked my lucky stars that in all these years we have been spared until now.

I have been cutting back hard when things have been smashed, to regenerate plants that I think can take it. Where the foxes have changed their habits and moved on elsewhere, the sanguisorba are back and gleaming with fresh new foliage, as are the geraniums and the astrantia, which are throwing up a few new flowers. Fresh foliage at this time of year is a bonus as the garden has also struggled with the dry weather and is looking shabby in places. It is the usual August slump, but there are always ways around it.

Foxes aside, a good crop of foliage keeps things looking fresh and lively when the garden is over the first flush and not yet relaxed into autumn. The *Clerodendrum bungei* are a good example and over the years this suckering shrub has jumped through the beds to appear spontaneously and in combinations I never would have planned. You have to watch this unruly behaviour if it decides it likes you, and I'll pull the suckers where they are misplaced. Those that aren't are pruned back hard in March, like buddleia, and then hard again in early July to keep the foliage coming. Left to their own devices, the *Clerodendrum bungei* would be in flower by now but the second cutback delays the sugary domes of flower until the autumn. The leaves, which are heart-shaped and made larger by pruning, are about the size of an outstretched palm. They are fetid, foxy even, if you brush them, and the colour of copper beech.

Pruning hard to encourage dramatic leafage is not a new thing; the Victorians were masters and used it in their extravagant bedding schemes. 'Architectural' plants such as the castor oil plant and canna were often the focus of these schemes, but they used shrubs and trees, too. *Ailanthus altissima*, the tree of heaven, will produce leaves that are almost a metre long if the plants are 'stooled' to the base at the end of the winter. You will barely recognise them when you see this effect for the first time and by the end of the year the plants will form a many-stemmed mound 1–2 m high if your soil is hearty.

Pruning hard is only advisable after plants have been in for a couple of years and are strong enough to bounce back because they have their roots established. You should remember that, with such severe treatment, they require a good mulch and a feed if they are to reward you. In a friend's garden up the road, we have punched up the scale of things by 'stooling' a small group of the foxglove tree, *Paulownia tomentosa*. The scale of the leaf is further heightened by the fact that this is a small London garden. Soft and velvety with fur, each leaf expands to the size of a child's umbrella.

I do this here in the garden with the *Vitis coignetiae*, whose leaves I use for serving plates at summer parties, as well as the *Melianthus major*, which never looks finer than in this run-up to the autumn. Each leaf is grey-green, with a jagged edge to the margin, as if it has been cut with pinking shears. They cover for a multitude of sins elsewhere; for this year the sins have been many.

24 August, *Peckham*
TALKING HEADS

At this quiet time in London I like to make the most of the difference in pace. The hollyhocks are at a tilt, the dahlias doing their absolute best, the tomatoes are colouring fast, and sitting plump and comfy in front gardens across the city is a magnificent display of hydrangeas.

They are uncoordinated by default, one garden unrelated to the next, but somehow their sheer blowsiness unites the streets. They are mostly leftovers from another era and some spill out through the railings and over walls like loaves trying to escape the tin. Colour is the domain of the mophead hortensias and I can see why they have been so out of fashion for many years. Occasionally, there is one flushed an otherworldly cobalt, where proud owners have dutifully applied sequestered iron or a handful of treacherous rusty nails, but in the main they are every shade of Barbara Cartland.

They have been building towards this moment for a while. The hydrangea undergoes a remarkable transformation as it moves through the summer, and the first signs appear early in June, when leaf buds give way to the ultimate goal, the inflorescence. This starts small, like a bunched-up knot of fabric, and it is some time before it starts to show any sign of colour. First green gives way to cream, then usually pink, but most are as dynamic as amethyst, a fusion of lavender and violet.

There are a goodly number of named varieties that can supply you with a look you can depend upon. *Hydrangea* 'Preziosa' is one of the nicest of the red hortensias. A small bush of not much more than a metre with modestly sized flowerheads no larger than a grapefruit, it is raspberry-red when at its best. This plant is completely reliable and never attempts to steal the show. *H.* 'Ami Pasquier' is similar in stature, but with darker cherry-red flowers that can colour blueberry-blue in acid conditions. *H.* 'Madame Emile Mouillère' is possibly the best of the whites and instantly adds an air of opulence in the right situation. We grow it in giant pots in Italy in a shady courtyard clad with Virginia creeper and it gives this area of the garden an air of sophistication and glamour. A reliable supply of water is a necessity if you want to keep things looking smart, and a good mulch early on in the year works wonders.

The mophead hortensias need the comfort of domesticity to look the part, but there is a wealth of hydrangeas that cast a very different mood and work beautifully in a more naturalistic setting. The lacecap hybrids are just as reliable, but they vary dramatically, with a flattened whirl of outer florets surrounding the inner constellation of tiny flowers. *H. serrata* 'Grayswood' is one of the most beautiful, starting out a silvery-white and shifting slowly towards pink. *H. macrophylla* 'Lanarth White' and *H. macrophylla* 'Veitchii' also add a pale sparkle to a shady corner. *H. macrophylla* 'Blue Wave' is pure electric blue if you have an acid soil, but it is just as pretty fading to mauve in an alkaline soil.

I have *H. quercifolia* at the front of my own house, which I first saw in full autumn colour in America, where it grows twice the size with the heat. Here it forms an open shrub not much more than a metre across, but with considerable sprawl if you let it. Oak-shaped leathery leaves are its main feature, that and the fact that, of all the hydrangeas, it is tolerant of some dryness at the root. In sun it blooms more profusely with creamy, wedge-shaped flowers; in shade it produces a larger leaf and less flower, but is every bit as lovely. *H. quercifolia* 'Snow Queen' is my favourite, with simple, single, ivory-white blooms.

Of those that have a wilder edge, I would not be without *H. aspera*, one of my favourite foliage plants. There are several groups of this species, all with differing habits, but all are united by a bristling leaf that, in the right conditions, easily reaches 30 cm in length. The largest-growing of all is *H. aspera* subsp. *sargentiana*, with stems and young foliage so hirsute they appear mossy. It is a sturdy, upright shrub, easily twice my height, and it takes off and suckers if you give it shade and moisture. In sun it dwindles and scorches, so make the most of that fact and put it in a dark corner where you will have flowers the size of dinner plates. By comparison, *H. aspera* 'Mauvette' has small flowerheads and is the neatest and best-behaved of the tribe, but my favourite is *H. aspera* Villosa Group. This is a plant that settles easily into woodland without seeming to be out of place, and will be at its happiest in the dappled light. Flat lacecaps, produced later than most, towards the end of August, are an eerie violet-blue. Hovering in the shadows, they could not be more different from their tarty, blousy cousins, but I'm pleased that we have both ends of the spectrum to brighten the holidays.

SEPTEMBER

September sunflowers are racing up and blazing away over our heads. They make you look up and out and map the summer season. If, as I have, you have dabbled with dahlias, they are now making a riotous display that you can only submit to. Restraint is out of the window, so fill your vases and keep picking.

Meanwhile, and in sharp contrast, the ornamental grasses are at their best, knitting the garden back together with gauzy flower. Down in Somerset, we are pleased to have them in the garden now that the meadows have been cut, and welcome their presence amongst the later-flowering perennials. They are host to later summer's longer shadows and the tallest are silhouetted against the backdrop of pale blue skies. I cannot imagine gardening without them, for they soften a blaze of black-eyed Susan and, weighted with dew, arch over the path to drench your morning passage. Give yourself the time to see them catch the breeze.

A new flush of weeds suddenly announces that it is time to grow again and heralds a fresh planting season. It is the perfect time to sow grass seed and make the most of the warmth and moisture in the ground. Autumn-flowering bulbs respond to the new season; cyclamen awaken and light dull corners, and out in the sunshine colchicum and autumn crocus appear in a new push of life. The garden is at its most relaxed in this often glorious month, one that might well see an Indian summer, but always brings with it some of my favourite combinations of flower, bulb and berry.

2 September, *Peckham*

MOOD INDIGO

———

The light is never more beautiful than it is now, sliding into the garden at an ever-increasing angle to tease out the detail. It feels like there is time on our hands to take it all in, the rush of growth slowed, the fear of losing control diminished. Rosy-faced apples weigh down branches and lazy wasps have the remains of the plum harvest. Sunflowers will never be taller, berries are hanging heavy on the once-blooming roses, and the butterflies, which have had a hard time of it this summer, are making the most of the asters and the last heat in the sun.

Over years of garden-making I have come to see the benefit of playing to this season. Spring is automatically exciting and we are spoilt for choice in summer, but leaving room in the borders for this window has many benefits. It provides us with anticipation and the contrast of fresh life among the remains of what has come before. It is interesting to use shrubs as the building blocks around which the more ephemeral annuals and perennials can ebb and flow.

You have to be sure when you commit to the long-term investment of a shrub, and I like the way this concentrates the mind.

In open, sun-filled situations, few things work harder than Russian sage. *Perovskia atriplicifolia* hails from the arid lands of Central Asia, and if it doesn't sit wet, in heavy clay soil, it is hugely adaptable. It has a long season of flower, when pale spires rise up to colour violet-blue with the lavenders. Where lavender is ready to be cut back to its winter framework by the end of summer, *P. atriplicifolia* will branch and re-branch with new spurs and spikes until well into autumn.

'Blue Spire' is the typical form on offer, and where I have room I will leave it to loll about under its own weight as the spikes topple across paths and neighbours; but for the neater minded, 'Little Spire' is a better option. It will keep the vertical better and will grow to 90 cm at most. Russian sage is a beloved plant of bees and butterflies, which easily access the nectar, and the violet-blue makes a good companion to the hot pink of late-flowering *Nerine bowdenii* or autumn-flowering *Colchicum*.

Buddleia also bridge the high-summer gap and move gracefully into autumn. Secondary spikes of flower, which are smaller than the first, provide the impact now. Some might argue that *Buddleia* have a railway-siding mood once they go to seed and that by now they are bringing the tone of the garden down rather than providing the focus.

The darker-flowered varieties tend to be lighter on their feet once the first flowers are over, and I favour the smaller-flowered forms for the same reason. Velvety 'Black Knight', fine-leaved 'Nanho Blue' and silvery leaved 'Lochinch' are all good. I will team them up with *Caryopteris* × *clandonensis*, which like the same pruning regime. *C.* 'Arthur Simmonds' is a good dark blue, forming a deciduous 90 cm shrub. Like *Buddleia*, they are tough and adaptable.

I found *Vitex agnus-castus* in hot black sand dunes in Greece this year, and having seen it in context I can see why it favours a warm position if it is to flower well. The fingered foliage could be confused for hemp or cannabis, but the flowers emerge as tapering spikes at the tips of the extension growth. The true form is silvery-blue, but, if you can find it, 'Silver Spire' is a shimmering white selection with light limbs.

I plant it with *Ceratostigma willmottianum* at its feet, as they both love the same conditions. *Ceratostigma*, known as the hardy plumbago, is a small wiry shrub which performs late. Indigo and violet flowers stud growth that colours vividly crimson as autumn advances. The flowers will outlast the nerine, the acers and the latest of the asters until they are finally silenced by frost.

10 September, *Peckham*

SPLENDOUR IN THE GRASS

———

In the early twentieth century, the German naturalist and gardener Karl Foerster wrote that 'Grass is the hair of the earth.' I love that description, and the fact that grass is no longer banished from the garden for fear of the wild. The ornamental grasses are at their best now, capturing the breeze on a blustery day and the light as it rakes ever lower across the remains of the last season. They are the personification of the naturalistic movement. When I was a child and I first saw their potential, my choice was almost entirely limited to pampas and the toothpaste stripes of gardener's garters. The odd, brave nursery stocked a limited list of *Miscanthus*, because they were powerfully architectural and, like yuccas, were used as exotic full stops and exclamation marks; but I had the advantage of working in a rather wonderful garden as a Saturday job.

It was the creation of the late Mrs Frances Pumphrey, and Greatham Mill was, in the mid-seventies, an unusual and much-loved garden. Aged ten, I went there religiously every weekend for a whole summer. Mrs P. was a spirited woman, often replying with enthusiasm 'Well, bugger me,' which I rather liked because it gave her an edge. She was a gifted plantswoman, combining colour, form and texture with a natural flair and informality. After my constant presence and endless questions, she offered me the Saturday job, which I kept until I left home at seventeen.

She had an eye for a good thing, and had *Miscanthus* in her garden to inject architecture into the borders, and a bed of the rampant blue-grey dune grass *Leymus arenarius* – a lovely thing if you can curb its running habit. She had it sandwiched between the stream and a strong clump of *Cornus*. She gave me *Molinia caerulea* 'Variegata' for my yellow border and several slips of *Miscanthus*. I put *Miscanthus* 'Silberfeder' in front of a west-facing window at home to catch the evening light in autumn plumage. She knew about things like that and passed on her tricks with ease. *M. sinensis* 'Zebrinus' also became a mainstay when I started out. With its unusual horizontal slash of gold in the leaf, it was perfect for plantings that needed an exotic air without being too tropical. I used it with tall devil's walkingstick (*Aralia elata*) as a backdrop and lime-green *Alchemilla* at its feet.

Whereas I used grasses as punctuation, now I select plants that can be used as an underlay or gauze into which a combination of other plants can be woven. They allow me to filter and diffuse colour and to imbue plantings with a mood that is reminiscent of somewhere far beyond the garden. Pale, ever-shifting *Stipa tenuissima* conjures up an open, airy plain; the lofty rustle of *Miscanthus floridulus* makes us feel small and summons the jungle. Shimmering *Melica ciliata* and shiny *Luzula sylvatica* form the cool green eiderdown that keeps the woodland floor from feeling parched or naked, while soft, mist-like *Deschampsia* makes the link from darkness to light on the margins.

With their rise in popularity, grasses are in danger of over-saturation. Plant too many varieties of grass together and they become a collection which is not cohesive, a jumble of which one can easily tire. So I have introduced some self-imposed rules to avoid over-egging, because I do not want to tire of them. I only ever use grasses where they feel right and not just because I love them. I use clump formers almost exclusively to ensure they stay put, and I never put more than three different grasses in any one space, because they each suggest something that is individual. This way I can tap into just one mood in each place. The greatest asset of grasses is their subtlety, and subtlety needs to be handled with kid gloves.

The Japanese see the late plumage of their native *Miscanthus sinensis* as a signature for autumn, but earlier-flowering selected forms make their presence felt in July. I choose them for flower over foliage, as this is easier to work into a soft aesthetic. 'Ferner Osten' is a favourite for its plum-coloured tassels and 'Kleine Fontäne' for its silver flowers in September, but far more subtle and still rare, because it is not hardy, is *M. nepalensis*. I am growing this well in Guernsey and in the warmer counties where it will come through the winter easily, as long as it is not wet at the root. Its flowers are white gold and quite exceptionally beautiful. Burnished and light-reflecting, they make me gasp when they are in their moment. Neil Lucas at Knoll Gardens in Dorset is the man to go to for plants, and the garden is well worth a trip to see the grass collection.

The line of a grass is also important, and though I love the bolt-upright plumage of *Calamagrostis* 'Karl Foerster' – it is impeccable in winter, with its pure verticality – I would much rather choose those grasses that have a less immediate presence. I want them to be gauzy in a planting and for them to be something you stumble upon. You might find them when they halt and hold light at a certain time of day, or when they capture movement in the breeze and give substance to something usually unseen.

The group I am most excited about is the North American panicums, not least for their fantastic names, such as 'Squaw', 'Warrior' and 'Cloud 9'. When you see them wild in the prairies they are one of the plants that create the haze through which echinaceas, eupatoriums and prairie dock emerge. They like plenty of light and are tougher-growing if they are kept on the dry side once they are established. Forming a tight basal clump, *Panicum virgatum* carries its foliage along its delicate stems until it reaches two-thirds of its height and breaks into a mist of flower in late summer. There is a lightness about the growth even in the 2 m, grey-leaved 'Cloud Nine' that means they can be worked in with ease among other plants. 'Shenandoah' is a beauty too, with maroon-tipped foliage that darkens to black-purple in the autumn. I have yet to combine this with the aptly-named 'Heavy Metal' for darkness and light in the same place.

Although they do not hold their form well much after November, the molinias are also a delight. *M. arundinacea* 'Transparent' was sending out its almost see-through flowers in July, but now it is an open cage of dark filaments through which I can suspend the white tapers of *Actaea*. *M.* 'Windspiel' (wind play) reaches a very mobile 3 m by September, but right now I want to explore something new.

I saw *Sporobolus heterolepis* last autumn for the first time when I visited Piet Oudolf and his recently replanted garden. Known as the prairie dropseed, this is another grass with a smoky quality that is light on its feet and flowering no more than knee height. What singled this first meeting out, for I love a new discovery, was the sweet perfume of this grass when flowering. It was the perfume you noticed first, but then your eyes refocused upon the shimmering cloud of flower. It was a moment where everything was soft and sensual and full of light. A moment to remember.

14 September, *Peckham*
FOR GOODNESS' SAKE

———

Up and down the country there are harvest festivals and late summer flower shows taking place in church and town halls. If there was one in the area I would be submitting my dahlias and some produce from the allotment, just for the joy of the gathering together of all those different passions and peoples. Metre-long leeks from old-timers and unnaturally straight runner beans mark the seriously competitive, as do the onions with beautifully turned over tops artfully tied with string. There are pears of all shapes and sizes, and melons that mark how good the summer has been – or not. Unblemished damsons scent the air, their powdery bloom bearing not the slightest fingerprint, and single-stem hybrid roses, as old-fashioned and immaculate as fifties hats, sit alongside chrysanthemums with petals groomed into position. In contrast, and for those of us a little less interested in perfection, bunches of 'Mixed Garden Flowers' reveal the contents of their owners' gardens, with each as particular as handwriting.

There is something pagan about the gathering of the summer's produce and the joy in the harvest. It must have been celebrated in some shape or form for as long as we have been cultivating ground. The feeling runs deep and I have been living it several times over since the spring. First it was with the mustards (frilly red and green, giant red and giant green), the mizuna and red pak choi in the salad beds. These were sown with the lettuce as soon as the ground was warm enough in April. The oriental greens were in the salad bowl little more than a month later, showing up the lettuce as a dawdler. I have been struggling to keep up with them ever since. Re-sowing short rows every three weeks has kept us in good supply and I am just about to sow my last crop in the hope that I can keep them under cloches and enjoy some greens well into autumn. I will be minding the slugs now that the garden is providing them with a multitude of hiding places.

Next were the elderflowers turned into cordial. We missed our chance due to a busy week when they were at their best on the fringes of the cemetery, so friends brought a bucketful up from the country. It sat in the pantry for twenty-four hours, steeping with sugar, lemon and citric acid and scenting the whole of the kitchen before it was strained through muslin and bottled. Though I have yet to try it, I wonder if the liquorice-leaved elder *Sambucus* 'Black Lace' will produce pink syrup to match the tone of its flowers? Next year I will try to persuade the friends who are trialling the plant I don't have room for to part with some. Bartering is the order of the day and they will get a bottle of the nectar in return for the favour.

It took a while for things to come to fruition on the allotment because I had to wait for the green manure crop to decompose after I turned it in in March. This meant that I was a whole month late putting my spuds in, but of course they caught up. I used two blight-resistant varieties, 'Lady Cristl' – a perfect, waxy tuber – and 'Robinta' – much less space-hungry in its top growth and a little later. It is mealy in comparison to 'Lady Cristl', but marvellous for soaking up lashings of butter. There is nothing quite like that moment when you turn up the first spuds of the season, the dirt coming away from the pale, unblemished fruit. We ate a whole bowlful of that first harvest with nothing more than butter and sea salt.

I planned ahead with several winter brassicas that were sown in early June, but I got the timing completely wrong as, by the time all the spuds came out, the brassicas were far too big to transplant to the newly cleared ground. The Russian kale was the fastest and we simply ate it early along with the broccoli tops and the 'Cavolo nero' in salads or lightly steamed. I then re-sowed further rows to plant up for winter. I am now hoping that my timing doesn't work against me, because I would like the pleasure of passing by the greens at the market for at least some of the coming winter. The leeks were better behaved and were perfectly sized for planting out (pencil thickness) alongside the greens, but it was a close thing, with the courgettes threatening to take over the nursery bed, reaching out their great fleshy limbs like giants stretching in the morning.

In the herb bed things soon got out of control and, to resolve the spread of the sage, we harvested all the tips of one of the three plants and made it into pesto. I have done this with sorrel to fashion a tart garnish for fish, but the sage pesto was a very good complement to a well done pork chop. Despite the cool summer, cosseting in the cold frame also gave me enough basil to convert into pesto, which was given a spicy undertone by the red- and green-leaved 'Violetto Aromatico' from Seeds of Italy, which has a peppery punch with a hint of clove and is the best thing in the world with a sun-warmed tomato. The climbing beans were late, because I had to re-sow them after a slug attack, and then we suffered the predictable glut. 'Meraviglia di Venezia' is a flat, stringless yellow, and delicious braised Spanish-style with onions and *jamón*. Equally lovely were the plum-coloured 'Cosse Violette', despite the fact they lose their colour when cooked.

Bottling, pickling and making preserves is one of the best ways of being able to carry the fruits of summer into the next season, and one day when I have more time, I will do more to make the most of the surfeit. Feast or famine seems to be the thing to avoid when you are managing a productive garden, but who could ever really complain about an excess of homegrown goodness?

15 September, *Hillside*
LATE TO THE PARTY

———

In Russia, this time of year is described as velvety: heavy dews and grass growing in a last rush before the frosts, soft light, lengthening shadows and bloom on cabbages and damsons. With this change comes the push of autumn bulbs and their out-of-season energy.

The annual return of the autumn cyclamen sparks the

memory of my mother and me on one of our adventures. We came upon an extensive colony growing in the unkempt garden of a nearby house up for demolition. They were hidden in brambles and we convinced ourselves that they were in the line of the bulldozers. Being a vicar's daughter, she sought permission from the contractors and in no time we were back with a spade and buckets.

They were just up, tilting back with pointed buds and the pink of opened flower a surprise in the tangle and leaf mould. Young leaves, which were waiting for rain, were coiled, tight and still embryonic in the centre of the corm. It was a shock to find that the corms were the size of tea plates and we felt like we had discovered treasure. I re-planted them lovingly in the dappled shade of a laburnum where they thrived and were soon seeding themselves to prove that they were happy.

Cyclamen hederifolium are a European native and the best colonies I have ever seen were in nut groves on a derelict section of the Appian Way in Italy. They were scattered in the hollows, where the leaf mould accumulated and where in the autumn they were free from competition. Their leaves, shaped like ivy but marbled in silver, had the run of the woods in winter when the light fell freely through the bare branches onto an empty forest floor. Find them a place that sounds something like this in a garden and they are easy, providing for you in the autumn and then retreating below ground in spring.

Their corms can live for years, but you should never buy them dry with other autumn bulbs. First, they may have been stripped illegally from the wild and, secondly, they are easy to raise from seed.

I moved some here from a group growing outside my kitchen window in London. They were a selected white form with good silver marbling on the foliage. I had them at eye level in the half-basement window growing among *Viola labradorica*, which covered for their dormancy in the summer months. I could witness their return close up from this vantage point when everything around them was spent at the end of the summer.

They are struggling here, as I have them in grass under my holly tree. If there was a little more shade, so the grass grew more thinly, they would be happy but I must move them as soon as their foliage breaks through. They will be found a home with a fleet of *Colchicum speciosum* 'Album', which I will plant under my young crab apples. Together, they will be a lovely celebration of this late flurry.

The white form of the autumn crocus is the best in my book, being spectacularly pure and standing proud and clean ahead of their foliage. Like the cyclamen, it is there for the winter. People complain about *Colchicum* foliage but I love its glossy winter presence and its ability to vanish when the garden kicks in at the beginning of the growing season. On my sunny banks, beneath the crab apples, the grass will cover for their absence and no doubt I will forget about them until I am in need of the tonic provided by their miraculous return.

16 September, *Peckham*
SEEDS OF HAPPINESS

———

A small part of me cannot help but associate sunflowers with a certain sadness. This is directly related to the return to school at the end of the summer holidays. The feeling of the impending loss of freedom in the last week with the trip to get a uniform brought on instant nostalgia for the carefree days of summer. I remember all too clearly the dragging of heels through the dew-laden grass in the last few moments of that final Monday morning, and lingering in the vegetable patch where the hot months had been marked by the growth of the sunflowers. They lined the road to school, too, towering over hedges and tied to stakes and drainpipes to prevent them toppling. Summer was over.

Of course, sunflowers are anything but sad, and I soon kicked the connection once I got school over and done with. Now I see them in a new light: one that takes pleasure in their convenience, their willingness to perform, and in their embodiment of a season. In France you drive through fields that stand to attention, the flowers tracking the sun in unison.

Anyone can grow a sunflower, even if they have never lifted a spade or fork or intend to do so with any regularity. They even crop up in gardens that are never meant to be gardened, in seed spilt from bird feeders that has found a niche and gone for it.

I know it is corny to say so, but sunflowers are wonderful for children; this is why we had them at home and why that trip back to school saw them in procession in the front gardens where the children lived. The seed is large and easy to handle, you can put it in the dirt on a sunny day in the early summer, and as long as it has room and water, it is a plant that grows before your eyes, making you feel small in the process. None of that magic wears thin once you become an adult, and I am right there with the six-year-olds staring in wonder at their lion-like faces.

On one of my cycle rides through London I passed a fantastic traffic island of sunflowers that made me get off my bike and laugh when it started to bloom. It had been planted by a group of guerrilla gardeners among the dreary council shrubs and is not the first to have cropped up in my neck of south London. The sunflowers were brilliantly brazen, standing tall over the rushing traffic and quite out of character with the bleakness of the season and the city. Pedestrians stopped to look, too, and were smiling as they moved on. So simple, so cheap and such great results from just a handful of seed.

I use them frequently also in young gardens, slipping a few seeds in here and there so that in the first summer there is height, volume and colour. Block plantings stifle young plants beneath them, but occasional groups or well-placed individuals rapidly rise above slower-growing shrubs that benefit from the shelter while they are putting roots down to do the big grow in their second summer. Today's sunflowers are far from limited to the giant single-headed yellows, which are still wonderful if you are running a competition for kids or wanting that cartoon quality in the garden. The multi-headed varieties provide with ease and bring drama – but repeatedly on one plant, and in a whole range of sunrise and sunset colours.

When I started my garden here ten years ago, and planted the tree brooms to provide a gauze of shelter from the pavement, it was multi-headed sunflowers I planted between them to provide interest in the first couple of seasons before they got away. I grew a variety, *Helianthus* 'Italian White', putting two or three seeds to a pot in April and growing them on until they were large enough to cope out in the ground. The seedlings were thinned to just one per pot and planted out at about 15–20 cm high and 45 cm or so apart. They grew fast, escaping the slug and snail attacks to which they are prone, and branching and re-branching until they were 1.5 m or so and covered in flower. The flowers are each about the size of a man's fist, with a dark centre and palest primrose-yellow petals. There is a delicacy about them for a sunflower, and this runs right through from the seed (which doesn't germinate as readily as most) to their requirement for plenty of light and good living. Most sunflowers will 'do' if they have the simple ingredients of sun, food and water, but *H.* 'Italian White' is a bit of a prima donna. The key to my success in growing them this first year was in the open, newly prepared position. Though they did perform in the second year, there was already competition from the broom and they were half as good.

In the back garden during the early days here, when the planting was still young and there was plenty of light, I played around with a multi-headed variety, *H.* 'Velvet Queen'. I had grown this for several years up at Home Farm, rearing one plant per pot to slot in once the oriental poppies were over. This was usually some time towards the middle of June, so the sunflowers had to be grown in decent soil in 22 cm (9 in) pots to keep them going. By the time the poppies were cut back and the slot was empty, they were well above your knees and needed a strong stake to support them for the future. The rate at which they grow and their lust for life usually demands that most sunflowers are given some additional support. The combination of rain and wind can easily topple them, especially when their weighty flowers are in full swing.

The 'Velvet Queen' were a great success, reaching well over head height among the hip-laden *Rosa moyesii*. The foliage is a dark inky green and the flowers, emerging from dark buds, range in colour from rusty copper to the deepest, most sumptuous mahogany. I grew them here until I discovered 'Claret', which I think is a better selection. It is more reliable and less variable, so you can depend upon the darker wine-red.

Although sunflowers are slender in their lower regions and can be fitted in among other plants if they are low, they are bulky at shoulder height and not easily placed in the garden now that it has grown together more thickly. The fig has taken their space at the end by the veggie beds, so next year I will be setting out a few in my newly acquired allotment. Here I can grow the aptly named 'Lemon Queen' and 'Double Shine', which is like a child's drawing of a burning sun, and know they will not just be enjoyed by the passers-by or the odd child sorry to be going back to school. I will pick them for the house to stand in stout jars, and when I am tired of the display and wanting to move on, I will leave them to moulder and turn brown. It will then be the turn of the birds, which wait until just the right moment for the seed to ripen before descending upon them to gorge and keep up their fat deposits for winter. Now that's nothing to be sad about.

REAL MEN GROW DAHLIAS

———

The green is remarkable here and all pervasive. It rolls on and off into the distance and sweeps up to the house to meet the concrete footprint. My instinctive move is to create a colourful counterpoint. I feel a joyful need for contrast, and the subtleties I played to in the garden in London have been replaced by brilliant rows of calendula and towering sunflowers of gold and bronze and rich, rusty red. It is the dahlias, however, that are the stars of the show. There are fifty-six plants lined out in rows and the garden is now a kaleidoscopic island.

When I was a child, submitting my garden-in-a-seed-tray to the local flower show, I remember quite clearly the pride with which the dahlia growers would present their wares. The dahlias were the domain of the men in string vests, who specialised in the biggest and best of everything. Aside from the monstrous onions and metre-long leeks, the dahlias were the beasts of the show. They were like dragons spitting fire and, lined out on the show bench, they held your attention accordingly.

Back then it seemed like the dahlia was as much vegetable as it was flower, for they were an allotment plant or a specimen – a man's plant for all their glamour. It took some time to come to this point as the dahlia has been in Europe for more than 200 years. It came from Mexico to the Botanical Gardens in Madrid in the eighteenth century, but horticulturists quickly found that it produced a rich and varied offspring when crossed and grown from seed.

The National Dahlia Society was formed in 1881 to communicate such excitement, but dahlias went through an unfashionable slump until Christopher Lloyd, among others, started combining them in his borders. He was never a man afraid of a bit of colour; the dahlia provides that and more, beginning its season in high summer and continuing relentlessly until blackened by frost.

Today, there is a dahlia to suit most tastes. My own selection is made up of favourites from the past. The waterlily-flowered 'Moray Susan' – a complex mixture of butteriness and peach – and new varieties such as the liquorice-leaved 'Twyning's After Eight' with single flowers of pristine white. 'Soulman', with flowers of the deepest red, reflexes back in a stretch of petals, while 'Julie One' is as dark on the underside of the petals, but banana yellow on the inner side. I have pompoms and spiders, cactus- and anemone-flowered dahlias. Once you get a taste, the sweet jar seems bottomless.

Like bulbs, it is worth ordering them while they are in flower so that you are not disappointed by stocks being sold out the following growing season. I urge you to see them in the flesh at a garden near you to make the selection. Of those I ordered this year several are misnamed and bear no resemblance to their namesake on the website. Never mind, there are as many successes as there are horror stories and it really doesn't matter if you remember that a favourite might be awaiting you next year.

In London, I used to risk it and leave the tubers in the ground with a decent layer of mulch over winter. They would survive for three to five years before ground slugs got them, but best practice is to lift after frost and store in just-damp compost, or to do as I did and buy in rooted cuttings from national-dahlia-collection.co.uk. This was incredibly exciting as they arrived in May packed in plastic cylinders. They were planted out directly after all risk of frost was past, into soil improved with manure and guarded from slugs until they were established. Being hearty animals, they like to feed and the south-facing slopes coupled with a damp summer have reaped rewards here.

The fields surrounding my plot seem greener for the cacophony of colour. To keep them blooming I have picked to promote the flower, and the house has been as bright and light-filled as any Mexican festival.

OCTOBER

October gathers autumn together in its finest month. The asters are at their best, a constellation of tiny flowers, spun with cobwebs and covering for the multitude toppling all around them. *Rudbeckia laciniata* 'Herbstsonne', at a tilt from the weight of its own flower, flares its pool of artificial sunlight. The dahlias look like they have partied long and hard. They have out-flowered your will to keep on top of the deadheading and the mould has set in. It is not a mould that I mind by this time of the year, for there is so much to see and so little one can do to control the inevitable pull of the season.

My orchard in Somerset is now in its sixth autumn. The trees are tall enough to stand under and the fruit weights the branches. This is a good feeling for it is the beginning of a place that will only get better. We do not have a glut yet as the trees are young, but the same cannot be said for the blackberries in the hedgerows and the last-but-not-least of the autumn-fruiting raspberries. It is a race now to get to them before the damp-loving botrytis mould, but not a great hardship, and the last are destined for the freezer or jam.

Foraging and stocking the larder for the months ahead are key parts of October. It is a rich month and a profuse one, with hips and haws spilling from the hedgerows and lighting up trees and shrubs that have apparently been in repose. Colour smoulders as foliage turns: butter-yellow elder, russet-brown oak and, if the weather holds, for a memorable week or two the burning yellow field maples. Autumn has a tidal pull that touches everything in its path; it can make you feel very small and insignificant. Best to stand back, not worry about the leaves on the lawn, and just enjoy the moment.

6 October, *Peckham*
THINGS FALL APART

———

The beds at the front of the house are planted with bronze fennel. The south-facing position and a dry summer have suited them perfectly and they are standing taller than I am. From inside you look into their airy cages and on the warm days of autumn the ripening seed has wafted the smell of aniseed through the windows. Though their foliage has turned cinnamon-brown and ginger, they have plenty of life in them yet. When the birds think you are out, they descend upon the seed, and the stems are filled with a network of cobwebs.

It is tempting to wade into the beds where they appear to

be falling apart. Weighted down by seed and autumn wetness, the topple might at first appear to be something that needs managing, but a little patience is timely. This is the moment to stand back and enjoy the autumn, and wait. In a month or so you will see the keepers in the wreckage and a new order will assert itself. Hit by frost, the apparent bulk of nasturtium will wither and make you realise that they were not much more than water. The lush rosettes of hemerocallis foliage will also succumb, but they will leave behind the upright bones of flower stem and seedcase. Let the worms drag the rotting foliage to the ground, where it will be converted to humus.

Bare is the most unnatural state for soil to be in. Exposed and raked clean, it is open to desiccation and to erosion, so a little untidiness now is a good thing for a garden.

Of course we do need to assert some control if it is not to be taken from us, but the moves are strategic ones. I would prefer to let the rot happen and the birds to have the windfalls I cannot cope with in the kitchen rather than spend my energies battling an enormous wave. Very quickly the autumn will be in retreat, so I am enjoying the colour while I wait to pick over the bare bones once the leaves come down.

I took two weeks off at the end of last month and based myself at home as an antidote to a summer of busyness. After allowing myself to settle I adjusted to the new order and saw beyond the topple of sunflowers and the browning dahlias. A little tidying to reveal the paths allowed me a way in and the clarity of a free head to order my thoughts for a winter's work ahead.

Crazy though it may sound, I am planting weeds again. Not weeds I plan to let go, but a couple of forms of blackberry I have been meaning to grow for an age. *Rubus fruticosus* 'Himalayan Giant' is a cutting from a friend who is slowly being engulfed by the beast, but she can pick a large bowlful of succulent brambles in a matter of minutes, the fruit is that plentiful. It can easily be wall-trained if you have a fighting spirit. The second? A far more sensible choice for being thornless and of moderate vigour: the parsley-leaved bramble. Next autumn when I am beginning to feel like things are out of control, I will have my distraction. A crumble or two of seasonal windfalls.

7 October, *Hillside*
THE BERRY BEST

———

Thank goodness for the glorious light of September spilling in. It eased the feeling that we were short-changed on summer. Suddenly the garden was dry and it was warm enough to lie out on the grass and enjoy the miniature worlds of the cyclamen at their level. It was a bad year for produce, the plums and damsons offering up a smattering and the apple trees light-limbed. It is not a bad thing: the occasional year off 'rests' the trees.

The wet summer suited the autumn-fruiting raspberries, however. We picked until our fingers were stained red and the weight of fruit in the bowls started to squash those at the bottom. Though the 'Allgold' are tart and without the perfume of the 'Autumn Bliss' I was pleased to have the pale-yellow fruit in the mix. I like the autumn-fruiting raspberries as they perform on this year's growth, not last year's, and can simply be razed to the ground at the end of the winter.

The blackberries were later than last year but they rose to the harvest once the weather warmed in September and we were pleased we hadn't cut the hedges. The birds will be happy, too, for the sloes, hawthorn, rosehips and the scarlet berries on the honeysuckle are a valuable addition to their autumn larder.

Next year I plan to add to our own larder by diversifying the fruit we are growing here still further. A dud year with the tree fruit would be eased with more soft fruit, which I plan to work into the vegetable garden as fruit hedges, to ease the wind that whips up the valley.

Parsley-leaved blackberries are something we had at home when I was a child and I like the way their prettiness allows you to warm to a bramble. 'Oregon Thornless' paves the way to a relationship with a plant that more usually demands a set of gauntlet gloves. It needs good soil but the biennial limbs are a lovely rich red and easily manipulated. We trained them up sculptural chestnut wigwams to punctuate a pumpkin patch in one garden. The foliage, cut deeply and curling upon itself like its namesake, is a welcome foil to a flush of pretty flowers and the fruit are good and juicy and as blackberryish as any blackberry might be come September.

I will be trying the same thing with tayberry – a cross between a raspberry and a blackberry. 'Buckingham Tayberry' is a thornless variety that makes training and pruning that much more pleasurable. When you remove the spent biennial canes to replace them with this year's growth, you can do so without cursing. It is important to break your own rules so I will make room for Japanese wineberries as I love the red bristling on their stems, although I have yet to be convinced by the substance of the fruit.

Our soil is acid at the bottom of the hill and alkaline at the top. The garden, which lies in the middle, errs just on the chalky side of neutral and the raspberries have shown a little chlorosis this summer with yellowing in their foliage to indicate that. I will not let this deter me from growing blueberries, which require an acid soil to do well. Fortunately, the blueberry hybrids are adaptable plants and we have been using them with great success in containers where the soil pH can be kept on the acid side of neutral.

Like raspberries and hedgerow blackberries, blueberries are woodlanders by nature and more than happy in a little shade. Put them out in the sun and you will have to watch the watering but they will produce more fruit, which will be sweeter and come over a longer period. If you grow more than one variety they will help each other in terms of pollination and provide for you over several months. Early 'Earliblue', the mid-season 'Bluecrop' and the late-season 'Liberty' should see the season covered. The fruit store well, too, so that you can build up a bowlful in the fridge before gorging yourself. Come the autumn, their foliage colours a wonderful crimson, bringing the berry harvest to a spectacular close.

9 October, *Hillside*

TURN ON THE LIGHTS

———

The first spring here at the farm revealed a marked absence of spring bulbs. We were without snowdrops or bluebells, but a perfect line of electric blue *Muscari* lined the concrete path to the front door, providing handsomely for the early bees. Up behind the house, where the tip of the field became impossible to graze, a clutch of florist daffodils poked from the base of the hedge. But it was far from a golden host, more a token contribution to spring – a farmer's dash of unpretentious colour.

Having left a fleet of bulbs in the garden in London, I was pleased that I had brought along my pot-grown narcissus, as it was good to steal a march on spring. Bulbs are good for that, providing hope in the bleak half-light of February, with new shoots spearing ground and an almost guaranteed display while most other things are still slumbering.

Delightful though they are, unless I am planting them in pots I like to take my time with introducing bulbs permanently into their setting. I'll let a new planting settle in before weaving them among it, as it's frustrating working among their newly emerging shoots if you are making changes. Though they soon disappear once they have flowered, their early foliage can be surprisingly overwhelming if the plants don't have the resources to rise above it. Without a garden to speak of yet, I am also faced with the conundrum that a 'show' in farmland would clearly look odd. Save a drifting of snowdrops that I will weave into the hedges, the solution will be to grow this year's bulb order in rows in the vegetable garden.

Practical rows will allow me to see what fits and what does well and provide for posies in the house while I am planning for the future. I will start with the *Narcissus* and the tulips for a guaranteed display. The ground is still warm and perfect for promoting root growth, but the tulips can be left as late as November, so should be saved until last.

Of the *Narcissus*, I favour those with fine, grass-like foliage, as they are easier to work into both meadow and mixed plantings. The *Narcissus cyclamineus* hybrids with their flung back petals, the jonquil hybrids and the *triandrus* group will be a discreet presence until they flower and then die more easily in company, leaving behind nothing of the weight of foliage that the larger-flowered hybrids produce.

By the end of March I tend to lose interest in the golden daffodils that dominate parks and gardens, so I will opt for the early-flowering varieties, such as 'Jack Snipe', 'Peeping Tom', 'February Gold' and 'February Silver', and then move into the small-flowered primrose, cream and ivory varieties such as 'W. P. Milner', 'Segovia' and 'Petrel'. The scented jonquil will follow on late in April and into early May when the 'Pheasant's Eye' join the apple blossom.

I will also indulge in pot-grown treasures that can be loved up close by the house. Hard-nosed though it might sound, these will be treated as annuals, as the early-flowering *Iris* and tulips rarely last more than a couple of seasons in our wet climate. Blue-flowering *Iris* 'George' and the deep purple 'J. S. Dijt' will be out late in February, the buds rising sharply in a day or two once they decide they are ready to go. Tulips rarely return as reliably a second year in the ground, but treated sacrificially in pots, their colour will go a long way to brighten spring.

Burned red-brown in the body of the bloom with the relief of an orange rim, 'Abu Hassan' is on my list, as are the orange, sherbet-scented 'Ballerina'. I've even given in to a few stripy varieties, 'Pinocchio' and 'Johann Strauss', for a fun-fuelled ride into spring. As autumn strips us of one growing season, it is good to have the next so clearly captured in these nuggets of potential.

14 October, *The Studio*
IT'S CRUNCH TIME

———

Autumn, or more to the point, the smell of autumn, must be one of the most distinctive times of the year. There is rot waiting in the wings and damp hanging in the air, and with it the slow and certain decay that comes now the energy of the growing season is dissipating. With that smell comes an instant and indelible link back to the orchard I grew up with. At this time of year there was always fruit on the ground and a rich, cidery aroma hung among the trees as the windfalls got the better of us and collected in the hollows. It was a mysterious, moody place, complete with a bluebell carpet in the spring. The remains of it are still there, although the trees are old now and shattered by bumper years that have brought the twisted branches crashing down under the weight of fruit.

Though the apple plucked by Eve was almost certainly a pomegranate or a fig, the true apple has been cultivated since

1500 BC. However, they have not been cultivated in the British Isles for that long as they were introduced by the Romans, who found the wild apples here too sour. They had developed skills in propagating trees through grafting and budding, and soldiers were given land to plant orchards as an inducement to stay.

In the first few weeks as new students at Wisley we were put on apple-picking duty as it was September and several crates had to be taken from each tree to be stored, sold, or taken up to the Great Autumn Show at the RHS Halls in Vincent Square, London. There were some 650 varieties and, needless to say, we tried most of them as they ripened over the weeks; the earlies followed by the mid-season and the lates running on into December, by which time the fruits hung naked in trees blown free of their foliage. We started to prune the moment the foliage came down as it was a winter's work to make our way through the rows. The trees were all grown on a semi-dwarfing MM106 rootstock, so that they remained accessible and in reach of the ladders that were used to tend them. These trees were managed so that you could see through them, with no crossing limbs, an open centre to allow plenty of free air movement and a well-developed spur system. We pruned out the canker, the water shoots and the leaders of all those varieties that were spur-bearing and pruned those that flowered on the tips of the fruits (such as 'Beauty of Bath') to retain the fruiting wood, working each tree according to its own particular growth habit, while making sure it was done by the book.

The RHS publication, *The Fruit Garden Displayed*, became our bible and it came complete with images of Hayden Williams, our supervisor, toiling in the same windswept fields, so we felt we were living the book. But I must admit that, in the twenty-five years since I graduated from Wisley, I have never pruned another apple tree with such dexterity and doubt I ever will. This is not to say that I have drifted away from the idea of the orchard – on the contrary, I love the principle of a grove of trees that is productive, the repetition, the spring blossom, the way you can tailor an orchard to produce for you over months, if you choose your varieties correctly. I also love the fact that you can weave local varieties into an orchard that have been bred or singled out to do well in exactly that locality and make connections with a rich seam of peoples who have also enjoyed getting their food for free. But I am happy for an orchard to evolve on its own and to see it as a place that strikes that happy balance between agriculture and production and ornamental garden.

I have planted at least one orchard a year. They are places that can be tended easily with livestock to graze the grass if there is room but, even in quite modestly sized gardens, it is possible to add the cool atmosphere that they engender in the knowledge that they will provide far more in terms of atmosphere than many other, higher-maintenance areas. Apples may be prone to a wealth of problems, but if you choose your varieties well you can select those that do well in your locale and might be scab- and canker-resistant. The Thornhayes catalogue lists more than 150 varieties and the nursery is happy to advise you as to which varieties suit your particular part of the country. Apples like free drainage, but an M25 rootstock can cope better than most in a heavy wet soil and this is the rootstock I favour to grow a larger tree.

Selecting a range of varieties to provide early, mid-season and late-cropping fruit is worthwhile, and there is nothing like going to one of the many apple days set up across the country to savour the fruit first-hand and to talk to the growers about the vigour. I like to get a good range into an orchard, too. Nutty russets with textured flesh, waxy-skinned 'Cox's Pomona' for that wonderful red on one side, green on the other. I want cookers that can double as a tart eater such as 'Blenheim Orange', and cookers to keep on a cool shelf until Christmas or to make into spicy, baked apples as a welcoming treat for the autumn. I always try to weave in a 'Bramley', because I love the weight of the tree which has gravity in a garden and is still one of the most lovely of spring-blossoming trees.

Formative pruning is all I ever advocate to establish a tree for balance so that it has a good structure that can bear the weight of fruit later in life. Some additional maintenance to remove cankers and broken limbs and retain good structure helps later on but, if space is a limitation, I am just as happy to look into trees that can be pruned as a means of training them into a space.

I draw the line at the pixie rootstocks, as I don't like to see a tree that looks like it has the equivalent of bound feet. If you want to grow apples in a small space, cordon and fan-trained trees that are grown on an MM106 or M27 rootstock can be hugely productive, and trees can be trained to form arches and arbours. 'Step-over' apples are a great example of a space-saving device, and I have been using them to edge potager beds in several gardens. On the whole, the more dwarfing the rootstock, the better the growing conditions it needs. Soil needs to be free-draining and nutritious, so roots should be kept free from competition and the plants given an open, warm position to do their best. That said, the Romans were on to something when they planted their orchards here, for our cool winters and moist summers are what make apples one of our best and most easily cultivated fruiting trees. Trees that I will always come back to and want to have near me.

15 October, The Studio

GOING OUT ON A LIMB

———

Some years ago, I was in the Chelsea Physic Garden for a function in January and, innocently enough, plucked a solitary mahogany-red hip from one of several thousand that were festooning a *Rosa brunonii*. For those of you unfamiliar with this eclectic little garden in the heart of London, I will describe the scene for you. An old and hunched *Catalpa* near the entrance has become the climbing frame for this interloper which, in the past, must have been planted at the base of the tree into which it was intended to scramble. Several limbs with cracked and fissured stems, each the thickness of an arm, rear up to lasso the host in a muscular ligature, and today, when you look up into the canopy, it is not the *Catalpa* that you see but an enormous weight of criss-crossing rose branches. I wonder how long the *Catalpa* has before the rose gets the upper hand, but it is a marvel in June, with its Milky Way of blossom. Each bunch of flower holds a mass of creamy white blooms and the hundreds of bunches perfume the lawns around the tree.

The blossom is short-lived by today's rose standards, and you have only two to three weeks from start to finish but, like the best cloud formations, you have to make special time to take in the event. Several months later, you become aware of the rose again. By this time it is starting to fruit and, from here, the rose-hips go from strength to strength, igniting the tree red among primrose autumn foliage. In January at the Physic Garden, the rosehips were still there, providing the pleasure I was seeking out on a dim winter's day.

The pocketed hip stayed put for a month, but not before I had played with the idea of several trees I know of garlanded with a second generation of this rose. So it was early March when I broke open the withered fruit and liberated the seed into a long tom of loam, top-dressed with some sharp grit to prevent it from rotting. I put it in a cold frame, covered with a small pane of glass to keep the squirrels and mice from rummaging, and forgot about it until I was clearing up in April, when I noticed that the seedlings had already germinated. I potted out a dozen seedlings in May and, by August, I was beginning to wonder if I had been foolhardy. The plants were striving to reach the sky, barbed against the world and pretty damn ready to get into it.

I have a particular fondness for the species climbing roses. I love their exuberance, and they bring another season or two to a garden and one that takes place way over your head, allowing you to get on with things at ground level. This fondness goes back to a *Rosa multiflora* that was planted on my parents' balcony at Hill Cottage. When we moved there it was threatening to take the rotting balcony down, but it was a delight in June when, for a week or so, it would festoon the balustrade. In the summer of 1976, we slept out as a family for six long weeks on a line of mattresses with this rose tickling our feet, and I remember watching the hips evolve. By the time we had to move back inside at the end of that long, hot summer, they were bright red and being feasted on by a frenzy of birds.

If you are talking about a rose to cover any unsightly object, *R. filipes* 'Kiftsgate' always comes to mind, but it is a prime example of how you need to know what you are doing when you play with plants that are hard-wired to get the upper hand. The reason 'Kiftsgate' is good in trees is that it has evolved to scramble, ascend and conquer. Go to the garden of the same name and you will see 'Kiftsgate' filling a skyline some 20 m up. It has conquered several mature trees and shows no sign of settling into old age. This is a plant that I have only planted once, but in three years it had already put out growth that, if you got in its way, held you by the hair and threatened to take your eye out. I wince when people talk enthusiastically about their first 'Kiftsgate' and never recommend it unless clients feel like a tussle.

Vita Sackville-West was one of the great exponents of sending ramblers up into the fruit trees in her orchard, where they looked their most romantic above the long grass. But even Vita had some learning to do, as I understand this is one of the main reasons there are so few elderly apples in the orchard at Sissinghurst today. The trees have long since been overwhelmed by roses mismatched in vigour to their hosts. You need a fruit tree on a large rootstock, such as M25 or MM106, to support a vigorous species rambler, or you need a tree that has already made some headway to be able to support the extra weight.

When planting, you also need to set the rose a metre or two from the tree's trunk, so that it is away from the immediate root zone of its host. Despite their muscle, the young plants do need a good start in life. A good trick is to dig out a hole the size of a bucket and then cut the bottom out of a large plastic pot so that the roots of the new rose can have at least a couple of seasons before they get out of the bottom. This way a tree's hungry roots will be kept at bay until the rose has made some good top growth. You should also plant so that the rose will grow into the light. Bear in mind that if you are planting into a tree, the rose will grow towards and flower where the light is.

Of the more moderately vigorous species, *Rosa* 'Wedding Day' is one of the first to bloom. Reaching a graceful 8 m, this powerfully scented rose has large, single ivory flowers that turn a wonderful dirty pink when they age, and good hips, too. *R.* 'Francis E. Lester' is even more prone to a pink blush and is of a similar size, but its flowers are semi-double. *R.* 'Seagull' is less vigorous and more cottagey, with double white flowers – a sensible choice for a smaller garden. But if you have the room, I would go for the glossy-leaved *R. mulliganii* with its massive sprays of cream flowers and crop of bloody hips in autumn. This can reach 11 m, as can *R.* 'Bobbie James', another semi-double white. The doubles and semi-doubles tend to be longer-flowering than the single-flowered roses, so *R.* 'Paul's Himalayan Musk', which is blush pink, is a great addition to *R.* 'Bobbie James' if you are wanting the longest possible season.

'La Mortola' is a hardier selection of *R. brunonii* that has a bluish cast to the leaf and larger, lusher flowers, but I am holding out for my seedlings. Eleven were given away last year to friends and clients with a robust approach to gardening, but I kept one seedling that had a promising red flush to the leaf. As I write, it is straining to escape from its pot and should really be planted out this autumn. Do I dare let it loose in my own garden? I think not, but one thing's for sure: I will find it a home where I will be able to take my time one day and sit under its vast dome of autumn hips, and marvel at its tenacity.

21 October, *Hillside*
FANNING THE FLAMES

———

A sulky summer can be made good by the mood of a pretty autumn; heavy dew marking the tracks of animals that have been up and about before daylight, asters catching low sunlight and windfalls lying in excess and making the air under apple trees smell of cider. The best, when still weather combines with a sharp start and then sun, will see a ramping of colour that will cause you to look beyond the confines of your garden. Motorway embankments will flare with the red of hawthorn berry and the brief but ambered *Prunus avium*, while street and park trees will remind you that they are capable of more than just greening. For a wonderful interlude, things are capable of taking your breath away, like blossom might at the opposite end of the growing season.

We may not have the 'fall' of north America – a colouring that is visible from satellite – but our season here can be lengthened with the addition of ornamentals. Many of these hail from the Americas, Japan or China – and the best will reward us with a second season. Turquoise *Clerodendrum* berries will follow scented blossom in August, herbaceous peonies flash scarlet in the leaf before collapsing and Virginia creepers can colour a building crimson for a fortnight.

More and more I plan an autumn flush into gardens, combining several trees and shrubs specifically for this moment. Where we were lucky enough to have space we introduced a grove of *Acer palmatum* 'Ozakazuki' into one garden. If you haven't seen the maple glade at Tetbury's Westonbirt Arboretum in its full autumn spectacle, I urge you to go: it is an unforgettable sight.

I wanted our own glade to be such an experience and needed to know that we would have a form that would colour reliably. Although there are many Japanese maples that colour dramatically, the best-colouring forms tend to be green during summer. The copper-leaved forms, such as 'Bloodgood', are dramatic in their summer guise, but pale next to the spectacle of 'Ozakazuki'.

We have also planted a succession of trees selected specifically for their autumn climax: *Ginkgo biloba* and *Metasequoia glyptostroboides*. Both are Chinese by origin and the Metasequoia is unusual in that it is a deciduous member of the conifer family. Ginkgo is a lean tree in its youth and surprisingly adaptable to street living. The leaves colour butter yellow and have the peculiar habit of dropping all at once to leave a yellow skirt underneath.

Once you have mastered saying *Metasequoia glyptostroboides*, you will almost certainly want to plant one. The feathery foliage colours copper. They are speedy and easy, soaring upward with a gentle flare of limbs swooping low at the base and a spire reaching skyward.

If you have damp ground or a high water table and room, *Nyssa sinensis* is very hard to beat in terms of luminosity of colour. Autumn is its season, and a well-grown tree will form a dome with its lower branches arching to the ground.

The North American *Liquidambar* is perhaps the most persistent of all colouring trees come the autumn. Deep red, crimson and purple all at once and for six to eight weeks in a season, it is one of the longest-colouring of all autumnal trees.

The spindle bush is a native with candy-pink fruit rupturing to reveal bright orange seed.

I have become increasingly fond of *Euonymus alatus* – the winged spindle. This is a neat shrub with a clear sense of organisation in its dome of branches. These radiate up and out from the base and each is encrusted with an extraordinary armour of bark that becomes increasingly winged as the limbs age. In winter the foliage colours vermillion and crimson. They are happy in a large pot, too, if you need to scale a spectacle into a smaller garden – for no garden should be without a flash of drama before the winter kicks in.

21 October, *Peckham*
FANTASTIC MR FOX

Shortly before departing on my September holiday I entered into a small war with the foxes. They have always been in and out of the garden and I know where the den is, several doors up the road. It is within the roots of an old conifer, a mass of entrances and exits in a garden that is dominated by their dusty tracks and bawdy behaviour. We have gone through ten generations in the ten years I have been here and got to know their habits, which from year to year vary according to the number of cubs that survive or decide to stay the summer within this area.

This has been my toughest year in terms of fox activity, made so by a particularly lively group of cubs that took it upon themselves to make my garden their playground. I have been woken by their dancing up and down the broken-slate path at dawn and by their bone-chilling, childlike screams. I have also watched them running helter-skelter around my pots, in, out and over the box hedge and deep into the borders with total disregard for my precious plants. Lobbing an old shoe from my bedroom window is usually enough to scare them off temporarily, but they treat this as a game, too, and return soon after I have slipped back into sleep.

I have tolerated the neat run they have made across the vegetable beds, the sunbathing in the stipas and the musky, foxy scent. I have also put up with the odd spate of wanton vandalism. I went down one morning to find all the hemerocallis buds nipped off alongside the chair on the deck. A cub had obviously been using the chair, and I could imagine exactly how it had lain there nonchalantly snapping at the plump buds and casting them on the decking. The problem was resolved by moving the chair, but things worsened shortly before I went away, with dog foxes leaving telltale 'gifts' in very prominent and premeditated places. A fetid turd appeared first directly in front of the cat flap, then at the back door and then at the top of the steps into the garden. These offerings were signs that they were marking their territory, but one day I noticed light beneath the fence.

It had been years since they had burrowed between gardens, as the last few generations had been content to hop up on to the wall in an effortless exit, so I plugged the hole with a large log. Though there is little that one can do in reality to control the urban fox, one thing I have learned is that you need to break their habits before they start to adopt space and discourage digging immediately. Holes under fences can quickly lead to burrows if they start to feel settled. I started to patrol my boundaries to check for holes and several times found the log, or whatever obstacle I had inserted, cast aside like a plaything. Each time the hole got larger, and it went on like this for a month until it was the last thing I was doing just minutes before having to leave for the airport. On this occasion the dirt they had thrown up was strewn over my propagation area, the pots toppled and covered in fox-smelling dirt. It was a moment of high anxiety. What would I return to a fortnight later?

On returning, I gingerly set out into the garden. No more holes had appeared, but they had obviously been partying. There were fish-and-chip wrappers under the box hedge, animal bones on the terrace and three different trainers (not mine), one complete with a dirty sock. I wondered if they were trying to tell me something, but worst of all were the full nappies, several of them strewn about the beds and in different stages of being pulled apart for the contents. There were nests, too, that had been made under the hydrangea and runs through the beds, the eucomis had been toppled, and several of the newly emerging spikes on the nerine had been snapped off and spat out. I have a soft spot for wildlife and like to see my garden as a haven, but at this point my blood was boiling.

In terms of control, foxes' stealth, intelligence and nimble light-footedness will outwit you every time, and barricades are as good as useless. You only have to see them leap over a 2.5 m wall like a gymnast, squeeze their dog-like frame through the tiny openings in trellises or witness what they can do to an irrigation system to know that the city is now their domain. The population of foxes is now so dense in urban centres that trapping them is discouraged since the territory will immediately be filled, and relocated foxes have problems re-establishing new territories. They get used to sonic devices, and in my experience lion dung (yes, I have tried Silent Roar and products with names like Get Off My Garden!) has zero effect.

I cannot give you a satisfactory solution other than always to clear up after them and discourage them from feeling like your garden is home. Never feed or encourage them. Using bone meal and other fertilisers which smell like food encourages them to dig in the belief that they will find a meal. Using plants that are tough enough to survive their games is the advice of the RHS, but I think you have to get into the mind-set of dealing with a naughty child, to outwit and to keep your cool. Plants have a way of coming back, and the fox has a short attention span.

City gardening or country gardening both have their problems, but just because an unwelcome guest might be present doesn't mean that you have to set yourself a warring agenda. I lived with deer as a child, which have the most impeccable taste and invariably go for the rosebud at its most delectable moment or your most treasured, irreplaceable plant. We couldn't possibly have fenced our woodland garden (an effective deer fence is 2.5 m high or electrified in extreme cases), but we kept them at bay with string and well-placed rags dipped in creosote. They are also reputed to hate the smell of human hair, and a friend says that leaving out a sweaty T-shirt once a week in the vegetable patch is just as effective.

I have also lived with rabbits, and in the end the most sensible course of action is to decide upon a pest-free zone in which you have the treasures and then to fence out the problem if you can afford to. A rabbit-proof fence need only be 1 m high, the gauge no more than 2.5 cm. There is no need to dig the wire into the ground, as some advice might suggest – the secret is to fold 30 cm of the wire outwards just under the ground. The rabbits will dig at the base of the fence and quickly stop where they cannot make headway.

Out in the open, rabbit tree guards (taller for deer) are essential in areas where they are present, but both are most interested in young plants, and after three years the guards can be removed. The RHS also provides extensive lists of plants that deer and rabbits favour less, such as hellebore, *Cornus sanguinea* and aster, and you can garden quite extensively if you give young plants initial protection. In one garden where it is impossible to keep the rabbits out, we have a stack of wire hanging baskets. These are upturned and placed over the crowns of new perennials and those that are prone to attack early in the season, and this is enough to bring them through the vulnerable periods. As usual, prevention is better than cure.

26 October, *Peckham*
GOLDEN SLUMBERS

––––––

The autumn is so much bigger than we are, and as humble gardeners it is unwise for us to try to fight it head on. Goodness knows how many tonnes of leaves there are to come down yet or what profound but microscopic activity we are missing as the life in the garden prepares for the dormant season. There is the smell of rot in the air, a spill in the beds and the paths are a slew of rampant nasturtium, and if I want to hang on to let as much goodness as possible be drawn back to earth, I have little choice but to let it all happen and take solace in the relief of not having to keep up appearances.

Though I'll let most things go in the beds, I have been more industrious in the allotment, and yet I've kept things on track with only two hours a week. A small amount of time applied regularly has been the key to keeping the weeds at bay, the tomatoes tied in and the courgettes from straddling their neighbours. I have not kept all the courgettes from turning into marrows, nor have we managed to eat (or give away) as many beans as were provided for us, but I keep the rotation up, so there has been little empty ground. The potatoes gave way to the now-extensive leek and broccoli patch and the weekly vigil meant that I was able to pick off the cabbage white caterpillars without them getting the better of things.

But with rot taking hold, it is time to move on, so after taking out the last of the tomatoes I make a start by clearing where possible. The courgettes-turned-marrows only seem to have the tiniest purchase on the ground, and they leave a sizeable hole when piled into the barrow. I like to let leaves fall in the borders so they can be recycled back into the system, but it is best to keep the vegetable garden 'clean' to avoid a build-up of disease, and any spent vegetable plants are removed and composted.

The bamboo tripods are the first to come down and the vines of the tomatoes are dissected and pulled from their now-tenuous hold on the ground. This would be easier if they had been wilted by frost, but I take satisfaction in there being bulk to feed the compost heap. I was lucky enough to escape the blight this year, but I don't want to take chances, so all the rotting fruit that split and fell or never ripened is swept away and mouldering weeds pulled. Though the tops of the climbing beans are cut and taken to the compost heap, the roots will be left in the ground where the nodules will release stored nitrogen back into the earth.

I chose not to plant green manure on the plot this year because I still have edible chard, rocket and celtuce (a cross between lettuce and celery, and new to me) in the ground. Once these crops are used up, I will continue the clearance and begin winter cultivation, spreading home-produced compost over the surface of the newly forked ground. If I had a heavy clay soil

I would be turning the ground now and trenching the compost to let the frost break the clods down on the surface. As the soil here is a silty loam, or if I was gardening on chalk or sand, the protective eiderdown of compost will help to keep the soil in good condition. Over the winter the worms will once again be my allies by helping to work the eiderdown in, so that all I have to do next spring is lightly fork it over.

By emptying the compost bay in the autumn, I will make way for the first of this season's additions. I turn the heap twice a year to make sure that any dry and uncomposted areas are mixed with those that are lying wet. This gives the bacteria an injection of air to help turn debris to compost. The upper crust of the most recent deposits is turned back to the bottom of the empty heap beside it and a shovelful or two of the best compost thrown in to keep the new heap 'live'. Along with the beneficial bacteria, there are worms in the old compost, and they are all part of the re-cycling cycle.

As a token, and to make me feel like autumn doesn't have the upper hand entirely, I will clear certain areas to add a contrast of neatness – the equivalent of ironing only the front of a shirt that a suit will cover elsewhere. Though it works for me at home on the terraces, if I had a lawn I would be clearing the foliage once I have enjoyed it, and before it starts to lie wet and suffocate the grass. This slow, methodical sweep is one of the treats of the season, and leaves are best stored in a heap of their own. Leaf mould is a very different thing from compost, as it retains an open consistency that is so loved by the likes of lilies and other woodlanders.

In the hottest spot against the fence, I will plant my garlic.

'Thermidrome' is good for planting now; 'Printanor' can be put in as late as February. I will harvest and eat it green next year rather than dry it, as it's harder to get hold of in this luscious state. As the nights draw in and I battle with the feeling that it's all falling apart, I will hold that in my mind as reward.

28 October, *Peckham*

FALL'S FINAL FANFARE

———

There is part of me that wants to put everything on hold at the moment, to leave the remaining bulbs I have yet to get in the ground and to risk not bringing in the tender perennials in their pots. I want to leave the gutters to fill with leaves, the runner beans on their tripods to topple, the compost heap unturned and the veggie patch to moulder. I want to ignore all the tasks that stop me looking up and to put gardening aside for a while to enjoy the magnitude of autumn.

I would find it impossible to live without seasons. Each year I fall in love again with the scale of the change that we are in the midst of just now. Whole landscapes shifting as if growth is in reverse, foliage drawn back to earth, and that yeasty smell that comes with the damp and decay. Skylines change from green to brown or russet, red and gold in a good year, and then suddenly to transparency if we get a storm to rattle the branches bare. The countryside is the place to be – or on a drive into the landscape to feel it, to smell it and to kick through fallen foliage. Without an autumn walk or a forage for nuts, mushrooms or blackberries,

I feel we have failed to prepare ourselves properly for the winter.

I want to invite the season into the garden, too – vividly and in layers. I use asters, autumn crocuses and gentians at ground level, and shrubs that perform for this season to take the eye up and away, to straighten the back. *Sambucus* turns a buttery yellow, which might be brief, but kicks off the season early and with the addition of contrasting berries hanging jet-black by the bunch. I weave berrying trees and shrubs into the garden as much for their jewel-like fruit as for the birds which flock down to gorge when the fruit is ready for feasting upon.

Berry hedges (they also have their moment like the blossom hedges in the spring) are a good way of doing this, and I weave them into gardens up and down the country whenever possible. Rebecca in my studio calls them 'crumble hedges' – they are comprised of sloes (for sloe gin) and dog roses (for rosehip syrup), and always have room for the odd bramble. There are many other fruits, and in some cases droops and berries, to steer well clear of. You may find that bryony and belladonna have woven their way into the mix, deposited there by birds flocking from one feeding ground to the next. They are poison to us and worth telling apart. There is honeysuckle, too, with its crimson berries, hawthorn for its darker-red clusters of fruit, and *Viburnum opulus* for its bloody-red droops. These are the first to go, but many fruits last until long after the leaves are down. In alkaline areas, add the spindle *Euonymus europaeus* to the mix – its pink capsules rupture to reveal tangerine seed – or *Cornus sanguinea* and *Rhamnus* for almost black fruits. If you live by the sea, plant sea buckthorn, *Hippophae rhamnoides*, whose orange clusters of berries completely clothe the black thorny branches.

NOVEMBER

N

November provides us with a breathing point. Colour is going, if not gone, and branches are newly naked, revealing the bones of things. Scarlet hips are left starkly alone in the hedgerows, and the floor is littered with the fruit of a growing season. Birds are moving seed about, windfalls pecked to little more than skins. We may well have had the first frost by now; if not, it is sure to hit before the end of the month. With it the dahlias are suddenly blackened, to leave behind just a trace of their autumn bulk. The brick-red schizostylis and lipstick-pink nerine continue to flare for a while, yet in stark and diminishing contrast to the decline around them. There are few other flowers out – perhaps a rose or two looking out of place and left behind – and so they are doubly welcome.

We are surrounded by rot and decay, but it is a not a death to be disturbed by but rather celebrated as the cusp of this annual cycle. It's an appropriate time to pause for thought, as there is a new season opening up and, with it, the potential for new planting.

I wait until the garden starts to feel on the wrong side of neglect before imposing any order, and even then I favour a less-is-more approach. Sweeping the mouldering leaves from the lawn or the terrace imposes a little order on the chaos and allows you to stand back for a while to assess the departure of the growing season. But the pause is brief: there are the tulips to put in the ground, plants that need their winter protection, and the season for planting bare-root trees and shrubs opens up again as nurseries start lifting them before the ground freezes. Use the time well to plant before the year is out and new plantings will be settled before the worst of winter arrives.

7 November, *Peckham and Hillside*
PERSONAL GROWTH

———

Late last year, at a book signing in Bath, I tacked a day onto my trip to stay with friends just north of the city. It was an excuse to take some time walking their fields and we spent the day in the landscape, taking it all in. It was something I do far too little and, in idle passing, I asked them to keep their eyes open in case land ever came up in the area.

It has been a long-term dream to have sky and fields and nature up close but I had no idea that things would happen quite this quickly.

In January, Jane called to say that the smallholding on the

other side of the valley was coming up for sale and before we knew it we were committed and it was ours. It sounds so simple but, believe me, it was a struggle to get the keys to the farm. There were bridging loans to arrange and buyers to find to make it all possible, but finally the SOLD sign went up on the house here in Peckham and the realities of our actions were complete.

So, here I am, looking out of my Peckham window at the autumn light raking through the last thirteen years of growth. Growth that maps many hours of daydreaming, plans and actions, and all the associated memories of the things that have happened here.

In truth, this is a garden that is straining at the seams and the wisteria represents the feeling most strongly. It was the first plant that I introduced when we arrived here and every year I have trained it further, planning the lay of the limbs and the cascade of flowers around the windows. Today it has a stem as thick as my arm and branches that have travelled four floors and would happily continue if it could.

This is a garden that has offered us sanctuary, a place that protects and provides. The boundaries are frayed with growth now, my roses and vines leaning into my neighbour's garden, their Virginia creeper and bramble leaning into mine. It is good ground that has reared vegetables, herbs, flowers and fruits and it has given me back far more than I have put into it.

I have moved gardens before and know better than to try to re-create them in another place. The plants that we moved to Home Farm all those years ago from my friend Frances's garden in London took more space in the removal van than her furniture, but few of the plants survived the transition. It was not that they were too tender – indeed, they thrived – but it was more a case that they spoke the wrong language for a place that was influenced by such different boundaries.

It is perfect timing for the move, so I have been able to lift and divide in textbook fashion to sample just enough of this place to form a stepping stone and no more between the two worlds. The nerines that my old friend Geraldine gave me when I was a child, and the *Paeonia* 'Late Windflower' which was a present from Beth Chatto, have sentimental attachment. But there are also plants like the *Tulipa sprengeri* that have taken me years to raise, or special selections such as my hellebores with freckles or picotee edges that I know I will never come across, or will forget I ever had, if I don't take them with me.

A strong friend came last weekend and helped me move my pots and garden furniture. We emptied those pots that we could, and stacked them carefully for the removal men, and brought the treasures down to the terrace to be carefully packed for the journey. By treasures I mean my collection of Asian epimediums, my favourite lilies, and all the cuttings of the plants I have been busily propagating over the summer.

The black *Paeonia delavayi* that I gathered from Edinburgh Botanic Gardens when I was nineteen will have to stay behind because it is too much part of the garden, but I have saved the seed along with my black opium poppy and my favourite 'Mahogany' nasturtium. When they emerge from germination in spring, they will find themselves in another world and I have a feeling that I will embrace my new ground as readily as I know they will.

3 November, *The Studio*

A CRAB APPLE A DAY

———

Gardening is so much more than reading about it. It is in the doing and the growing and the experience of seeing for yourself that you really learn. A paragraph pored over is a good start; knowing where a plant comes from and how, in theory, it might grow is a useful part of the puzzle. Seeing it *in situ* and talking with the owner of the plant is better still, but there is nothing like growing it, living with it and having the time to see it develop to get to know its habits. Insider knowledge is the best knowledge, the information you need to give you the confidence to adapt and commit yourself in a garden.

One of the great joys of making gardens for other people is that I get to experiment. I can do this on a large scale in gardens that are far bigger than mine. Sometimes I think of it like building a country-wide plant collection in a range of wildly varying conditions that could never come together in a single garden. I can play with Judas trees, figs and mulberries as far north as Yorkshire to see if they will do well there in our increasingly mild climate. I can attempt to naturalise trilliums in a wood in the Midlands or really push the boundaries to see if my favourite *Datura* might possibly be hardy in a sheltered corner in Guernsey. On an educated guess I discovered that eryngiums do especially well in this mild, maritime climate and I am trying out a new and as yet untested palette there to broaden my experience. I carry out this experimentation within reason and always with a calculated risk, but it is good to get to know familiar plants better, and also to discover new ones to widen my knowledge of what might be possible.

I have passions that run through this path of discovery and one group that I am getting to know through my clients' gardens are the crab apples. The interest in these wonderful flowering trees started several years ago, with a grove that we planted in a garden in southern Italy. They are planted in a small, high-sided ravine so that you can walk among them and be lost in the experience of blossom in spring. The blossom then is sweet, heady and incandescent with captured light, but the trees also go on to fruit, and from late summer the boughs hang low with miniature rosy apples. This display lasts for months, well after the foliage is down, and it only ends once the birds start to hunger and strip the trees in a few days around Christmas time.

Sadly, I have no idea what the trees are and I try every year to get them identified. If I am there in blossom season, I can never get a flowering branch home intact to ask an expert, and photographs only give up part of the story. The Italian nursery that supplied the plants is notoriously relaxed about what a plant really might be. I waited years to discover that the 'white' wisteria they supplied, which they swore was what I had asked for, is actually blue. 'Does it really matter, if the plants are beautiful?' is their response when quizzed. Well, yes, because in the case of the crab apples, I want to repeat the experience.

The frustration over their identification has only heightened my quest, and over the years, in an effort to match these lovely trees, I have been planting what I glean to be the best varieties whenever the chance arises. I have planted up groves in several gardens up and down the country with the aim of creating a place within the garden that sings at a particular moment and does it en masse. In one garden I have interplanted wild hazel with a dozen *Malus hupehensis*. This is one of the best of the crab apples, a strong grower, with branches that ascend in the early years and then broaden out to form a dome-shaped tree as much as 12 m in height and width. When in flower, and they flower late towards the end of April, they eclipse most things around them and half a year later their branches hang heavy with small red fruits. I have underplanted them with late-flowering *Narcissus poeticus*, the pheasant's eye narcissus, so that the clouds of white are taken up from ground level, and in autumn there are autumn crocuses to complement the fruits.

Crab apples also make good urban trees where space matters. Clean white 'Evereste' is ideal in its upright space-saving habit, but I have also seen this used as a compact hedge at Harlow Carr gardens in Harrogate. The fruits are a rosy orange and it adapts well to pruning if you start it young with a multi-stemmed plant. In contrast, *M. × zumi* var. *calocarpa* forms a low, wide-spreading tree with brilliant bright red fruit. It is wider in the beam than it is high, but light enough to allow ground-covering perennials to establish under its skirts. *M. floribunda* from China is softer in character with fine, numerous branches and a froth of pink flowers in the spring. This is early and the buds are a bright, lipstick pink before they blow to something altogether softer in tone. I have heard it said that this tree is a martyr to canker, but I have been lucky so far and keep it well away from hawthorn hedging, as this is where the canker spends some of its life cycle.

A variety such as *M.* × *robusta* 'Red Sentinel' often hangs on to the fruit well after the foliage is down. Each miniature apple is the size of a marble and a deep uniform red, which lights up brightly when illuminated by winter sunshine. Its yolky yellow equivalent, *M.* × *zumi* 'Golden Hornet', has similar habits and oddly the birds leave them both until the going gets really tough. Before that happens, there is a wonderful moment during a gentle autumn when you get the fruit of crab apples combining with luminous foliage. The best of them colour pale golden yellow which, combined with fruit, is a gift in a garden. *M. transitoria* is a treasure in this respect, with foliage laced at the margins and colouring reliably. (*M. transitoria* 'Thornhayes Tansy' is even more dissected.) The tree has a wild, hawthorny quality about it and the leaves are the perfect foil to the tiny orange fruits.

M. transitoria is also reputed to be resistant to honey fungus and is happy on a heavy clay soil. Crab apples are not such distant cousins to the culinary varieties and favour similar free-drained conditions in the main. Not all are suitable for crab-apple jelly, but if you do decide to add to the depths of your autumn larder, 'John Downie' is a good candidate. One of just many that I am sure will be just as good for the purpose – I'll have to wait another ten years or so to know with confidence, once I have tried for myself, but here's to getting to know!

4 November, *Hillside*

GARDENING LEAVE

———

Late autumn, with its death and decay and dwindling light, should be a melancholy point in the year, but I rarely find it so. I like the feeling of withdrawal, the garden retreating into itself, offering views of the sky through newly transparent twiggery. Though there is always something to do in the garden, it feels like there is a natural pause around now – a taking stock while the windfalls are picked over by the starlings.

I like to take advantage of this change to reacquaint myself with the garden before it completely loses its framework. The blossom wood on the hill, which I planted two years ago, is not quite bare and, walking among it, the change is remarkable.

I planted whips, some of which were no higher than my knee, but already I'm walking through maidens that are standing easily as tall as I am.

The hawthorn, eglantines, bird cherry and mountain ash have their roots down now, and next year I will be able to fill my pockets with their fruit, which can be grown into future generations. It is not all success and there are the inevitable stragglers too. The guelder rose have only done well where the ground runs deep and moist, so I will be ordering more *Pyrus pyraster*, for they have loved the hot, dry ridges.

My notebook fattens with plants that need to be ordered now to take advantage of the planting season ahead of us. One of the apples in the newly planted orchard is obviously a martyr to canker. It already has three infestations on its young trunk where the other trees are clean and currently healthy. I will dig it out rather than soldier on and waste another year. A 'Discovery' will provide me with a good crisp early apple and hopefully prove my mantra that if you fail with one variety try another before quitting. The 'Manaccan' plum in the new orchard has for some inexplicable reason refused to perform while its neighbours are racing away. I will ponder this a while yet and probably give it another season.

My notes encompass plans for next year as well: move the pumpkins to a position with a little more shelter, remember to plant only early potatoes, as they escaped the blight, and give the tomatoes a rest. Two years of tomato blight are demoralising but my failure has triggered the desire for a polytunnel. Will the fact that I can grow a whole new range of winter salads and have confidence in growing tomatoes blight free and under cover cancel out its ugliness? Time will tell.

I will leave the leaves where they fall in the beds and take a lesson from how things naturally occur. Get down on your hands and knees and you will see that many of the fallen leaves are upended in the soil. This is where earthworms are pulling them into their burrows and where they will be converted into humus to improve the soil for next year. You have to ask why it is necessary to intervene in a natural cycle that is already providing for us. The excess that lies on the ground is protecting it from the wind, rain and frost that has blackened the last of the dahlias. Sweep a patch free and the soil looks friable and moist underneath.

I will only clear where I need to, to rake leaves from the lawns so that the grass isn't starved of light and to clear paths.

Areas where nature is left to take its course can be cleared gently and over the coming months, pulling the perennials away only when required, letting the foliage rot into the ground and the seedheads stand for the frost and the birds.

If I wade into the beds this early in the season it is to instigate change. Tired planting can be enlivened with something new or by division of exhausted perennials. It is also a timely moment to tackle an area infested by weeds. You will need to dig deep to remove every strand of fleshy-rooted bindweed or maybe start again where you have ground elder or couch among your perennials.

Like nature, we are not meant to sit still for long.

5 November, *Peckham*
RAINBOW WARRIORS

———

Autumn is the perfect wind-down after a full summer, when everything in the garden seems to happen at such a pace. Now there is time to savour the last fling before the garden sinks back into itself. Evidence of the big retreat is apparent on every bough, in every hedgerow and everywhere underfoot, as last season's growth goes to earth. It is a time to look and to take in the muskiness of decay, the otherness of curious fungi revelling in the damp, and the very last of the year's autumnal flowers.

In the country, where there is room to let autumn lie around for a little longer, fallen-leaf litter is something to savour. Kicked underfoot and eventually raked into piles so that it doesn't smother the grass, leaf litter is a precious bounty that should never be burnt on an autumn bonfire. Bonfires are best kept for prunings and for anything that you don't like the look of that may be diseased or simply exhausted. Roots of perennial weeds, such as ground elder and bindweed, can also be thrown on to the fire, but a pile of home-made leaf mould is the best-possible additive to compost for lilies. Mixed at a proportion of about 25 per cent leaf mould, it opens up a good loam to just the right consistency. It works because it's light and soil-opening, yet moisture-retentive. Leaf mould also makes a wonderful mulch for woodland treasures, such as trillium and wood anemone, because it re-creates the conditions of their native forest floor.

If you have the room, a simply constructed cage of posts and chicken wire makes the best place to store autumn leaves. Pile them high and then put your whole weight on them to reduce the bulk. However, air is what they need to rot effectively, so never compress wet leaves to the point of compaction. If you bag them in plastic sacks these must be well perforated so that the bacteria that decompose the leaves can breathe. The leaves can then be left for a year to break down quietly.

Although the monochrome of the next season is already making itself apparent, the garden is still surprisingly rich once you take the time to look beyond the wreckage. Brick-red and pink schizostylis are at their peak and the rudbeckias, which have been with us since August, bring sunshine on even the dullest day. Yellow is best when used with confidence, and I like the rudbeckias when they are used boldly – reflecting the raking light and adding fuel to the fire for the other colours of autumn. I have grown the giant of the group, *Rudbeckia laciniata*

'Herbstsonne', in various gardens and I like its presence, standing 2 m high by the time it flowers. It has a deep-green laciniated leaf and gangly stems that need support in good ground. If you grow them hard, with plenty of sunshine and no feeding, they can stand on their own, but it is best to assume that they will need staking. For this reason it makes sense to grow them towards the back of the border, but I like to put them in front of a window, where they illuminate the interior when backlit by sunshine. I have always fancied a long path lined with them on both sides. It would have to be wide enough not to drench you if they overhung too much, but it would be like walking down a sunlit avenue, and all the more dramatic in this low autumn light. I might weave in the odd tawny miscanthus and back it with the brilliant orange of *Rhus typhina* or *Cotinus coggygria*.

The asters introduce another colourway for those who are a little wary of the yellows, but you need to know what you are doing with asters if they are not to disappoint or, indeed, overwhelm. The railway embankments that you see strewn with their lilac drifts at this time of year are testament to the rogues that must have been hurled over the garden fence and never made it on to the bonfire. Those asters that run do so with a vengeance; you need to drive in tiles or a board to contain these varieties, but it is better to stick to the clump formers. Mildew also loves an aster and can ruin a plant early in the season so that you are bothered by it long before it flowers; but again, there are selections that are chosen for their ability to resist this blight.

The *novae-angliae* group of asters may have been bred for mildew resistance, but their dwarfishness lacks elegance. In my book, they look best suited as institutional bedding, possibly with heathers. When you see asters in the wild they are airy and light, their colours misty and effervescent, which is what makes them so perfect for the soft light and dewiness of this season.

So, with good manners, good breeding and grace in mind, I have whittled the vast list of asters down to a handful of good clump-formers. Of the well-behaved asters, few are better than *Aster* × *frikartii* 'Mönch'. A plant of about 60 cm high, with large lavender flowers, 'Mönch' comes into flower in August, at the beginning of the aster season, but it continues for months if it is happy. While most asters actively prefer a poorer soil, 'Mönch' likes a handsome mulch of compost in the spring and division every five years or so to replenish clumps with the best and strongest offshoots. I like this variety most with the bright bubblegum-pink of *Nerine bowdenii*, but they are just as lovely against the neutral silveriness of lavender.

Very different in feel is *A. lateriflorus*, with massed sprays of tiny off-white flowers. *A. lateriflorus* var. *horizontalis* forms a low, self-contained mound about 90 cm across and high – Christopher Lloyd used them as a perennial hedge to divide up the topiary garden at Dixter. A tight grower with coppery foliage, it develops slowly over the summer, remaining neat and healthy looking when many a perennial is starting to flag. *A. lateriflorus* 'Prince' is another selection with deep brown-purple foliage and a looser, more open habit.

My long-term favourite is *A. divaricatus*. This is also an exception to the aster rule in that it is quite happy in a little shade. It is a sprawling plant, forming a low mound the size of *Alchemilla mollis*. You might not notice it much for the first half of the year, but when you do tune in you will see that among its pale green shiny foliage is a network of liquorice-black stems which go on to produce the most delicate, airy flowers. Pale but not white, spacious and long-lasting, they are the perfect foil for *Cyclamen hederifolium* and *Colchicum autumnale*, for which they cover in the early summer when the winter foliage of the bulbs is dormant. A toughie that demands little in the way of energy on your part, it is a plant that is perfectly placed in a season that should really be about just that – standing back and taking it all in.

6 November, *Hillside*

A MOMENT ON THE HIPS

———

The last fortnight has been marked by the memories and flavours of moving here a year ago. The weight of dew in the grass, the length of shadow elongating away from the poplars and the nights drawing rapidly in. The first frost has already hung in the hollow by the stream, and with it the tumble of foliage from high up in the branches as a bright thaw starts a still, crisp day. Once again, we are at the turning point, one season shifting into the next, the landscape opening up to reveal the bones of the winter ahead.

The farmer is already cutting the hedgerows along the lane but we will resist the urge until the birds have had their fill. The elderberries have already gone, as have the last of the blackberries, but the inky sloes, the crimson hawthorn and the rosehips are still spangling the hedge lines. Arching out to catch you if you walk the line too closely are the dog roses. We have three native roses on the farm. Higher up the slopes where there is plenty of sunshine is the domain of the common dog rose, *Rosa canina*, and where the hedges dip low into the shade of trees you find the field rose, *R. arvensis*. The habit of the field rose is more like the brambles among which you often find it, its long limbs using its neighbours for support. Its flowers are white, where the dog rose is pink, and they come a little later in the shade. Their deep red hips are currently darkening to black.

Last winter, I introduced the sweet briar to the hedges to add the third of these lovely creatures. In terms of habit, it is hard to tell *R. eglanteria* from the dog rose until you catch the delicious smell of its foliage, which is sweet and clean, like apples. I am planning more at openings by the field gates so that every time we pass through, their perfume will catch us unawares, and I have already placed an order for a bundle of bare-root seedlings for this planting season.

The hips are handsome compensation for the fleeting shrubs and climbers, and they will often take you by surprise, colouring up at the end of August and taking you into early winter when all the foliage is down. Rosehips are hugely variable: the Scotch briars stud the thorny bushes with jet-black beads, every bit as lovely, but far more durable than the ephemeral June flower. The scarlet hips of *R. moyesii* are like flagons, while 'Scabrosa' are the size and shininess of a ripened tomato. Those on the tree-scaling climbers such as *R. mulliganii*, 'Kiftsgate' (beware, it's a monster!) or 'Sir Cedric

Morris' come in their thousands, a spray of tiny beads. They form sparkling cages for the autumn-feeding birds, which flit among them until they have had their fill.

R. glauca – a rose I grow more for the glaucous pink of its foliage than its flower – is one of the first to fruit, producing drooping clusters of mahogany-red fruit beloved by flurries of tits that will strip them clean while the asters are still blooming. Why some hips are more attractive to birds, I have never fathomed, but it is worth complementing one variety with another to keep the relay going.

The species roses are often incredibly tough, and this year I am weaving a walk of roses through meadow in a client's garden. Most are single-flowered dog roses, some species, others hybrids, but all are up to the challenge of growing 'rough'. They will be given a head start, with a metre kept weed-free for the first three years, and then they will fend for themselves. The roses will come with the wafting meadow grasses in June, but the hips will come later for a dual experience once the meadows are cut. *R. virginiana*, the toughest of the lot, will be eased in under the canopy of trees as it is a pioneer species often found in waste places.

The ferny leaved *R. willmottiae* is one of the most lovely, with showers of small red hips, but I will leave room for the impressive 'Scharlachglut' or 'Scarlet Fire'. Wide, single roses will glow in the June green and the hips will take on the mantle to ease the shift into winter monochrome with a last bolt of colour.

16 November, *Peckham*
IN WITH THE NEW

———

I have been pulling the garden apart now that the fragile beauty of autumn is crumpled. Seed from the *Tagetes patula* 'Cinnabar' has been saved and the summer pots turned out and soil revitalised with seaweed meal to make way for the bulbs and perfumed wallflowers that replace them. Next spring, I will treat myself to some new *Fuchsia* 'Thalia', so the last of the flowers are cut for a jug and the plants guiltily consigned to the compost heap. If it isn't me, the frost will get them and I have vowed this year that I will attempt to cut down on the number of plants that I try to over-winter in the garage.

I took cuttings of the pelargoniums in August so that what I do keep is smaller and easier to look after, and they developed well in the frame, so I can part with the elderly plants that I have been hanging on to for several years now. Youthful vigour – and the health that comes with it – goes a long way in the right places.

With that in mind, I have some young daturas coming along and have made plans for my fifteen-year-old plant to be liberated into the ground. It is old and woody, exhausting the compost that it occupies in the summer, so this will be the last year that it is hauled into the garage for the winter. Next year it will have to take its chances in a corner by the house as the mild winters here in London are always worth pushing to the limits. If I lived out in the country, there would be no way that I would behave in such a risky manner. I would be digging up the dahlias and storing them with the cannas in a frost-free corner immediately after the frost had blackened their tops.

I have to admit I enjoy the first frost of the winter, for it cuts to the chase and makes the decision for you. Once it strikes I no longer have to worry about the seemingly endless spread of the nasturtiums nor when to wade in and remove the last of the annuals. If after a proper freeze they aren't entirely done for, at least they are damaged enough not to have to worry about clearing the ground they have occupied. The new gaps in the border that are exposed like missing teeth can be seized upon to inject new energy for next year.

Though I have already planted most of my bulbs to take advantage of the heat held from the summer in the ground, I have yet to do the tulips. They are happy to go in as late as December and I work a few in every year for the lift that they provide among the fresh growth of the perennials. The hot orange 'Ballerina' and the dusky 'Abu Hassan' have been confined to pots, crammed like commuters, thirty in each for decadence, but in the beds a smattering is all that is required. Though they never really come back with conviction for a second season, I love the pale flames of 'White Triumphator' among the honesty, but a couple of years ago the bulb company wrongly supplied me with what I later identified as 'Sapporo'. Over a fortnight, the pale primrose flowers faded out to ivory white in a delicious shift. Mistakes are nearly always interesting and I am now favouring 'Sapporo' for its subtle transformation.

I really don't mind wading in and cutting back what is already over, for things have to be done if we are to provide for the spring. The *Persicaria amplexicaulis* 'Alba' that are in the bed where I have winkled in the 'Sapporo' have no stamina in terms of keeping a good winter skeleton, and their growth is collapsed but still sturdy enough to make a satisfying crunch when the secateurs are taken to them at their base. Pulling this newly cut vegetation away, I see that the rhizomes have run more than I had realised in the coverall of summer, and they are now encroaching upon my precious 'Late Windflower' peonies and making a dent in the hellebores. Though they can live for many years without disturbance, in a garden as densely planted as this they need to be kept within bounds but in good condition too, if they are not to let the side down in the summer.

The persicarias have been in this position for a decade now, and three years ago I curbed their enthusiasm by reducing the outer rhizomes, to decrease their spread. This is not good practice as it leaves the old, less vigorous growth behind. The rapidly increasing asters or the likes of bergamot would hate it as their tendency to spread outwards and die out in the centre would mean I'd be removing the very growth that I needed for flower next year. I try to avoid these live-fast, move-on perennials because they need to be dug up and divided every third year to retain good vigour, but the slower clump-forming perennials, such as the persicarias, also need attention once they start to show signs of tiring.

So, levering them up with a border fork and the care of a surgeon, I removed the knot of roots that had developed under the hydrangea. Fresh compost was worked into the ground with some blood, fish and bone for good measure. I then divided up the knuckles of growth, removing the best young shoots with a sharp knife and putting these on one side for replanting.

The strongest material should have a healthy clump of roots and vigorous shoots waiting tight for next year. The old growth, sad though it may be, is best thrown away as the new blood of youth is what you are after to revitalise a planting. Carefully firmed in so that the roots can easily gain a new purchase, they will be ready for action, as I will, when the pendulum of spring swings back.

17 November, *London*

BETWEEN THE LINES

———

We have just completed the planting of Handyside Gardens, a public park that is part of the redevelopment around the new Central Saint Martins art college in King's Cross. It is a strip of land wedged between a modern building and the old train sheds. The site couldn't be more urban: underneath it run the lines of the London Underground.

The site was once an industrial hub and a terminus for the grain from the east and coal from the north. We drew from the previous network of railway tracks to provide us with linear paths and beds that helped to slide the park between the buildings. I also wanted it to suggest a place that was reminiscent of railway sidings, with a planting of garden escapees that to this day use the infrastructure of the industrial revolution for their own migratory purposes. Asters and shrubby willows feather their way through swathes of grasses to give the feeling that the planting has evolved in this newly created space.

As per usual with a site that is still in flux, the planting dates got pushed back and the guys were working in the rain, with ever-shortening days. Despite the hold-up, this window between summer and winter is my favourite time of year to plant, because there is warmth still in the ground. If you tip a pot carefully upside down and give it a sharp tap on the rim to set the root ball free, you can see just how ready the roots are to escape and make their own way in the ground. Although plants may appear to be dying back for the winter, as soon as they come into contact with the soil they make their move towards independence.

All our plants were pot-grown or containerised, as our original plant date was too early to use bare-root or root-balled material. It was important that the perennials were checked over before planting. The roots should not be twisting their way out of the bottom of the pot, but there should be enough root growth to hold the soil together so that when you tip it out, the root ball stays firm enough not to be disturbed as it goes into the hole.

All our trees were grown in air pots – a modern system that uses pots with perforated sides so that as the roots hit a hole in the pot, and air, they terminate and branch to form a more fibrous root system. A good root system on a plant will mean it is able to draw upon minerals and water in the soil and establish itself quickly.

The soil in the park was all imported and it has been important to get it right. This goes for any new plant. A hole should be a third as big again to twice the size of the rootball so that you can backfill with friable soil enriched with compost. Planting at this time of year requires little watering but pots that are dry should be plunged in water then drained before being planted. A handful of blood, fish and bone to every square metre and a top dressing of mulch will set a new planting up for the coming months so that, by spring, everything is ready for the off.

22 November, *Peckham*

CONKERS FOR KIDS, PLUMS FOR A CRUMBLE, NUTS FOR THE SQUIRREL

———

Look under an oak of any size and the ground will be littered with acorns. I stoop to pick up a pocketful whenever I see them and press them into a bare patch of ground the next time I come upon one. It is a game of sorts, but I do it in the hope a life might be lived should the many obstacles that lie ahead be hurdled. This is the point that many of our plants have been working towards, the object of the exercise, and you will find the produce of the growing season wherever you look. Beech mast will carpet the ground in a good year, turning it a cinnamon red under the canopy, and conkers provide the focus for children who flock to trees that for the remainder of the year go unnoticed.

I often cycle through Hyde Park, and was amused this year to see city foraging in action. A line of young sweet chestnuts (*Castanea sativa*) has been planted to the south of the Serpentine, and they have become a focus now they are old enough to produce. People with sticks, umbrellas and a steely will to get to the prickly cases were going at the trees with a fever, and where the cases had fallen to the ground and escaped the foraging, the geese were doing their best to finish the shiny remains.

Castanea sativa is a tree that often refocuses my attention at this time of year, and for more than the obvious bonus of the fruits, which, when pulled from the coals of an autumn bonfire and cracked open, steam sweet and savoury. Chestnut is a tree with substance, and this comes into its own now that the leaves are down – the fissured bark of a mature specimen looks like the trunk is being twisted from the ground by its branches. It takes time to reach this stately position, but *Castanea* is a fast tree and one that is being recommended by arboriculturists as a safe bet for the future. Being of Mediterranean origin, they are tolerant of summer drought and the vagaries of global warming. Since they are long-lived, and have all the gravity of an oak, I use them as an alternative in clients' gardens, where it is appropriate to do so.

The fruit of most trees is produced in quantity to ensure a certain amount escapes the animals that flock to it to build up their reserves before winter. That said, there are never enough cobnuts to escape the squirrels, but there is a wealth of fruiting plants to bring this extra interest to our gardens. You have only to look to our native hedgerows to see that there has been a steady succession since late summer. Mountain ash and *Viburnum opulus* as shiny as bloody beads were ripening early in September, and they were soon stripped along with heavy-trussed elder. Tart and in need of a sweet syrup, the elder fruit is rich in vitamin C and makes a delicious cordial – if you manage to get to it before the birds. Jet-berried *Cornus sanguinea*, inky-blue sloe, blackberries, bryony, juicily berried honeysuckle, rosehip and hawthorn, and a lacing of deadly nightshade ensure the show continues until the leaves are blown.

Look up into the branches of trees you might associate with another season entirely and they will often be providing us with the fruits to follow blossom at the back end of the year. *Cornus mas* is one of the loveliest, with acidic yellow-green flowers in February. The fruits, though small, are another source of vitamin C, and delightful once you retrain your eye to see them. Sloe will not be far behind and, though I love the blossom in early March, the inky fruits of *Prunus cerasifera* are equally lovely.

Most years I make it a mission to plant a berry hedge; this year we are including varieties of the cherry plum into a run that forms a boundary to a public right of way. The idea is that there will be enough for the birds, my clients and the passers-by, who we hope will feel that they can scrump as they go. 'Mirabelle Gypsy' (appropriate on this wayfarers' route) has red fruits rather than the more usual inky-black, and 'Mirabelle de Nancy' is a yellow form of the cherry plum and will cover itself so abundantly that its branches hang heavy under the weight. Each is the size of a quail egg and makes a good jam, or a tart addition to crumble if balanced with a sweet cooking apple. Mirabelle 'Golden Sphere' is a new form of the above that we are giving a go for good measure.

On the same property we have planted an orchard of crab apples that will eventually be underplanted with woodland plants once the trees are large enough for the canopy to close over. I have used two of the best, with *Malus transitoria* by the field entrance, not far from the hedge. This is a tree that at first glance you might mistake for a hawthorn, with its tiny, divided leaf and similar domed habit. The branches are graceful, as are the sprays of delicate, creamy flowers. Amber fruit, no larger than peas, follow on with good autumn colour, and the birds go mad in this tree when they are ripe. The main body of the orchard is formed from a stand of *Malus hupehensis*. This is said to be the best-flowering crab, with just-pink bud giving way to scented pure-white blossom. But right now it is the fruits that draw your eye: a deep wine-red, shiny, and cropping so heavily that on a bright late autumn day, the last thought on your mind is that winter is nearly upon us.

25 November, *The West Country*

JOINING THE ROTTERS' CLUB

———

On one of those lovely autumn days in October, I spent a day with a new client, walking their land. The night before had been the first cold one and it had broken the short spell of the Indian summer. We travelled down on the train, through a smog that muffled the suburbs, but soon, as we moved into open pasture, I realised that the fog was not the shroud it had appeared to be in the city but a magical, mysterious mist. Your framed view of the sky is so reduced in the city that it can feel like a lid on the world, whereas in the country the same grey skies can be seen to their full extent, turning seemingly oppressive weather conditions into things of great beauty. And so the day opened up as the train sped towards our destination, the cover becoming more luminous and then breaking into brilliant pockets of sunlight, one of those perfectly still autumn days when you can hear every leaf drop.

My client's land has been 'neglected' since shortly after the Second World War; only modest fields had been maintained, with small flocks of sheep looked after by a reclusive shepherd. These meadows were tussocky and full of variety, but most of the land had been consumed by woodland; first by birch and then hornbeam and oak. The birch margins, which were gauzy and apparently fragile, were filled with a golden light given off by the myriad tiny leaves colouring in the cold. Beneath them, and reaching out into the eiderdown of fine fescue grasses, were rafts of heather strung with dewy cobwebs. And you could see, punctuating the gaps, the red stab of the wickedly poisonous fly agaric and the tawny conurbations of fruiting honey fungus.

We talked about the head of 150 wild deer that had made the woods their sanctuary, of the wild boar that you could only ever see if on horseback. These shy woodlanders sense only the horse, not the rider, and had never been spotted by anyone walking the woods on foot. Great crested newts were in all the ponds, badgers in the banks, and rabbits were a given. If we were to do anything here, it would have to be with all the beasts, bugs, flowers and fungus in mind. We would have to tread lightly to be part of the ecology.

My trip coincided with a fleet of emails from readers prompted by the mushroom season and a panic that always seems to accompany anything that implies rot and decay. The tell-tale fruiting bodies of the honey fungus were their primary concern. Will the young apple trees survive in an orchard where a cluster of mushrooms had sprouted? Do the bootlace-like strands in the compost heap mean that the compost cannot be used on the beds? Will mulching with bark be a problem, and should rotting stumps in the garden be dug out to remove the host of the fungus?

It has to be said, gardening is not a discipline that is truly in tune with ecology, and I found myself replying, 'Healthy, young apple trees should survive, but apples are particularly prone to *Armillaria*.' Although there are seven species of *Armillaria* present in the UK, only *A. mellea* and *A. ostoyae* will infect and kill healthy plants. To avoid panic it is important to remember that you may not have a species of honey fungus that is lethal. Young and healthy plants are best equipped to resist attack, so you have to grow for strength and vigour and take an optimistic approach to gardening.

The characteristic bootlaces in the compost heap are *Armillaria gallica*, a saprophytic species that only damages a plant if it is sickly. The rhizomorphs are one of its conduits through the soil and I have it in my heap at home. It can attack woody plants and perennials but, once again, it is less likely to be a problem in soil that is healthy and free-drained. This form of the fungus is also partly responsible for breaking down organic matter and releasing it into the soil as useful nutrients. With regard to mulching with bark, the RHS trials found that a 10 cm layer of coarse bark is more likely to allow the fungus to survive, whereas with a 7 cm mulch, it died when it dried out in the summer. In fact, it was found that adding bark chips improved the soil conditions to the benefit of the plants.

In terms of digging out rotting stumps that might be a primary host to the fungus, this question re-affirmed the battle I have between 'sound horticultural practice' (my gardening hat) and what might be best ecologically. With my wildlife hat on (and this is one I am wearing more and more as time goes on) I am resisting this need to tidy everything up. A recent trip to Kew Gardens was a good reminder, and I was just as impressed by the ecological areas they have been developing over by the river as I was by the autumn colour in the botanical collections. One display answered this question unequivocally. A stumpery of rotting tree trunks plunged in part into the ground was demonstrating the home they provide for the stag beetle. The grubs live below ground in the decomposing wood and are just a fraction of the fauna and flora that also make a home amid the rot and decay. So, in the long run, the balance seems to tip towards the ecology. Leave the stumps, but couple that with keeping your soil, and consequently your plants, healthy.

More and more, I am being approached to work on schemes that include the natural world and preclude the need to order it by gardening, but gardens are ideal places in which to balance the two. In this spirit I will be allowing the leaves to stay where they fall this autumn, unless they are smothering a lawn or vulnerable plants, or collecting around those that like free air movement, such as lavender and thyme. If they fall on the lawn I will mow the lot with a cylinder mower and collect the cuttings in the box. These will compost in half the time on the heap and can be returned to the ground in targeted areas.

I will also be encouraging my clients to make log piles where they don't need the wood for the fire, as these are wonderful habitats for fauna and flora. We have been making sculptural log heaps in the forest garden I am working on in Japan, to form enclosures where people can perch and take in the scenery. At Kew there were also 'dead hedges' made of brushwood and coppiced material surrounding a wildlife pond which provides shelter for creatures such as newts, toads and hedgehogs. This is a great way of creating wildlife habitats if you have the space and don't want to burn or chip the wood.

You can help in the battle against honey fungus by reading up about those trees that are particularly prone. Avoid malus, birch, privet, rose, willow and wisteria if you are of a nervous disposition – although all of these should survive quite happily if they are healthy. The RHS lists a range of more resistant species on its website that are enough to stock any garden. Catalpa, bamboo, phlomis, yew, walnut, oak and Judas tree are just a taster, but, and I feel this with certainty, it is a combination of the two hats, the gardening and the ecology, that is the best way forward.

DECEMBER

D

A smattering of winter-flowering cherry lights this darkening run to the shortest day of the year. Their pale blooms, suspended in cold, dark branches, seem incongruous at the beginning of winter, but they are as welcome as bonfires.

We might be lucky to get a Christmas rose by Christmas, and you can rely upon a bowl full of paperwhite narcissus or hippeastrum from an autumn planting, but this is really the season of evergreens. Their weight is apparent again now that deciduous plants are laid bare. Piebald darkness appears in mixed hedges with the shimmer of holly and ivy, and the steadfast ornamental evergreens give our gardens depth and lustre.

Providing structure for a garden in winter enriches a season that, at first, might appear to be static. Depth and proportion have changed again now that the leaves are down, and your eye is drawn to the straight run of a well-clipped hedge, standing alone or in contrast to the perennial skeletons that you choose to leave for the weeks ahead.

Perennials that keep their foliage and may have been eclipsed by summer colleagues now earn their keep again; mottled lungworts and marbled arum, tellima darkening to its winter colouring. You will be pleased that you made room for a cluster of winter-flowering *Cyclamen coum*; their foliage is fresh and new and ready to take advantage of the light that their sleeping companions have made way for.

2 December, *Peckham*
SKELETON CREW

———

Some people love the beginning of winter for the bite in the air, the hunkering down and the promise of fires. Some like it for the simplicity that comes with a landscape stripped back and drained of colour, and some like it for the fact that they can turn their backs on the garden. It is true that the garden appears to go into hibernation and to loosen its grip on us for a while. It is a blessed relief to many gardeners that they can ignore the slug-ridden vegetable patch and the remains of a summer garden that never came to much in the first place because summer never really arrived. But I like this time of year, and after a brief spell of inertia when I let the leaves swirl on the terraces and the autumn have its shambolic way, I am out there, fired up and enthusiastic for change. I want to redefine my grip and set up the garden for the months ahead, for there is no reason, no reason at all, for it to be anything less than beautiful.

Once the steam is up, I want to move the garden on, to address the things that didn't work and to take with me and refine those that did. An initial de-cluttering is usually triggered by the threat of frost. London is always milder than outlying areas, but I am amazed at just how localised warm pockets are. When I lived in Vauxhall, a stone's throw from the Thames and within earshot of Big Ben, we often went the winter with nothing more than a tickle of frost, but here, just a couple of kilometres further south, we usually get the first snap around now. This freeze puts ice on the copper in which I grow the water lilies and withers tender annuals overnight. The nasturtiums hang in ghostly, gelatinous strings, leaving the fat seed that has been nestling under their foliage like grain on the ground. I gather this up quickly as it is soon consumed in the general decay and I like to have a good stock of this lovely variety. It is shocking to think that, just the day before, they were vivid green and pulsing with life. The dahlias, too, are blackened as if by a blowtorch and reduced to a phantom of their former glory. All that life, bulk and vigour extinguished in an instant. Back to base and to their chosen method of coming back another summer.

Where the nasturtiums provide for next year with seed and the dahlias retreat into their tubers, succulents and half-hardy perennials are altogether more vulnerable. If the frost gets them before I do, the succulents succumb beyond the point of salvage and the tender fuchsias wither. Although I only grow the dark-leaved, long-trumpeted *Fuchsia* 'Thalia', I hate to lose a plant that has developed some bulk. It provides much more of a show the following year if it can be kept ticking over in the frost-free garage. I remember vividly a frost disaster in the garden I worked in as a child, which was the ruin of Jim the gardener's fuchsia collection. Mrs Pumphrey, who owned the garden, indulged him in this fantastic show, and his dripping standards were the talk of the county. As a rule, as soon as the nights got a chill in them, the fuchsia collection was lifted into the greenhouse along with the pelargoniums. Here, they were kept on the dry side to put them into a state of partial dormancy. Then one year, an early cold snap caught Jim out and his prize plants hung black and in tatters. It took years to rebuild the collection to its former glory, but he made a point of starting again with new and untried varieties that he grew alongside his trusted favourites. Out of the ashes came something rather new and wonderful to compensate.

Frost has a way of cutting through the clutter and once the datura, the pelargoniums, the salvias and their tender friends are carried, like the vegetable cousins of Noah's animals, into the protection of the garage, I make inroads into the beds. Some plants cope better than others after a frost. Dahlias are a good example of those that don't, as they leave behind so little structure. I reduce them back to 15 cm or so, so that I can see where they are next spring, and then leave them rather than lift and store them inside. They are quite hardy below ground in much of Britain if they are given a 15 cm mulch of compost or bark to prevent the frost penetrating to their tubers. A reader in East Yorkshire wrote to inform me they have left their tubers in the ground every winter for the past twenty years. Cannas can be treated in much the same way, although ornamental gingers

(*Hedychium*) are so slow to get off the blocks if they do come through outside that I now prefer to grow them as pot plants and keep them in leaf inside over winter. Last year's foliage can be cut to the base once the weather warms up some time in May.

Editing the garden is a gradual process of elimination, and I like to let nature take its course and for foliage to find its way back into the ground in its own time. *Geranium* 'Patricia' collapses quite rapidly after a cold snap, and once the worms and the rot have done their bit, there is little above ground worth looking at by the end of the year. I gather the remains in one hand to leave next year's buds showing at ground level. These are bright red and are already being joined by the bronze leaves of the celandines, *Ranunculus ficaria* 'Brazen Hussy'. The same can be done with *Persicaria*, but I savour many perennials for their winter seedheads, form and structure, and this is what I edit back to so that there is plenty for the winter sunshine to fall upon. Jagged *Eryngium*, the last of the lacy umbellifers, the russet spires of *Veronicastrum* and soot-black *Echinacea* are what you should be looking out for. A brilliant place to see these gorgeous skeletons at their best is in the Piet Oudolf borders at Wisley. This is the season for these borders, and they are a wonderful reminder that there is life and beauty out there still.

Removing the clutter lets you see things in a new light, but you need to retrain your eye in winter to see things in a more economical way. It is good to understand the structure of a garden and to aim for it to be as handsome as it can be. Deciduous hedges that got the better of you in the wet summer can be trimmed to reintroduce a good line. The fine outline of a handsome shrub or tree can be made a focal point by clearing around it. It's a gentle process, this editing, but one that gets you back to the best and the most trusted winter forms. When the bulbs start pushing through in February, you can clear up the garden for good. In the meantime, err on the side of restraint. The more time you take to look, the more you see.

5 December, *Hillside*
DEALING WITH DEADWOOD

———

It won't be long now until the shortest day of the year. The leaves are down and swirled into corners. The colour is drained from the autumn and, through newly naked branches, low light falls to the floor for the first time in months.

I love this time of year for the counter-movement it provides to the rush of the growing season. There are signs of what is yet to come in the embryonic catkins already formed on the hazel, but for a brief window the garden relaxes. Toppled borders might appear chaotic, with stems akimbo and shadows of spent foliage flung to the floor, but the remains of the growing season are far from ugly if you take the time to see the beauty in the natural cycle.

Selective clearing will juxtapose the disorder. Leave things a while for the worms to take the leaves back to earth and you will see that many of the perennials are as beautiful in death as they were alive. Cinnamon pods on the lilies will dry once they have jettisoned their seed to reveal silvered interiors, while fennel stands tall to catch frost on its umbels. It will smell deliciously of liquorice on a bright day in January, and when the weather gets cold the seed that weights the *Verbena bonariensis* will draw birds to feast.

Cut the miscanthus to the base and the light that illuminates it will simply fall to the floor. Clear the beds and the homes that the stems provide for overwintering insects will be swept away in a moment. Take the breathing space the season is naturally offering us and clear only what is needed to keep chaos in check.

Trees and shrubs are showing you their limbs now that the foliage is down. There are mixed opinions about the viability of dead wood in a garden – some say it is a vector for honey fungus – but I prefer to take the risk. Healthy trees and shrubs will not be prone if they are kept in good condition and there are plenty of other beneficial fungi that need a place to call their own.

Our neighbour down at the farm believes in the same principle. From time to time one of his elderly poplars has come crashing across the brook that divides us. Although I have been happy to have the wood, I left the first tree that came down for the air of wildness that it lent the field. We cleared the smashed-up wood to burn, and made the remains into twiggy cairns. Three years on and the wildlife has moved in, revealed by rustling from within and hedgehog tracks. The fallen tree is home to verdant moss, with ferns and even an elder seedling growing in the clefts.

Not everyone has the space to allow such evolution, but even the smallest garden should have an area of stillness that is left to itself. An eco-pile is nothing more than a decomposing heap where the woody clippings can make their way back to humus.

If you cannot have a bonfire or access to a chipper, a carefully stacked pile in a shady corner will provide a home for slug-eating ground beetles and a host of other beneficial inhabitants.

8 December, *Chicago*

A WAY WITH THE PRAIRIES

————

I have just returned from a lecture tour of the USA, where I caught the fall at its best and spent longer than ever before in Chicago, the City of Broad Shoulders. When I asked the origin of this nickname, it was proudly announced that the city believed that it should be able to carry the world through industry and innovation. After all, Chicago was home to the first skyscraper and to Frank Lloyd Wright, who developed his Prairie Style architecture in its suburbs. I had only known his wonderful, iconic Fallingwater, cantilevered over a cascade in woodland, so I was shocked to see these vast, low-slung Arts & Crafts family homes littering crisp expanses of lawn in the wealthy Oak Park area on the edge of town. Not a prairie in sight, but impressive nonetheless.

In the city centre, an industrious new wave of architecture has been revitalising the downtown area. On the way into Millennium Park, the beautiful Cloud Gate by Anish Kapoor reflects the spectacle of the city centre on its polished stainless-steel surface, capturing passers-by, skyscrapers, clouds and Frank Gehry's Jay Pritzker Pavilion rearing up over the park like a silver dragon. Beyond the Gehry, and behind the dramatic

Shoulder Hedge (to reflect the broad shoulders), lies the Lurie Garden, designed by Gustafson Guthrie Nichol, a celebrated new addition to the park. Piet Oudolf devised the planting for the garden and, among the glittering architecture, the essence of the long-lost prairie has been brought into the city.

Today, skyscrapers and concrete and lawns in the suburbs roll out from one to the next in a pristine carpet that has left no room for what gave Illinois its name as the Prairie State. The vast prairies once covered 570,000 square kilometres, from Canada to Texas, Indiana and Nebraska. In just over fifty years in Illinois alone, prairie that was seen as being rich for cultivation was swept aside to make way for industrial farming. The Lurie Garden, lovely as it is, with its tawny grasses and seeded perennials, could not have been a greater contrast to what lay around it.

Feeling inspired, and in need of some real landscape, I met up the next day with Roy Diblik, the man behind Northwind Perennial Farm, a pioneering nursery that specialises in native American plants. Roy had grown all the plants for the Lurie Garden and knew all there was to know about North American perennials. How brilliant that the garden has reactivated people's interest in their own natives again, but how much more amazing to be taken to some of the restoration projects outside the city. Here, in relatively small pockets of land, a growing movement that started in the early sixties has seen prairies re-established by teams of volunteers. These nature lovers saw the need to act before all was lost, because today the original prairie only exists in slivers of land, rocky places that can't be turned by the plough, and railroad embankments. Pointedly, and rather poetically, I thought, the pioneer cemeteries had also acted as an oasis for the plants that were swept away by the settlers, and it was the seed gathered in these sanctuaries that enabled the new reserves to be colonised.

I was shown one of the first restorations at the Morton Arboretum, an open area of about eight hectares. I felt so small with the grasses and eupatoriums standing at well over shoulder height, and it was ravishingly beautiful, with the only true green at that time of year being the 'artificial' green of the mown lawns of the gardens that lay beyond. Here there was every shade of brown, fawn and parchment white. In certain places, the hot cinnamon stems of *Rudbeckia* with coal-black seedheads and the grey-green of long-gone baptisia formed an undercurrent. Prairie dropseed, *Sporobolus heterolepis*, a grass that has a sweet, sugary perfume when flowering, formed low clearings where it had developed into a colony. Among the grasses, in a combination that it would be impossible to better in a garden, were jagged *Eryngium*, or rattlesnake master, and soot-black *Echinacea*. *Sylphium perfoliatum* rose half as tall again as me. Its scalloped foliage had turned a leathery brown, and I stood for some time marvelling at the sculpture of it, thinking of my solitary plant in Peckham and how very far it was from its natural home.

Later in the day, Roy and I met up with Tom van der Poel, a charismatic leader in the contemporary prairie movement. He took us to Flint Creek, a six-year-old project of some twenty-five hectares. The land was purchased by Citizens for Conservation, a volunteer group which now owns 160 hectares. We plunged in after Tom as he took off along a tiny path, scattering handfuls of seed where he knew each species would have the best chance of thriving. As I followed, I asked how best to go about re-establishing an environment that had been erased well over a hundred years ago. 'The restorations are a combination of science and art,' he proclaimed. 'The larger your perspective, the greater your understanding.'

He went on to explain the intricacies of the grassland as he showered seed into areas that were 'ready' for it; where the brome grass, the grass sown by the settlers for grazing, had been weakened enough by the other prairie plants. If they're set free and given the room to thrive again, the process of reviving the natives is possible. Using the most vigorous species first and then inter-sowing weaker species such as the prairie dropseed and the bottle gentian, it has been possible to create microclimates to suit a wide range of plants. In just six years, 260 species have been re-established on this site alone.

Each site is sown according to the local conditions, which are often wildly removed from their original state – farmed and infertile, drained of the ground's natural resources; but the volunteers are keen for diversity, so they 'undo' the sterile farmland by breaking the land drains to create a range of conditions again. The culture of burning sections to clear the thatch that builds up in time, as the Native Americans did, is still practised at the end of winter before growth starts. Tom said they only burn the prairie in sections, to allow the wildlife that has flocked back room to escape. 'Building the food chain is just a small part of this work,' he explained.

Every year another site is brought back in for re-colonisation by the efforts of volunteer groups such as these, and I hope that in our lifetimes this will be a chain reaction we can all be touched by.

10 December, *Peckham*
MAKING THE CUT

———

It is just a matter of days now until we have endured the longest night, which always feels like a major hurdle jumped. However, the truth is we have yet to suffer the worst of the winter: weeks of cold and darkness. But it is important to try and make the effort to attempt a mental flip, as winter in the garden should be one of the most industrious times. The leaves are down and very little is growing above ground, so we can forget about watering and tending. With time on our hands we can stand back and imagine our small green worlds as better and much-improved places for next year. Failures can be swept aside and, with a little effort, images of Eden easily summoned.

In terms of what can be achieved, the weather is rarely so bad that it is difficult to get out into the garden. We are seldom under snow and it never rains as much as we think it does, though you do have to watch your ground if it is heavy and lies wet. You can do untold damage working a heavy soil if it is muddy for it compacts and ruins the soil structure. You instinctively know when the damage is being done, because the soil smears and leaves behind a boot-shaped depression that holds water. There are ways around a heavy soil and you can spread your weight by working off boards, but in the main it is best to get on with the pruning and leave the soil work until it is dry.

Frost is also something which comes in batches and, if you have a heavy soil, a frosty day is the perfect time to get onto the beds to cut hedges or to start pruning the hardier shrubs and trees. Top fruit, such as apples and pears, and most soft fruit is hardy enough to be pruned in the winter, although it is always best to wait a while with roses, because their comparatively tender branches can suffer from dieback. Soil resists weight when it is frozen, but you should never think about turning the ground when there is a freeze in it, as the cold soil stays where it is put and that is bad for root growth.

I like to see this window before Christmas as the best time to get all my woody plants into the ground. This is an ideal, I know, for in a late year such as this, many nurseries will not even start lifting until all the leaves are down on bare-root and root-balled specimens. In truth, we have until early April to put in trees and shrubs, later in a cool year, but early action is always better in terms of the long-term establishment of the plant. Although you might not think it, root action is happening below ground in all but the most frosty periods, so the sooner a plant can make this growth, the better equipped it will be to take in the water and nutrients that it needs to flourish next year.

Things are never quite as simple as you might think. Plant a deciduous hedge at this time of year and it is simply a case of putting in the effort to prepare well and standing back to wait until spring, but with evergreens the story is different. Unlike plants that lose their foliage, evergreens continue to transpire at a rapid rate, drying like sheets in the wind in a dry winter. In a windy position, keep them checked and damp. A perforated screen to protect them from the prevailing wind will also help to get them through to the spring. If you are happy to water more frequently in the summer, to make up for lost time gained over winter in root development, waiting until March to plant the evergreens does take the worry out of the equation.

As part of a need I have to feel that my garden is always productive, I make a point of getting my hardwood cuttings taken this side of Christmas. The energy that is still 'up' in the woody plants can be used to our own ends for a whole range of woody cuttings. By energy up, I mean that the sap is still high in the branches – it tends to retreat to the roots later in the season, making the wood less supple. I came to understand this best when I visited some hurdle makers on the South Downs who live in the woods in caravans and under tarpaulins for the winter. It is important to them that the hazel coppice is cut in the first half of winter as the rods have give in them then and are less prone to splitting. Wood cut earlier also lasts longer, so if you are lucky enough to have a supply of hazel pea sticks on tap, the early part of the winter is the best time to get them. In terms of hardwood cuttings, which have no foliage to feed them, the rich sap is the energy source that the cutting needs to regenerate itself.

The hardwood cutting is the next easiest thing to an 'Irishman's Cutting' – a slip or a heel from the base of the plant that has roots already on it. A hardwood cutting is an easy option, because the cutting is without foliage, and half the battle with conventional cuttings is keeping the foliage damp enough to support the cutting while it initiates its own roots, without rotting. Propagating this side of winter ensures that the roots have initiated during the so-called dormant period and the young plant will be equipped enough to support its own foliage next growing season.

Vines are a prime candidate for a hardwood cutting, and each year I take a dozen or so to spread my strawberry grape further afield. *Vitis vinifera* 'Fragola' is a great open-air grape in this country, for it has a short ripening period. The flavour of the strawberry grape is curious in that it has a taste of something else – could be wild strawberries, but there is also a hint of bubblegum, which sounds horrible, but is not. My plant originally came from my Italian client who had kept it in the family through several generations in just this way. As it is relatively hard to get hold of (Reads of Loddon in Norfolk stock it), this was how I got enough plants together to plant up the courtyard at the British Library in London. The plants were fruiting away there three years after taking the cuttings, giving passers-by the opportunity to pinch some grapes, as intended.

Willow, which can be planted direct if you are growing a willow hedge, is easy; poplar, *Cornus alba* and several of the more vigorous species roses are also easily propagated in this manner. The method is simple. Take 25 cm lengths that are about a pencil in thickness, certainly no less and not much more, and make a horizontal cut immediately below the bud at the bottom. This is the means by which you will remember which way is up and which way is down, because the cut immediately above the top bud should be gently sloping away from the bud to shed the water that might lie there over the winter. Insert the cuttings to half their depth in a pot of free-draining compost and tuck them in a cool, sheltered corner where they should be kept moist, but not wet. If you have a heated mat in a frame you will be laughing, as this promotes root-growth still faster. If not, there is no need to worry as nature will take its course while it would appear the garden is in hibernation. Come the spring you will not only be smug in the knowledge that you and your plants are ready for the off, you will be plant-rich and nothing is better than that.

16 December, *Hampshire and Peckham*
STUCK ON YOU

———

I grew up, as I'm sure many of us did, with ivy in close proximity. In the mid-seventies our home was festooned with it, as the old lady who lived there before us had become overwhelmed by her garden during the course of forty or so years. The ivy represented this demise perfectly and it had grown in strength as she had weakened. It had made its way over most of the windows to cast a dim, green glow over the rooms inside. You could see the tendrils and dusty leaves pressing on the glass, while in some of the bedrooms it had found its way under the skirting boards and was poking out from behind the abandoned wardrobes. It was even more sinister in the loft, where, without light, it crept among the rafters like a vegetable Nosferatu, pale, emaciated and etiolated.

Since the Picturesque movement of the early eighteenth century, when it was used to create an instant impression of ancient decay and ruin, ivy has had a widespread reputation as a melancholy plant, and its sinister, Gothic edge was loved by the Victorians. Indeed, the young Victoria was said to wear a wreath of Osborne ivy laced with diamonds in her hair. Yet its roots in the pagan religions of the north gave it the symbolism of eternal life, loyalty and devotion, for when the leaves are down it provides a rich foundation of greenery.

Ivy was in danger of submerging my childhood home and removing it was a necessity: we pulled away great mats of it like filthy fleeces. The shadow of its aerial roots traced its history over the brickwork from innocent seedling to the leafy summit of the eaves. The trunks at ground level were the thickness of your wrist, and where its head reached the sunshine and could climb no higher, it had mutated into the mature, flowering state. Birds lived up there.

As a result I was scarred for a few years, and to this day will never plant ivy near a house or a building. When I moved to Peckham ten years ago, my first job after the removal lorries left was to pull away a severed ivy that had made its way across the front of the house. It was strange that the vendor had cut it and then decided to leave it, for it only enhanced the feeling of neglect here, too. The leaves had browned but had resiliently clung on. Pulling it off was a huge relief.

While shaving this plant from the house, I became painfully aware that, despite its tenacity, a dead ivy is a far more horrible thing than a living one could ever be. It was late November and the mush of fallen foliage from the deciduous trees was rotting underfoot. I couldn't help but notice the gloss and the sheen of healthy ivy in neighbouring gardens. It reflected sunlight like tiny mirrors, bouncing it back from deep, lustrous greenery which, in the darkest months of the year, has something life-enhancing about it.

Ivy is our only native evergreen climber and is capable of reaching a height of 30 m in a tree and making its way patiently to the top before it decides to change character and branches out to produce fruiting wood. It thrives almost anywhere, up north and out west in particular, in a host of soils and often hostile conditions. It is ubiquitous, hence the rich folklore surrounding it, but I have come round to it as something that can make a handsome foundation. It can be the green against which you throw a light-catching *Clematis montana* 'Alba', or the dark foil for snowdrops, or the first of the hellebores.

Miriam Rothschild, a fearless environmentalist, grew it so heavily over her house that it had formed clouds of growth that magnified and bearded the gabled mansion. I lived there in the gardener's cottage for a short spell and learned that she loved it for the bees – she was an entomologist first and foremost. It flowered between September and November, providing the bees with one of the richest sources of nectar at that time of year. Its evergreen foliage was the perfect cover for the birds. It ripened in early summer to a wonderful blue-black, when the plant became a riot of activity as the blackbirds gorged themselves. This is how the ivy turns up as seedlings in the most unlikely places, but always a flight away from the parent plant.

Although ivy is not a parasite, the weight and volume of the flowering wood in a tree can act like a heavily rigged ship in full sail, so you have to choose where to leave it and judge if your trees are up to the challenge. I always like to leave it where I can and like it best for the fruiting wood. If you take a cutting from the mature flowering wood it will retain its shrubby character. When grown as such, it is called *Hedera helix* 'Arborescens' and this is how I have been planting ivy of late, to avoid the panic associated with its scrambling proximity to architecture. The shrubby form is most reliable grown in sunshine, which helps to trigger the mature wood. Grow it in shade and the odd branch will start to run along the ground, like it does when it is in search of a host to climb, and reach into the sun again. These strays can easily be removed to keep it within bounds, but it's best to be vigilant.

The Irish ivy, *H. hibernica*, is a variety loved by the landscape trade for the fact that it fails to climb and remains as a low, juvenile ground cover. It can be dull when used in a carpark planting, but it is pretty wonderful in the right place, and I have used it to smother weeds under the flame and golden stems of coppiced willows. It is 100 per cent weed-proof if you keep it weeded while it is in the process of forming its unbroken mat.

Sports, or varieties, of ornamental ivies are also propagated in this way and were, with ferns, one of the plants selected obsessively by the Victorians. Not all varieties are equally stable, but some are worth seeking out. The filigree forms of *H. helix* are particularly pretty – 'Sagittifolia' is an elegant, large-leaved ivy with elongated fingers, while the smaller-leaved 'Pedata' and 'Très Coupé' look like green lace. The dark-leaved forms, 'Atropurpurea' and 'Glymii', are the epitome of Gothic chic, with almost black leaves that provide the most reflective surface for winter sunshine. I also love *H. helix* 'Buttercup' for its variously coloured foliage, the yellow flash brightening a dark corner. This plant will be too yellow for me if planted in sun, though some people love it like this.

I am also not much good with the visual clutter of variegation and I seriously struggle with the brilliance of the large-leafed *H. canariensis* 'Paddy's Pride', which, like 'Goldheart', is a chunderous mix of green and yellow. There is also the ubiquitous, large-leaved green and white *H. helix* 'Cavendishii', which looks as if it has been colonised by a flock of incontinent pigeons and is thus also something I avoid. If you can find the simple, plain form of *H. colchica* it is the most lovely thing, with foliage that can be 15 cm across when it is happy and reflective enough to flood your garden with sparkling light in the depth of winter. Just remember (he said, suppressing old fears) to keep it from the gutters . . .

18 December, *Hillside*
HARD NUTS TO CRACK

———

We have been foraging away since the fruit started to ripen. The damsons were made into jam, the excess of blackberries and autumn raspberry and several bags of rosehips ferreted away into the freezer. Our neighbour Jane brought round apples by the sack, which were turned into a lip-smacking juice. The apple press is a new addition to our kit and we made a day of it, four of us chopping and crushing and pressing. We are happy with the results, despite the bruised colour of the liquid. I have a glass of it on my desk as I write. It represents so much: the anticipation of my own newly planted orchard, the nurturing it will take to make it flourish, the goodness of sun and nutrient and life come together in fruit. Every sip of the nectar is a delight and I don't want it to end.

With my foraging hat on, I have been collecting hedgerow fruits and seeds to grow my own hedging plants to plug the gaps in the hedgelines. The field maple will be lined out in shallow trenches in the kitchen garden where they will be grown for the three years it takes to get them to planting size. The rosehips, haws and sloes are put into a bucket of water and allowed to ferment to simulate the action of passing through the gut of a bird. It doesn't take long for the natural sugars in the fruit to start the process and for the pith to foam and start to decompose. Rubbing away the pulp after a fortnight will turn your hands red and leave them smelling bitter and yeasty, but it is necessary to free the seed, which by then will have been subjected to the acids of fermentation. When harvesting the fruit, I made a beeline for the hedge trees that exhibited the best berries in the hope that their genes will be passed on in the seedlings.

We missed the hazelnuts on the trees down by the stream by a long shot. The nuts on the ground were empty and there were none on the trees by the time we got there. I imagined the squirrels giving them a shake or sizing them up for weight, as we might a melon, before deciding to save their energy on breaking open those that bore the kernel. Undaunted, and perhaps in the mistaken belief that there are enough to share if I can get the numbers up, I have ordered a collection of cobnuts and filberts. If the squirrels get to the nuts first, at least we will have hazel rods and twigs for staking, but we're on a learning curve of getting to know our land and I remain optimistic.

It took my first year here to decide upon the position for the nuttery. With the exception of the hazel in the hedgelines, which must have arrived there by squirrels burying and then forgetting their bounty, the hazel favour the woodland. Try planting them out in the open and they will sulk for a good three to five years before gathering the strength to bulk up and out, but plant a hazel in a cool, sheltered position akin to their native habitat and they will flourish. The chosen site for the nuttery is to the bottom of the slope below the orchard, where the ground lies moist and the fingers of shade from the poplars keep the air cool. If I were to plant hazel in a more urban setting I would find a spot to the north or east of buildings, or in the shade of a tree where other plants might not do so well.

As I have the room, I have ordered four dozen trees of seven varieties. 'Kentish Cob' from the 1830s, 'Pearson's Prolific', a good compact variety (and hard to resist a namesake), and 'White Filbert', with its milky kernel, to name just three. They will be planted on a loosely structured grid of about 6 m so that it is easy to move between them. In time, when the canopies touch and the pasture underneath is shaded I will introduce bluebells and snowdrops, campion, primrose and, by the gate, to either side as markers, two trees inoculated with the spores of black truffle. Who knows if my foraging will run to such luxuries in years to come, but here's to trying.

20 December, *Peckham*
ALL YE FAITHFUL

———

Last year, on the shortest day of the year, the Christmas rose in the front garden produced its first flower. This was not any old hellebore but *Helleborus* × *ericsmithii*, given to me by Beth Chatto with the promise that it was a good plant and one to watch. Plants with special associations are the ones I treasure the most, and Beth was right about its performance, as the pale flowers were more than timely, appearing when the sun is at its lowest from the half-light of December.

The true Christmas rose, *Helleborus niger*, rarely does what it says on the tin and in my experience struggles to produce something by the end of January. It is a plant that needs just the right conditions to thrive, with plenty of sun, free drainage and preferably a cloche – not only to encourage the flowers but also to keep them clean in the winter months. *H.* × *ericsmithii* is the result of a three-way hybrid (*H. niger* × *H. sternii* [*argutifolius* × *lividus*]), and the hybrid's vigour has produced a much better plant. The flowers arch away from a rosette of pewter-coloured leaves, with the stems and protective hood to the flower stained as dark as green can be. What is more, these Christmas-time flowers are just the first, and they will continue on until they fade through dirty mauve to a curious metallic grey. By then, in February, the rest of the hellebores have kicked in and are beginning to bridge the gap from winter to spring, but in these first months of winter the life they give could not be a better tonic.

After this stellar performance and feeling smug in the knowledge that at last I could have a Christmas rose at Christmas, I must confess to buying out the stock of one small nursery so that I could extend the solitary clump in the front garden. The extras, of which there are five or six, will be Christmas presents for those friends and family who I know will appreciate something a little special. They will be given with the advice that their Mediterranean parentage means that they differ from the Lenten roses, as they prefer life to be free draining, with plenty of light. This is a plant that I expect we will be seeing a lot more of at this time of year. Though it is sterile, the nurserymen are producing it en masse by micropropagation.

The silvery sheen to their foliage, so timely at Christmas, set me off in search of other plants that could continue the theme, and soon there was quite a list to join the hellebores, or at least be used close by to prevent them from feeling out of place. Metallic foliage can easily feel too ornamental, but balanced with other greenery its light-giving properties are welcome when light levels are low. *Cyclamen hederifolium* 'Silver Cloud', selected for its pure silver leaves, is almost at its best now, and the foliage is easily as good as the autumnal flowers. If you are lucky enough to have the right garden for the winter-flowering *Cyclamen coum*, and by that I mean it's tricky and doesn't always take to an open position under deciduous trees, there are lovely forms selected for their foliage. Though I have failed here in Peckham, each year about this time I make a point of buying a few more to try them somewhere new. They are chosen for the silver markings on the leaf as much as they are for the flower, and I live in hope that one day I will crack the ideal position.

The land is only recently devoid of foliage when the shortest day of the year arrives, and it is now that you start to see the backbone of holly and ivy in the hedgerows. These are plants that shimmer on sunlit days, and it is no surprise that the pagan ritual of bringing in foliage to garland the house arose at this time of year. Evergreens were thought of as plants that represented immortality, and their enduring presence in a landscape stripped back for the best part of half a year clearly illustrated that certain things live beyond the natural cycle. I like this idea despite the fact that we still suffer from an evergreen overload, brought upon us by the Victorians. Too much laurel, aucuba and yew can be sombre, but in the right quantity and with room around them for ephemeral things to come and go, there are many evergreens that make a fine backdrop.

In my own garden I make do with bamboo and the plain-leaved *Hedera colchica*, which tumbles over the garages at the end, but it would be nice to have enough evergreen to gather for the house to keep up the pagan traditions. *Ilex aquifolium* is still one of the best, but as it is a tree that has both male and female forms, you need to know that you have bought a female if what you want is berries. *I. aquifolium* 'Amber' is a female form with yellow berries, and 'J. C. Van Tol' fruits heavily because it is self-fertile. Branches can often be so heavily festooned that it looks unnatural, but I get around this by planting it in shade rather than berry-promoting sun. This form is also easy to use as the leaves are entire, with just one prickle at the point of the leaf. I remember a childhood camp that was perfectly private for being evergreen, but it was far from perfect in that the seclusion came at a prickly price, so

I am also using 'J. C. Van Tol' more freely in gardens where there are children. When I have some land of my own, I will plant a ring of it to celebrate the power of endurance as much as for the joy of bringing something into the house that keeps us in touch with the natural side of Christmas.

24 December, *Hampshire and Peckham*
MRS CHRISTMAS'S PERFECT GIFT

———

When I was five years old, I was given a hippeastrum bulb by Mrs Christmas, who was our neighbour's mother. At that point I was making brick houses for my burgeoning troll collection. They were made from three bricks only, had a slate for the roof, and a roof garden made from mud and stones and houseleeks. I was also rearing snails in an old suitcase in the back yard. These two activities were enough of a sign that I might respond to things that grew. The hippeastrum was an inspired move – for grow it did, and apparently under my care. It was potted up and put on the kitchen windowsill where, after a few days in the sunshine, the slit at the top of the bulb parted to make way for what was to become the flower. This was the beginning of the alchemy; the fat green sheath emerged from the bulb and then ascended vertically on a stalk that lengthened with every day. Touching the stalk left a fingerprint in the powdery bloom that covered it.

I watched this metamorphosis with bated breath, for every day the plant had changed and things were a little different.

After a couple of weeks a pair of waxy leaves followed the stem, and after a month, when the flower stem stood a good 60 cm above the pot, the sheath that covered the buds began to swell and then to part, like lips about to utter something profound. Once the sheath became as transparent as onion skin, two crimson buds pushed up and then out and down in a well-rehearsed choreography as they fattened in readiness for flowering. Eventually, after what seemed like forever, the petals parted, opening out into a megaphone of a flower that glistened when you caught it in sunshine. I was just as fascinated by the withering and the decay that followed, but I see now that in those few weeks I became hooked on growth – snared by the magic of transformation and with a determination to repeat the experience.

Over the next few years I discovered that these incredible bulbs are programmed to perform, and that I was far less instrumental in the production of such a spectacle than I had thought. But that was no deterrent. The bulbs continued to hold a fascination when I saw them dry at the garden centre and I tried white-flowered forms with green sweeping down from their throats, pinks with names like 'Apple Blossom' and the appropriately named 'Red Lion'. In this case, the flower was dark and lushly opulent. It seemed an impossibility that such a show could emerge from what looked like little more than a large onion. I was always rather sniffy about the striped varieties, I might add, but things changed when I saw a big pan of several, all in full flower. There were seven or eight stems with flowers colliding above them like a fairground ride or circus performance in full swing. It was a moment of realisation. There is no point in dabbling in something as dramatic as hippeastrums when what you need is complete immersion.

Today I am still a sucker when I see the bulbs for sale. Only last year on a trip to visit friends in Amsterdam I managed to buy a clutch of the largest bulbs I had ever seen. They were the size of cantaloupe melons and part of a magnificent stall that was held on a floating barge. I saw my chance to do as Mrs Christmas had done for me and pass them on as gifts to those who would enjoy the surprise that was to come. I kept one for myself and looked forward to the scarlet flowers that would light up a dull January – I was assured that the bulbs were 'Red Lion'. They came up a garish salmon pink, with five huge, fleshy flowers to each stem and three stems that followed on one from the next like a Roman candle. Not at all what I expected – I like red to be red – but a spectacle nonetheless.

Looking after a hippeastrum after it has flowered is easy enough. They prefer a loam compost, such as John Innes, as it has more guts and is weightier, so the top-heavy flowers are less likely to topple a pot. They also like to have a restricted root run, which inhibits an excess of foliage that is produced at the expense of flowers. In summer they are happy to sit outside in a sunny position which feeds the bulbs, and they also respond to tomato food. I never dry them out, as books recommend you do, at the end of the summer when they are brought in, but keep them going on a bright windowsill. *Hippeastrum papilio* is a curious greenish-white finely striped with ox-blood red, and my all-time favourite, but it is never a plant that responds to the breeding programmes of the bulb merchants. It must be more closely related to the species and wild at heart, so it flowers when it wants to and you just have to wait patiently. But I'm happy to wait, for when they do I'm right back, as fascinated as ever.

Although I never buy cut flowers, I am quite happy to take advantage of the breeding programmes that encourage winter-flowering bulbs to perform without faltering. After they have flowered, I put them out on the street for passers-by to take them on, as I need my windowsills for seedlings and over-wintering tender perennials. Paperwhite narcissus are a good case in point, as they rarely do as well the second year round as they do off the shelf. I've had great success growing them in Italy, where they are up and flowering outside in November. There the early growth has the chance to live unharmed through the winter and dry out completely in the hot summer. Here you are best to treat them like cut flowers and get over the feeling of waste once they finish. Sometimes it is not so bad to be decadent in the garden.

I find that just one pot of paperwhites goes a long way, as the perfume is overwhelming in a closed room. I find hyacinths are the same, but these really need to be grown en masse, several to a pan, for them not to feel cumbersome. Part of the magic of forcing them is in growing them in a cupboard for the first six weeks after potting on. This promotes root action before stimulating top growth. Keep the temperatures down (below $7\,°C$) during this period before bringing them out into the light. Water carefully around the developing shoots, as they can easily rot at this stage, but once they are away and growing faster there is little to stop them being the prelude to growth out in the garden.

I like the ephemeral flush of these indoor bulbs and am not much good with the loitering quality of most house plants which just sit and gather dust. But, despite my prejudice, I do have a soft spot for a *Cymbidium* orchid. My early experiences led me pretty fast from hippeastrums into purchasing a *Cymbidium* from a lady up the road. As cool-growing terrestrial orchids, they do not require a hot house and humidity to do well, but are more than happy on a windowsill in a pot of open compost. They are happy to live as we do inside and with our temperatures, but you have to make sure that the house doesn't overheat when their buds are forming. I lost every last bud on my plant one Christmas when the house got too hot with friends, family and food on the go.

In summer, a *Cymbidium* can be put in the garden in a dappled corner and treated like any other houseplant on summer leave. Keeping them pot-bound is the best way to ensure a good supply of flower, as too much room and fertiliser makes them flabby and lazy. A trait you might tolerate in yourself and your loved ones for the next fortnight, but not one to aim for in your houseplants.

31 December, *Hillside*
PUTTING DOWN ROOTS

———

This winter's bare-root order has arrived from the nursery. The box is as tall as I am and pulling it apart is a thrill. The contents are unprepossessing enough, bundled carefully together with a twist of bailer twine and dampened down inside their bin liner, but in my mind's eye this winter's trees are already big enough to stand under.

Over the end-of-year holidays, they will be joining several generations of trees that go back as far as the remains of the elm stumps in the hedgerows and further to the twisted oak on the hill above us. Planting trees is said to require patience, but I have never found that to be so if you plant each winter as a rolling succession. I have been doing this over the past couple of decades for my clients and already I can lie in the shade of trees that were no more than whips when they went in. Trees grow faster than you think, not only skyward but out and down, gathering strength in their roots, their trunks swelling.

The tree positions, marked out in canes on the slopes behind the house, have been pondered over since late in summer. I have looked at them from every angle, moving around the canes so that I could see how they affect the land. Where would they cast their shadows over the course of the day, would they feel taller because they were perched on the banks? Capability Brown used trees on the tops of hills to give the hills more gravity and it is amusing to note that the old tricks still work.

The canes are placed next to a group of *Malus transitoria* – crab apples – which I planted here in the first winter. Though they were just a single whip when they went in, they flowered and fruited for the first time this year. The fruits are the size of a bead, glassy yellow and ripening to a deep apricot among golden autumn foliage. The birds loved them and that's the idea – I want the birds to enjoy the crabs as much as I intend to myself. Their small divided leaves make them look not dissimilar to the hawthorns, which are close by.

The canes represent a group of chequer trees that will be the crab apples' new partners. The chequer tree, *Sorbus torminalis*, a British native, is now rare but in medieval times it used to be seen more widely. Its fruits, which are tart when ripe but sweet when bletted by the action of frost, were once used for autumnal currency. This, and the fact that they were used like sloes to flavour alcohol, meant that they were often planted outside public houses; some pubs are named after them.

I first used *Sorbus torminalis* on coastal sites where it seemed all but oblivious to gales and salt-laden winds. Growing strong in these conditions, its silvery leaves might easily be confused with those of a maple until you came upon the cluster of fruit, each the size of a marble and looking like a Cox's apple. Up here on my loamy slopes, they will grow more rangy, liking my heavy soil and in time reaching 10 m or so.

There is some debate as to whether the soil should be improved in the planting hole of newly planted trees. One theory is that the improved soil doesn't encourage the tree's root system to break free of the planting pit in search of its own nutrients. I have adopted this approach on my soil here because it is hearty, simply excavating a decent sized hole – a third as big again as the spread of the roots – and adding a dish with the bottom broken up, to make sure it drains freely. But on poor soil, either very heavy or very light, I do add some organic matter, mixed into the topsoil and worked carefully in around the roots. So far I have found that the friendly bacteria delivered in an application of Rootgrow help in supplying the hair roots with water and nutrients by extending the surface area of the root. The wet summers have been good for the trees as well, and with the satisfaction of a not particularly patient man I can already stand beside them and look up, with hope, into their branches.

ACKNOWLEDGEMENTS

These writings wouldn't exist without the women who encouraged and taught me to garden and to write as a child: Geraldine Noyes, Frances Pumphrey and Joan Wiggins.

I owe much gratitude to Allan Jenkins at *The Observer* for his help with crafting my writing & for encouraging me to explore both my subject and my language. Thanks also to Ruaridh Nicoll and everyone on the editorial team there who made the column such a rewarding forum.

Thank you Howard Sooley and Jason Ingram for your sharp eyes, efficiency and skill in capturing the gardens in images for *The Observer*.

The team at Guardian Faber have made the process of assembling, revising and fine-tuning this compilation so easy and enjoyable. Thank you Laura Hassan, Katherine Ailes, Donna Payne, Will Atkins and Donald Sommerville.

Clare Melinsky, your beautiful, spare illustrations perfectly capture key moments of the seasons.

And finally, thank you dear readers for joining me on the journey.

Dan Pearson is now writing at www.digdelve.com.

INDEX

'Graham Thomas' 194–5
'Serotina' (Late Dutch) 194
similis var. *delavayi* 195
× *tellmanniana* 195
tragophylla 195
lords and ladies 27
lovage 142
Lucas, Neil 285
lungwort 76, 93–4, 146–7, 366
lupin 130, 153, 239
Lurie Garden, Chicago 373
Luzula sylvatica 284
'Marginata' 132
Lychnis 238
coronaria 234

Maggie's West London 130–3
Magnolia 14–15, 77, 91, 97, 216
'Atlas' 117
campbellii 15, 115–16, 117
'David Clulow' 116
denudata 116
'Elizabeth' 117, 158
grandiflora 20, 116
'Iolanthe' 15, 117
liliflora 'Nigra' 117
× *loebneri* 15
'Leonard Messel' 115
'Merrill' 116
obovata 115
sieboldii var. *sinensis* 117–18
× *soulangeana* 114
'Star Wars' 15
stellata 116
maize 148
Malus
floribunda 339
hupehensis 6, 339, 358
× *robusta* 'Red Sentinel' 340

transitoria 6, 340, 357–8, 395
'Thornhayes Tansy' 340
× *zumi*
var. *calocarpa* 339
'Golden Hornet' 340
maple 211, 260
field 85, 304, 385
Japanese 320
see also Acer
Marchant, Chris and Toby 134
Marchetti, Lauro 215
marrow 248, 326, 327
Matteuccia struthiopteris 139–40
Matthiola
longipetala 184
perennis 'Alba' 184
meadows
colour 208, 235
cutting 235, 239, 279
Fritillaria 101–2
Great Dixter xv, 234
in June 169, 185
Narcissus 310
Rosa 349
seed mixes 254–6
tulips 123, 136
wild flowers 268
in Yorkshire Dales 101
meadowsweet 119, 193
Melianthus 78
major 272
Melica ciliata 284
Mentha requienii 232
Metasequoia glyptostroboides 320–1
Michaelmas daisy 63
Middle Eastern gardens 98–9
Milium effusum 'Aureum' 188–9
Mimosa 173
Mimulus 190